No. 1396
$13.95

MICROPROCESSOR INTERFACING

BY JOSEPH J. CARR

TAB BOOKS Inc.
BLUE RIDGE SUMMIT, PA. 17214

FIRST EDITION

SECOND PRINTING

Copyright © 1982 by TAB BOOKS Inc.

Printed in the United States of America

Library of Congress Cataloging in Publication Data

Carr, Joseph J.
    Microprocessor interfacing.

    Includes index.
    1. Microprocessors. 2. Interface circuits.
I. Title.
TK7895.M5C37   001.64   81-18282
ISBN 0-8306-0064-7   AACR2
ISBN 0-8306-1396-X (pbk.)

Contents

Introduction

The microcomputer age is not a decade old, but seldom has any one component or concept so rapidly revolutionized the electronics industry! Engineering schools can now advise students that an electrical engineer who is not conversant with microprocessor design methods will not remain employable for long! At first we were told that this situation would be true "in five years," but history has shown that two years was nearer the truth. Everything from children's toys to complicated scientific instruments on-board space ships has been computerized.

The proper application of the microprocessor/microcomputer requires a person who is a synergism of the software and hardware people found on larger systems. With "dinosaur" computers there are completely separate engineering and programming functions—carried out by different people; but on the microcomputer level when you treat the microprocessor or microcomputer as a component in an instrument design, you as the designer must be good at both.

This book will bring you quickly up to date on the elements of hardware interface with microprocessors. Covered in this volume are methods for interfacing memory devices, creating I/O (input-output) ports, and interfacing with such devices as keyboards, printers, sensors, and the analog world.

Chapter 1

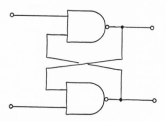

Introduction to Digital Electronics

Digital electronics is a general field that encompasses digital computers, including microcomputers. Before you try to solve microprocessor interfacing problems you must learn the basics of digital electronics. Whether or not you are professionally involved in electronics, you should learn this material because no one any longer can safely ignore the world of digital electronics. Even radio and television technicians find digital circuits in the products they repair. Computerized color-television tuning and stereo-FM tuning are almost the rule, rather than the high-priced exception.

Digital electronics is, however, often simpler than analog electronics because digital IC (integrated circuit) devices recognize only two states, i.e., on and off. This makes digital circuits similar to relays and switches. In fact some digital circuits are little more than high-frequency-electronics versions of simple switches. It is my opinion that anyone who can understand simple relay and switch-logic circuits can also understand digital electronics. Certainly anyone who can understand color television, SSB (single sideband), FM two-way radios, and certain other complex products can understand digital electronics.

LOGIC STATES

Digital circuits respond to only two different input states. These states are called 1 and 0 (after the two permissible digits of the *binary*, or base-2, number system), high and low, or (in older texts) true and false. These designations are merely representations of two different voltage states. In this book the high/low designation is used because it graphically describes what is happening to the circuit.

Transistor-transistor-logic (TTL) responds only to 0 and +5 V for the two logic levels. If any other voltage levels are used the TTL device either (1) fails to work, (2) works unpredictably, or (3) burns out. Figure 1-1A shows the TTL levels.

Complimentary metal-oxide semiconductor (CMOS) IC logic devices can use the same 0 and +5 V logic levels as the TTL devices but may also be

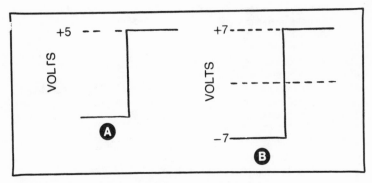

Fig. 1-1. (A) TTL logic levels and (B) CMOS logic levels.

used at any combination of voltage levels between ±4 V and ±15 V. In CMOS, illustrated in Fig. 1-1B, ±7 V is used. The voltage levels that represent high and low conditions in CMOS need not be equal. In fact many circuits use a positive voltage (i.e., +12 V), and 0 V for high and low conditions, respectively. Some CMOS digital devices, notably complex function devices, fail to operate properly and predictably if the applied voltage is less than 7 V. These devices sometimes refuse to operate properly on TTL levels of 0 and +5 V despite claims to the contrary.

POSITIVE AND NEGATIVE LOGIC

You may sometimes hear the terms positive and negative logic. These terms tend to confuse the newcomer and mean nothing more than how the high and low logic states are related to voltage levels. In *positive logic* the high is logical-1 and is a positive voltage (i.e., +5 V in the case of TTL). The low, logical-0, is 0 V in TTL. Logical-0 may be a negative voltage in some CMOS circuits.

In *negative logic* these designations are reversed (i.e., high = logical-0 and low =logical-1). In the vast majority of uses positive logic is specified. In fact the descriptive names given to digital IC devices reflect a bias toward positive logic. This potential confusion is why I prefer high/low designations. For the illustrations and truth tables 1/0 is used, but recall that positive logic is implied.

LOGIC FAMILIES

A logic family is a series of IC devices that may be interconnected without interfacing; they use similar technology in their construction. All of the devices within a given family have the same input and output circuits; so direct interconnection is possible.

The only major consideration is whether an output can supply sufficient current to drive all of the inputs that are connected to it. In any given logic family output voltage and current levels, also input voltage and current requirements, are fixed by agreement and defined in terms of *fan-in* and *fan-out*.

The unit used to describe these terms in most cases is the current requirement of a single standard-input at the fixed voltage level. Such an input has a fan-in of one unit. If a particular IC has a fan-out of five, this means that the device can drive five standard inputs. The device, therefore, can supply sufficient current to drive all five inputs satisfactorily. The total fan-in of all devices connected to any output must be equal to or less than the rated fan-out of the output.

The logic families considered are: RTL, DTL, TTL, HTL, ECL, and CMOS. Of these families CMOS and TTL are the most popular today RTL and DTL are obsolete and no longer used in new designs (although much of the older equipment, still in use, contains RTL and DTL devices).

SPEED VERSUS POWER

The principal factors governing the speed, or maximum operating frequency, of a digital IC are the internal resistances and capacitances. If resistances are increased, so that power consumption drops, then the resistance-capacitance time-constant of the device is increased. Long resistance-capacitance time-constants mean slower operating speeds. As a general rule, therefore, higher speed logic-families have high power requirements. CMOS devices, which require very little current (hence are low power), operate well only at 4 or 5 megahertz (MHz) with some devices operating as high as 10 MHz. TTL devices, on the other hand, usually work at 18 or 20 MHz, with some selected devices operating well over 80 MHz.

RTL DEVICES

Resistor-transistor-logic (RTL) is an obsolete logic family that was popular in the early to mid-1960s. Figure 1-2 shows a typical RTL inverter circuit, i.e., a circuit that produces a low output when the input is high and a high output when the input is low.

RTL IC devices use 0 V for logical-0 (low) and +3.6 V for logical-1 (high). If the input of the RTL inverter is grounded (i.e., placed low), then the output voltage is high, which in this case means +3.6 V. If the input voltage is high, the output is 0 V.

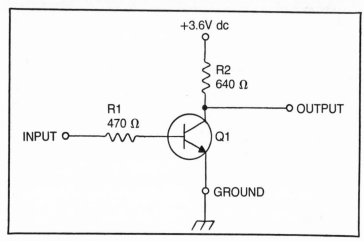

Fig. 1-2. RTL inverter.

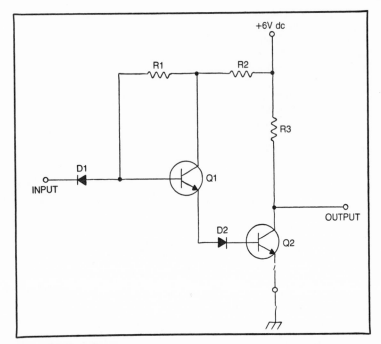

Fig. 1-3. DTL inverter.

RTL devices usually carry type numbers in the UL900 series (mostly 8 and 10 pin metal cans) and MC700 series (mostly 14 pin DIPS).

DTL DEVICES

The next popular IC logic family is diode-transistor-logic (DTL). These devices operate at speeds greater than most RTL devices. Figure 1-3 shows a typical DTL inverter.

When the DTL input is high, diode 1 is reverse-biased. In that condition resistor 1 forward-biases transistor 1, which in turn forward-biases diode 2 and transistor 2. Voltage levels in most digital circuits are selected to *saturate* the transistors; when transistor 2 (Q2) is turned on, it is turned on to full saturation. This means that the output of the inverter, which is the collector of Q2, goes within a few millivolts of ground.

When the input is low, the cathode of diode 1 (D1) is grounded. Since D1 is now forward-biased, the base of Q1 is essentially grounded. Under this condition Q1, D1 and Q2 are reverse-biased. With Q2 cut off, then, the output voltage rises to V_{CC} +.

Most DTL devices carry part numbers in the MC800 and MC900 ranges (Motorola designation).

TTL DEVICES

Probably the most widely used digital IC is the transistor-transistor-logic (TTL) logic family. When most people speak of digital ICs, it is the

TTL family of devices to which they refer. Most TTL devices carry type numbers in the 5400 or 7400 series. Those devices that are in the 5400-series are military equivalents to the 7400-series device (i.e., a 5447 is a 7447 in uniform). The principal difference between the 5400 and 7400 devices is the operating temperature range (−55−+125 degrees C for mil-specified devices).

Figure 1-4 shows the circuit for a typical TTL inverter IC. Like the DTL device, the TTL input acts as a current source, while the output acts as a current sink. The typical TTL input sources 1.8 mA (milliamps) and is low if the voltage is 0-0.8 V, and high if 2.4-5.0 V are applied. Performance at values of input potentials between 0.8 and 2.4 V is not defined; so operation of the devices is unpredictable.

When the TTL input is high, Q1 is cut off; so point A goes high. This condition turns on Q2 forcing point B high and C low. You find, that Q3 is turned on and Q4 is off. This forces the output low. Again, the transistors are operated either totally cutoff or totally saturated (on).

If the input is low, then exactly the opposite situation occurs: Q1 is turned on (forcing point A low), Q3 is off, and Q4 is turned on; i.e., it is connected to V_{CC} +.

TTL devices must have a regulated dc power supply of +4.75-+5.2 V. In fact there are some circuits or combinations of devices that require a more limited range of voltages nearer to +5 V dc. Voltages greater than +5.2 V often result in a high failure-rate of TTL devices.

Some TTL devices are described as being *open-collector*. They are essentially the same as regular TTL devices, except that the output circuit is modified, i.e., Q4 and D2 are missing. An example of an open-collector circuit is shown in Fig. 1-5. These devices require an external 1000-2000 ohm resistor between the output terminal and the 5 V dc power supply line.

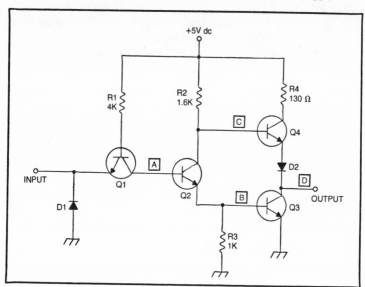

Fig. 1-4. TTL inverter.

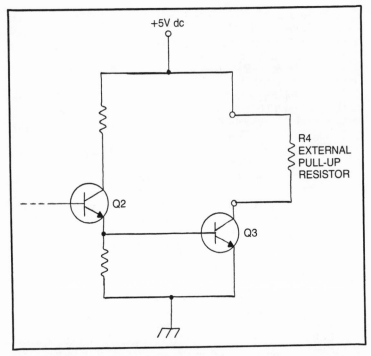

Fig. 1-5. TTL open-collector circuit.

CMOS DEVICES

Complementary metal-oxide semiconductor (CMOS) IC's use field-effect transistors (MOSFET), instead of the PNP or NPN bipolar transistors that are used in other IC logic families. CMOS inputs, therefore, offer very high impedance. Figure 1-6 shows a typical CMOS inverter circuit. Note that this family is called complementary because the output circuit consists of a complementary pair of MOSFET transistors i.e., an n-channel and a p-channel in series.

CMOS devices can use a monopolar power supply, like TTL or DTL, or they can use a bipolar power supply similar to operational amplifiers. When bipolar supplies are used, the positive voltage can be any potential between +4 V and +15 V, while the negative voltage can be −4 V to −15 V. In monopolar cases the V+ can also be +4 to +15 V, while the V− is actually 0 V.

CMOS outputs are not directly TTL compatible, although some specific ICs in the CMOS line are designed to have a TTL output stage (i.e., the 4049 and 4050 devices). These TTL-compatible devices are often used to directly interface CMOS and TTL devices.

Figures 1-7 and 1-8 show the equivalent circuits for a CMOS inverter in both possible input conditions (i.e., input high and input low). A p-channel MOSFET turns on when the gate is low, while the n-channel device turns on when the gate is high.

Figure 1-7 shows the situation when the input is low. In this case Q1 has a very low (i.e., 200 ohm) channel resistance. The output is equivalent to a 200-ohm resistor to the positive-voltage power-supply line.

In Fig. 1-8 you see the situation when the input is high. Q2 now has a very high channel resistance, and Q1 has a very low channel resistance (again, about 200 ohm). In this case the output looks like a 200-ohm resistance to ground; so the output is low.

The high/low or low/high output transition in a CMOS device occurs at a point when the input voltage is midway between the positive and negative voltages. If the negative and positive voltages are not equal, the transition occurs at a potential of $\frac{1}{2}((V+)-(V-))$. If, on the other hand, negative and positive voltages are equal, the transition occurs at 0 V. If the negative-voltage potential is 0 V, the transition occurs at $(V+)/2$.

The CMOS output stage always looks like a high and low resistor in series across the power supply (reexamine Figs. 1-7 and 1-8);so negligible current is drawn from the power supply (it sees a low resistance load) when the input voltage is at the transition point. The overall current drain, therefore, is very small.

But CMOS devices do have a problem: they contain MOSFETs; so they are sensitive to static electricity. All A-series CMOS devices (e.g., 4001A) have this problem, but it is less severe in B-series (e.g., 4001B) devices. The B-series has built-in diode gate-protection to bypass high static potentials around the sensitive gate structure. Nonetheless, they should be handled with care.

HTL DEVICES

Noise pulses are often seen by logic circuits as valid input pulses. This problem is especially bothersome in high speed TTL devices that are normally able to pass high frequency, short duration, pulses. The solution in noisy environments is to use a digital-IC logic family that requires a high

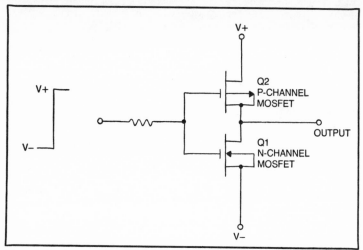

Fig. 1-6. CMOS inverter.

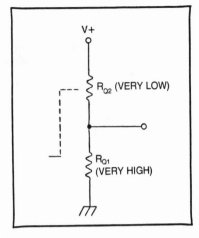

Fig. 1-7. Circuit model for low input.

input-voltage to trigger. CMOS, operated at high negative and positive-voltage values, meets this requirement, but an older, bipolar, *high threshold logic* (HTL) can also be used (Fig. 1-9).

HTL (also called high noise immunity logic, or HNIL), uses positive voltages of 12 or 15 V, depending upon the series. As a result, the logic levels are also high; so it requires a bigger noise pulse to cause trouble.

EMITTER-COUPLED LOGIC

Up until now I have talked about saturated logic families, i.e., the transistors in the ICs are either all the way on or all the way off (cutoff or saturated). *Emitter-coupled logic* (ECL) is called an *AC* logic family because the transistors are operated in a nonsaturated mode. As a consequence, ECL devices are capable of very fast operation. Most commonplace ECL devices can operate at 80 or 120 MHz, while some costly, special purpose, devices can operate at over 1 GHz (thats 1000 MHz!).

The usual *prescaler* for a digital frequency counter is nothing more than an ECL frequency divider that divides the 500 MHz input signal down to 50 MHz.

It is necessary to use VHF/UHF circuit design and layout techniques when working with ECL devices. The frequencies are, after all, in the VHF and UHF ranges.

GATES

A digital electronic *gate* is a circuit that either passes a signal or refuses to pass a signal, according to well-defined rules. The basic types of digital electronic gates are NOT, OR, AND, NOR, NAND, and Exclusive-OR (also called XOR). In the following paragraphs I discuss all of these basic gates.

NOT Gates (Inverters)

NOT gates, also called inverters, produce an output that is the opposite of the input signal. Recall that digital circuits respond only to high and low voltage levels. In an inverter circuit, therefore, the output is high when the input is low, and low when the input is high.

The circuit symbol for the inverter is shown in Fig. 1-10A Note that any digital symbol with a circle on the output produces an inverted output. Similarly, if one or more inputs have a circle, then they are inverted. The rules for the operation of the inverter are:

● A high on the input produces a low output.
● A low on the input produces a high output.

OR Gates

An OR gate passes a signal to the output if either input is high. The symbol for an OR gate is shown in Fig. 1-10B, while the truth table is given in Table 1-1B. The truth table shows the rules of operation for the gate. These are:

● If both inputs A and B are low, the output is low.
● If either input A or B are high, the output is high.
● If both inputs A and B are high, the output is high.

AND Gates

The AND gate is the opposite of the OR gate. The AND gate produces a high output only when both inputs are also high. The circuit symbol for the AND gate is given in Fig. 1-10C, and the truth table is shown in Table 1-1C. The rules for the operation of the AND gate are as follows:

● If both inputs A and B are low, then the output is low.
● If either input A or B is low, then the output is low.
● If both inputs A and B are high, then the output is high.

NOR Gates

The NOR gate is a combination of a NOT gate (inverter) and an OR gate, hence the designation NOR means "not OR." It is, therefore, an OR gate with an inverted output. The NOR gate is, in fact, sometimes represented in text books as an OR gate with an inverter following. The NOR

Fig. 1-8. Circuit for high input.

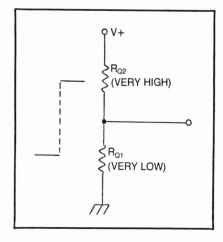

9

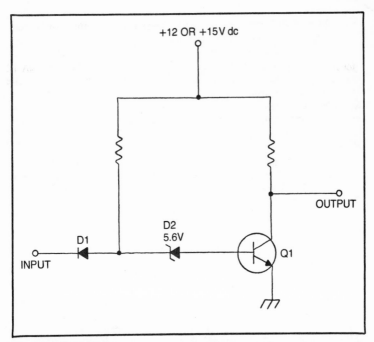

+12 OR +15V dc

OUTPUT

D2
5.6V

D1

INPUT

Q1

Fig. 1-9. HTL inverter.

gate symbol, shown in Fig. 1-10D, is an OR gate symbol with the circle denoting inversion at the output. The truth table for the NOR gate is shown in Table 1-1D and is also summarized below:

- If both inputs A and B are low, then the output is high.
- If either A or B input is high, then the output is low.
- If both A and B inputs are high, then the output is low.

NAND Gates

The NAND gate is a NOT-AND gate, i.e., an AND gate followed by an inverter. The symbol for the NAND gate is shown in Fig. 1-10E. This symbol is the AND gate symbol with the circle at the output to denote inversion.

The truth table for the NAND gate is shown in Table 1-1E. The rules are presented in summary below:

- If both A and B inputs are low, the output is high.
- If either input A or B is low, the output is high.
- If both A and B are high, the output is low.

TTL AND CMOS EXAMPLES

Earlier in this chapter, I introduced several different families of digital-logic ICs. Several of these are considered obsolete and are not covered further. The TTL and CMOS families, however, are very much alive and form the basis of most digital design today.

TTL/CMOS NAND Gates

In the TTL IC family the most popular NAND gate is the 7400 (see Fig. 1-11). This device contains four two-input NAND gates, and usually sells for less than 25 cents, or around 6 cents per gate. Each of the four NAND gates in the 7400 package is an independent entity, but shares a common power supply and ground connection (pins 14 and 7, respectively).

The 7401 is similar to the 7400, however, the pin-outs are somewhat different, and it is an open-collector device. This means that pull-up resistors are needed, i.e., one 2- 4-K ohm resistor from each output to the +5 V line.

The 7403 is also an open collector, but uses exactly the same pin-outs as the 7400. Of these three devices, the 7400 is by far the most popular.

The 7430 is an eight-input NAND gate (one per 14-pin DIP package). The 7430 device, therefore, has eight distinct inputs. All eight must be high before the output drops low. If any one of the eight inputs remains low, then the output stays high. Since most microcomputers today are eight-bit machines, the 7430 is often used as an address or I/O-port decoder.

The 7410 and 7420 are three and four-input TTL NAND gates, respectively.

In the CMOS line there are several different types of NAND gates. The 4011 is a quad two-input NAND gate, reminiscent of the 7400. The current required for the CMOS device, however, is a lot lower than that required for the equivalent TTL.

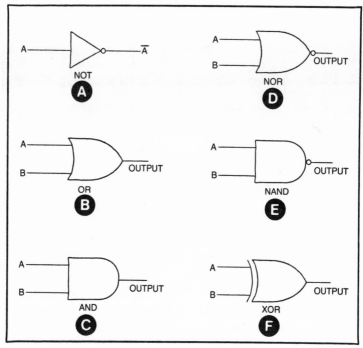

Fig. 1-10. Digital logic symbols for gates.

Table 1-1. Truth Tables for the Gates of Fig. 1-10.

A. NOT

INPUT	OUTPUT
1	0
0	1

B. OR

INPUT A	INPUT B	OUTPUT
0	0	0
0	1	1
1	0	1
1	1	1

C. AND

INPUT A	INPUT B	OUTPUT
0	0	0
0	1	0
1	0	0
1	1	1

D. NOR

INPUT A	INPUT B	OUTPUT
0	0	1
0	1	0
1	0	0
1	1	0

E. NAND

INPUT A	INPUT B	OUTPUT
0	0	1
0	1	1
1	0	1
1	1	0

F. EXCLUSIVE OR (XOR)

INPUT A	INPUT B	OUTPUT
0	0	0
0	1	1
1	0	1
1	1	0

The 4012 device is a dual four-input NAND gate. All four inputs of either gate must be high for its output to be low.

The 4023 device is a triple three-input NAND gate, while the 4068 is an eight-input NAND gate that is reminiscent of the TTL 7430 device.

TTL/CMOS NOR Gates

The 7402 TTL NOR gate is by far the most common example from the TTL line. It is almost as popular as the 7400. The pin-outs for the 7402 are shown in Fig. 1-12 (see Fig. 1-11 for comparison to the pin-outs to the 7400). Note that the pin-outs of the 7400 and 7402 are as different as their logic responses.

FLIP-FLOPS

All of the digital circuits I have discussed so far have operated in a transient manner. Once a pulse or any other input signal passes, the output state reverts back to its previous condition. Gates and inverters do not have any memory; so once the input passes, the resulting output also passes.

A *flip-flop* is a circuit that is capable of storing a single bit (i.e., a binary digit, either 1 or 0) of digital data. It remembers an input condition and holds the output after the data passes. There are various different types of flip-flop circuits, and they all operate on slightly different sets of rules. But, one thing that they all have in common is the ability to store a single data bit.

All common flip-flops can be made from various combinations of the basic AND, OR, NAND, NOT, NOR and XOR gates. The NAND, NOR, and NOT gates are used particularly often. Except for the two most simple flip-flops presented here, most electronic circuits use IC flip-flops instead of actual IC gates. It is simply too costly to make flip-flops from IC gates when the same manufacturers do all of the interconnection and offer the various flip-flops premade in IC form.

Reset-Set (RS) Flip-Flop

One of the simplest flip-flop circuits is the *reset-set,* or *RS,* flip-flop. Some textbooks call this type of circuit a *set-reset,* or *SR,* flip-flop.

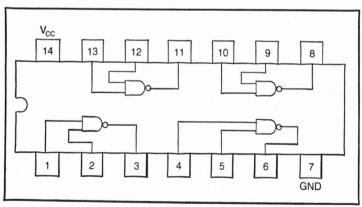

Fig. 1-11. 7400 quad two-input NAND gate.

13

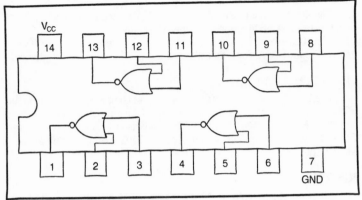

Fig. 1-12. 7402 quad two-input 7402 NOR gate.

The RS flip-flop can be made from either two NAND gates or two NOR gates, although note that the operation of the two versions is slightly different.

Figure 1-13 shows the circuit for RS flip-flop made from a pair of NAND gates (such as the TTL 7400 device, which contains four two-input NAND-gate sections).

There are two inputs required on the RS flip-flop; set (S) and reset (R). Also, there are usually two output terminals, which are complementary: Q and not-Q. *Complementary* means that one is low if the other is high. For example, when the Q output is high, then the not-Q is low. When the Q output is low, the not-Q is high.

The inputs of the NAND version of the RS flip-flop are active-low. Whenever you see an input that is designated as a not-input, or that has a bar over its symbol (i.e., $\overline{R}$), or that has a circle in the schematic diagram; it is an active-low input terminal. The circuit action of an active-low input occurs when the terminal is brought low. An example of the circled inputs as they are used in schematics is shown in Fig. 1-15, while the normal symbol for the RS flip-flop is shown in Fig. 1-14.

In most cases the absence of a bar over the letter, or of a circle at the input terminal in a drawing, indicates that the input is active-high. You sometimes see the exception when the RS flip-flop of Fig. 1-13 is shown as a square (similar to Fig. 1-14, but without the bars over the letters).

A momentary low on the set input of the NAND gate RS flip-flop causes the outputs to go to Q high and not-Q to low. Note that the term set usually means Q=high and not-Q=low. Reset indicates just the opposite: Q=low and not-Q=high. The flip-flop is said to have *memory* (and, indeed, solid-state computer memory devices use arrays of flip-flops); so the outputs stay in the set condition unless a reset pulse is applied to the R input.

The reset function is obtained by momentarily bringing the reset input low. This forces the Q output low and the not-Q output high.

The rules for operating the NAND-logic RS flip-flop are summarized in the truth table shown in Table 1-2. This truth table also lists two additional conditions. One of these is the condition in which both set and reset inputs

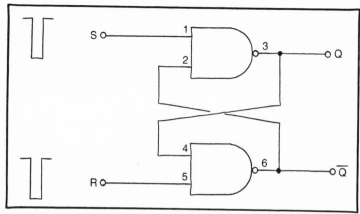

Fig. 1-13. NAND gate RS flip-flop.

are brought low simultaneously. This is a disallowed state, and the circuit does not know what to do; the output state is unpredictable. In the other condition both inputs are simultaneously high. In this condition you find that there is no change in the output state. The RS flip-flop simply remains in the condition present when the inputs were made high.

A NOR-logic version of the RS flip-flop is shown in Fig. 1-16. This circuit may be constructed from TTL 7402 NOR gates. Like the 7400 device, the 7402 contains four, independent, two-input gates (in this case, the NOR variety). The circuit in Fig. 1-16 performs differently from the NAND-logic version of Fig. 1-13. There are certain similarities, but a slightly different set of operating rules prevail.

The rules governing the NOR-logic RS flip-flop are summarized in the truth table of Table 1-3, but let's go over them briefly here:

●If both inputs are low, there is no change in the output stage.

● If both inputs are simultaneously high, there is a disallowed state and the output condition is unpredictable.

●If the set input is made high momentarily, the output condition is Q=high and not-Q=low.

●If the reset input is made high momentarily, the output condition is Q=low and not-Q=high.

Note the principal difference between the two forms of RS flip-flop (examine the truth tables in Table 1-2 and 1-3 again). The NAND-logic RS flip-flop has active-low inputs, while the NOR-logic RS flip-flop has active-high inputs.

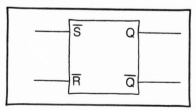

Fig. 1-14. Normal block diagram symbol.

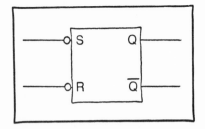

Fig. 1-15. Block diagram symbol using circles, an alternate.

Clocked RS Flip-Flops

You can sometimes get into trouble with flip-flops that are too simple. You see, for example, electronic versions of the old fashioned relay race. In this classic problem with digital circuits, two relays may have slightly different actuation times. If the time difference causes them to operate out of sync, sometimes catastrophic results occur. Many of these problems are solved in digital electronics by using *clocked,* or synchronous, operation. In the case of the RS flip-flop, you get clocked operation by using the *master-slave* flip-flop, also called the *clocked RS flip-flop.*

The purpose of the *clock* (a train of pulses) is to synchronize the changes in the output condition by allowing them to occur only at certain times: during, or immediately following, a clock pulse. Most large-scale digital circuits use synchronous operation in order to keep things straight.

There are two basic forms of clocking used in RS flip-flops: *level triggered* and *edge triggered.*

A level-triggered flip-flop is one in which the output state changes in response to conditions on the inputs only when the clock input is either high or low (depending upon the type). Some level-triggered circuits require the clock pulse to be low for it to be active; the more common types require the clock pulse to be high.

An edge-triggered flip-flop allows state changes only during one of the two transitions of the clock pulse. The pulse must be in the process of going from low-to-high, or from high-to-low (again, depending upon type). A positive edge-triggered flip-flop, therefore, allows output changes to occur only on the positive-going transition (low-to-high) of the clock pulse. A

Table 1-2. Truth Table for Figs. 1-13–1-15.

S	R	Q	$\overline{Q}$
0	0	(DISALLOWED)	
0	1	1	0
1	0	0	1
1	1	(NO CHANGE)	

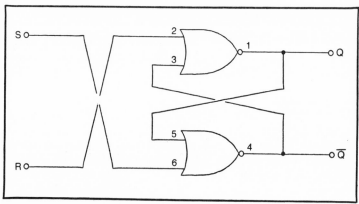

Fig. 1-16. NOR-gate flip-flop.

negative edge-triggered flip-flop allows output transitions only on the negative-going (high-to-low) transition of the clock pulse.

It is important to remember the differences between these two types of triggering; so I'll reiterate them:

Level triggering means that changes can take place only during the time when the clock pulse is active, i.e., either high (positive level-triggered) or low (negative level-triggered).

Edge triggering means that output changes can take place only during the transition period of the clock pulse. A positive edge-triggered flip-flop changes only on the low-to-high transition, while a negative edge-triggered flip-flop wants to see the negative-going, or high-to-low, transition.

An example of a simple level-triggered, clocked, RS flip-flop is shown in Fig. 1-18. The main flip-flop is the same as the circuit in Fig. 1-13; it is shown here in block form for the sake of simplicity. The S and R inputs are controlled by a pair of NAND gates. When the clock pulse is low, both inputs of the RS flip-flop section (i.e., points A and B) see a high; so no changes can take place.

Table 1-3. Truth Table for NOR-Gate Flip-Flop.

S	R	Q	$\overline{Q}$
0	0	(NO CHANGE)	
0	1	0	1
1	0	1	0
1	1	(DISALLOWED)	

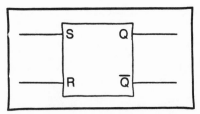

Fig. 1-17. Symbol for NOR-gate flip-flops.

But, when the clock input goes high, the levels at points A and B (i.e., the S and R inputs of the flip-flop section) are controlled by the other inputs of the NAND gates. These inputs are used as the S and R inputs of the clocked flip-flop. If you wish to double-check this, review the operation of the NAND gates in this chapter.

Master-Slave Flip-Flops

The use of clocking helps a great deal in taming the RS flip-flop. But several problems, again electronic versions of the old relay-race problem, can still pop up. Most of these are solved by using a slightly different approach, the so-called master-slave flip-flop. An example of the master-slave flip-flop is shown in Fig. 1-20. This circuit allows only one output state change per clock pulse (the clocked RS flip-flop allows continuous output-state changes as long as the clock input is active).

The master-slave flip-flop of Fig. 1-20 uses the clocked RS flip-flops of the previous example connected in cascade. The inverter shown in Fig. 1-20 allows you to drive the clock inputs of the two clocked-RS flip-flops out of phase with each other.

The clocked-RS flip-flop can change its output state only when the clock input is high, and then only in response to conditions on the R and S inputs. In the master-slave flip-flop, the main clock is kept high; so flip-flop 2 is active and flip-flop 1 is inactive.

When a clock pulse is applied, in this case a negative transition, flip-flop 1 becomes active, and flip-flop 2 becomes inactive. Note that the effect of the inverter is to make the clock input of flip-flop 1 high at this time. Any commands placed on the S and R inputs cause changes in the output of flip-flop 1 (i.e., points A and B in Fig. 1-20).

Because flip-flop 2 is inactive at this time (its clock input is low), changes at A and B are not yet reflected at its Q and not-Q outputs. Once the clock pulse has evaporated, the clock input of flip-flop 2 goes high again; so

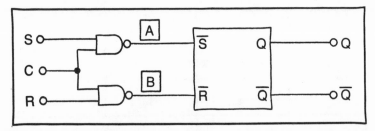

Fig. 1-18. Circuit of the clocked-RS flip-flop.

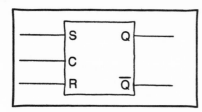

Fig. 1-19. Symbol for the clocked-RS flip-flop.

the changes that took place on A and B can be transferred to action at the Q and not-Q outputs.

The synchronization occurs by keeping flip-flop 2 inactive when the low input stage is being set. Then flip-flop 1 is rendered inactive (forbidding further S and R input changes from affecting the output), while the data is transferred to flip-flop 2. This part of the sequence is called a load-transfer operation.

ADDITIONAL TYPES OF FLIP-FLOPS

So far I have considered two versions of the RS flip-flop (NAND-logic and NOR-logic) and two flip-flops that are derivative of the RS circuits, i.e., the clocked-RS flip-flop and the master-slave flip-flop. In the following sections I consider some more complex types of flip-flop: type-T, J-K, and type-D flip-flops. The latter circuit, the type-D, is also called a latch circuit.

Type-T Flip-Flops

The type-T flip-flop (also called the *toggle flip-flop*) is shown in Fig. 1-21. This flip-flop circuit can be constructed by providing feedback connections (as shown) around an ordinary master-slave flip-flop. The master-slave flip-flop is constructed from a pair of RS flip-flops and an inverter stage. Note that the Q output is fed back to the reset input, and the not-Q output is fed back to the set input.

The type-T flip-flop functions as a binary divider, that is, the output signal has a frequency that is one-half (i.e., divided by two) of the input signal. The timing diagram for this circuit is shown in Fig. 1-22. Note that the Q output changes state only on negative-going transitions (i.e., high-to-low) of the clock pulse. At the first negative transition, the Q output snaps high and remains high until the clock input sees another negative transition. This condition occurs at pulse 2, at which time the Q output goes low again.

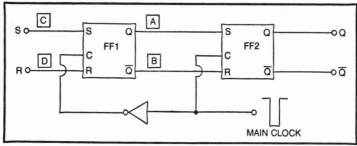

Fig. 1-20. Clocked flip-flop, type-T.

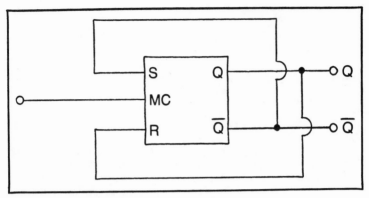

Fig. 1-21. Type-T flip-flop connection for binary division.

This is binary division of the input frequency; one output pulse is produced for each two input pulses.

There are sometimes differences found in terminal designations from one text or spec sheet to another. In Fig. 1-21, for example, I label the clock input MC for main clock. But, you are also likely to see T for toggle, or C for clock.

J-K Flip-Flop

One of the most useful, and perhaps most common, forms of clocked flip-flops is the J-K flip-flop. There are several advantages to the typical J-K flip-flop: (a) there are no invalid or disallowed states in the clocked mode, (b) it can cause the outputs to complement, and (c) in some IC versions it can provide nonclocked operation.

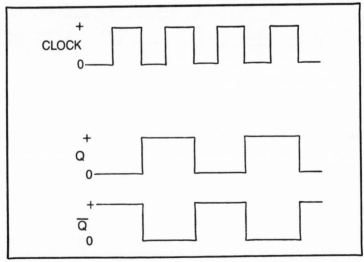

Fig. 1-22. Timing waveform of type-T flip-flop.

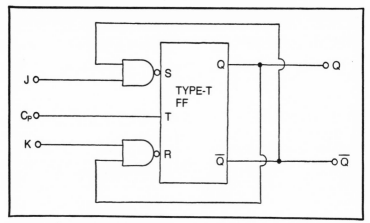

Fig. 1-23. Circuit for J-K flip-flop.

Figure 1-23 shows one of several popular ways to represent the J-K flip-flop. In this case, you see that it is a type-T flip-flop with the feedback to the set and reset inputs controlled by a pair of two-input AND gates. One input from each gate accepts the feedback lines, while the remaining inputs of the gates are used to form the J and K inputs of the flip-flop, respectively.

Figure 1-24 shows the circuit symbol for a J-K flip-flop. Not all versions of the J-K have the direct-mode input (*preset* and *clear*). However, preset and clear make it a more useful device. The preset input may also be called a direct-set input, and the preclear input called a direct-clear input.

Direct Mode Operation. The operation of the J-K flip-flops in the direct mode is very simple, and it is independent of conditions applied to the J and K inputs. The direct mode is controlled only by conditions on the preset and preclear input terminals. The rules are summarized in Table 1-5.

Direct mode input is active when low, so the only disallowed state occurs when both inputs are simultaneously low.

If the preset input is low, and the preclear input is high, then the outputs immediately go to a condition where Q is high and not-Q is low.

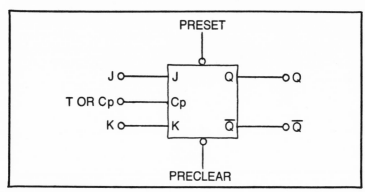

Fig. 1-24. Circuit symbol for J-K flip-flop.

Table 1-4. Timing Diagram for Clocked Operation of J-K.

J	K	CLOCK	Q	$\overline{Q}$
0	0		(NO CHANGES)	
0	1		0	1
1	0		1	0
1	1		BINARY DIVISION	

If the preclear input is made low, and preset input is high, then the outputs go to a state where Q is low and not-Q is high.

It is a general rule, when dealing with flip-flops of any type, that set or preset operations make the Q output high and the not-Q output low; while clear or reset operations work in just the opposite manner (i.e., Q low and not-Q high).

If both preset and preclear inputs are made high, then the flip-flop is ready for normal clocked-operation.

Clocked Operation. Whenever the preset and preclear inputs are simultaneously high, the J-K operates in the clocked mode. The rules for clocked operation are summarized in Table 1-4.

Like the type-T flip-flop, the J-K flip-flop (in the clocked mode) responds on the negative-going transition of the clock pulse. No output

Table 1-5. Timing Diagram for Nonclocked Operation of J-K.

PRESET	CLEAR	CLOCK	Q	$\overline{Q}$
0	0	(DOESN'T CARE)	(DISALLOWED)	
0	1		1	0
1	0		0	1
1	1		(CLOCKED OPERATION)	

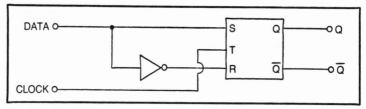

Fig. 1-25. Type-D flip-flop circuit.

changes occur, regardless of changes at the J and K inputs— until one of these negative-going clock-pulse transitions is seen. The outputs then respond according to the J-K input conditions. The rules for clocked operation are as follows:

●If both J and K are low, the flip-flop is inert and does nothing. No changes occur in the outputs.

●If J is low and K is high, the clocking makes Q low and not-Q high.

●If J is high and K is low, the clock-pulse transition makes Q high and not-Q low.

●If both J and K are high, the J-K flip-flop behaves much like a type-T flip-flop; clocking complements the outputs. This means that negative-going clock-pulse transitions force the outputs to go to the opposite state. The output waveform of the J-K flip-flop is then identical to the output waveform of the type-T flip-flop given in Fig. 1-22.

Type-D Flip-Flop

The type-D flip-flop circuit is shown in Fig. 1-25; an equivalent circuit is shown in Fig. 1-26.

The equivalent circuit consists of a clocked-RS flip-flop in which the set and reset inputs are fed by the same signal, but are 180 degrees out of phase with each other (i.e., complementary input). An inverter between the S and R lines accomplishes this neat trick.

The common line to the RS-inverter is called the data, or D, input instead of R and S. This input is usually labeled D on schematics.

The rule for operation of the type-D flip-flop is very simple: data appearing on the input is transferred to the Q output only when the clock line is high.

●If the clock line is high, the output follows changes in the input signal (i.e., changes on the data input). When the data-input line goes high, the output

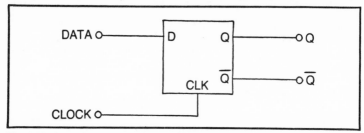

Fig. 1-26. An equivalent circuit for the type-D flip-flop.

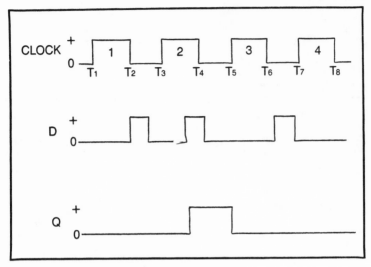

Fig. 1-27. Typical timing diagram for type-D flip-flop.

goes high. Similarly, when the D-input line goes low, the output follows by also going low.

●If the clock line is low, then the output retains the last data that existed on the data-input line at the instant the clock line dropped low.

These rules can also be seen in the timing diagram of Fig. 1-27. Read the description below, keeping in mind the two rules given above:

a. When the first clock pulse arrives (T1-T2), the data-input line is low; so the Q output goes low. (Internal timing in a microcomputer is kept by clock-pulse cycles; a complete clock-pulse cycle is a T-state, designated by T).

b. During interval T2-T3, the data input goes high; but since no clock pulse is present, it cannot affect the output conditions.

c. At the beginning of interval T3-T4, clock pulse 2 is high, but the data input is low. The output, therefore, must remain low.

d. About midway through clock pulse 2, however, the data input goes high, forcing the Q output to also go high.

e. The Q output stays high even after clock pulse 2 goes low.

f. At the onset of clock pulse 3, the data input is low; so the Q output drops low also.

g. The pulse on the data-input line during the interval T6-T7 cannot affect the Q output because the clock is low.

The so-called data latch is a special case of the type-D flip-flop. This device is used in digital readout circuits (i.e., in frequency counters) to hold current data until the new data is updated and ready for display. This gives the illusion that the data is updated instantaneously. In most cases the clock input is called a strobe input. Data at the input is transferred to the outputs only when the strobe line is high. The idea is to momentarily bring the strobe line high when the data at the input is valid, and then let the strobe line go low again until the next new data is ready.

24

MULTIVIBRATORS

So far, I have discussed the various digital-IC logic-families, assorted types of gates, and flip-flops. Now let's turn to the topic of *multivibrators*.

A multivibrator is basically a pulse-producing circuit. There are three basic forms of multivibrator: *monostable, bistable* and *astable*. It takes very little imagination to detect that these designations refer to the possible output states for each circuit.

The monostable multivibrator has only one stable state (usually the state in which Q=low—but not always). Triggering the monostable multivibrator causes Q to go high for a time, but since this is not a stable state Q drops low again when a predetermined time period has elapsed.

Monostable multivibrators are also called one-shot circuits, and also (erroneously, albeit graphically) pulse stretcher circuits. The latter label is a misnomer because the circuit does not actually stretch a pulse, but generates a new pulse that has a longer period.

The bistable multivibrator has two stable states. It can remain in either state (i.e., Q=low or Q=high) indefinitely. The RS flip-flop is an example of a bistable multivibrator.

The astable multivibrator has no stable states. It is incapable of remaining in either Q low or Q high states. The Q output of the astable multivibrator flips back and forth between the high and low states, producing a square-wave pulse-train output. For this reason the astable circuit is usually used to produce the clock pulse found in digital circuits.

There are several ways to produce each of these types of multivibrator. Let's examine a few circuits built from discrete gates and the integrated circuits. Some IC devices, like the 555 timer, operate in either the monostable or astable modes. Here, I won't consider the circuits in which discrete transistors and resistors form the multivibrator.

When people speak of bistable multivibrators they are actually talking about the RS flip-flop. The RS flip-flop can remain in either Q=low or Q=high states. These conditions only change when an input signal commands the circuit to change. It can remain in either state indefinitely.

The monostable multivibrator, or one-shot, has only one stable state. In most circuits the stable state is Q=low. When the input of the monostable is triggered, the output snaps high for a certain period of time and then drops low again. The monostable multivibrator, then, produces one output pulse for each pulse received at the trigger input. This is why the monostable multivibrator is sometimes called the one-shot.

There are a number of reasons why you might want a one-out-for-one-in circuit. One of the most common is to stretch pulses. A very rapid input pulse, even in the nanosecond range, can be used to trigger monostable circuits that produce output-pulse periods from nanoseconds to days. The duration of the output pulse is usually much longer than the duration of the input trigger-pulse. In so-called pulse-stretcher circuit-applications, the output of the one-shot is used to substitute for the shorter trigger-pulse.

Most monostable multivibrators do not respond to further input trigger-pulses until the period of the output pulse has "timed out," i.e., the output has returned to its stable state. Monostables that do not respond to further trigger-commands until the output duration has expired are called nonretriggerable monostables.

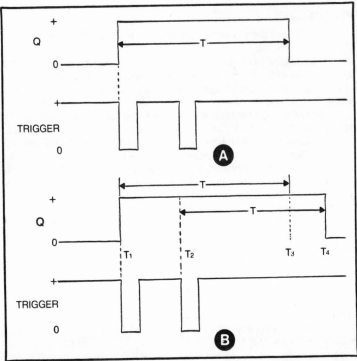

Fig. 1-28. Timing diagrams for monostable multivibrators, nonretriggerable (A), and retriggerable (B).

Some one-shot circuits are *retriggerable*, meaning that they respond to further input trigger-commands while the one-shot is in the unstable state, i.e., before it has timed out. Consider Fig. 1-28 to see how this might work. Figure 1-28A shows the operation of the regular nonretriggerable one-shot multivibrator. The first trigger-pulse causes the output to go high, and it remains high for period T. A second trigger-pulse has no affect of the one-shot because it occurs before T expires.

Now consider Fig. 1-28B. This is a timing diagram for the retriggerable monostable multivibrator. The output goes high when the first pulse arrives. But, before T expires a second trigger pulse is received. This second pulse causes the one-shot to retrigger; so the output remains high for an additional period T. Note that the total duration of the high state is not 2T, but T plus the portion of the first period that expired prior to the second trigger (i.e., $T + (T_2 - T_1)$).

An example of a monostable multivibrator built from a CMOS type-D flip-flop is shown in Fig. 1-29. Recall the rules for the type-D flip-flop: (1) when D is high, a high is transferred to the Q output when the clock line goes high, and (2) when the clear line goes high the Q output is forced low.

The operation of the one-shot circuit in Fig. 1-29, is as follows:
1. When the circuit is at rest, Q is low and any charge on capacitor 1 is drained off through diode 1.

2. When a trigger pulse is received by the clock input, Q goes high. When Q is high, capacitor 1 charges through resistor 1.

3. When capacitor 1 has charged to a potential of approximately 2 V, the CLEAR input thinks it is high; so the flip-flop forces Q low.

4. The period that Q was high, i.e., the period of the one-shot, is determined by the time constant of resistance-capacitance 1, the potentials of the Q output, and the point at which the CLEAR input thinks that it is high instead of low.

The circuit in Fig. 1-29A uses a diode (D1) across the timing resistor (R1) to discharge the capacitor (C1) during the period when Q is low. This diode i not strictly necessary, but serves to speed up the circuit considerably. Without D1 the charge on the capacitor bleeds through the resistor. This requires another resistance-capacitance1 time-constant before the voltage across C1 discharges enough to permit retriggering of the one-shot. The purpose of D1 is to rapidly discharge C1 so that retriggering can occur almost immediately after Q drops low (see the waveform in Fig. 1-30B).

But the use of D1 creates a little problem. The charge potential across C1 cannot drop lower than the function potential of the diode (200 to 300 millivolts in germanium types and 600 to 700 millivolts for silicon types). Figure 1-31 shows the circuit for a modified version that uses a switching transistor (Q1) to discharge C1. The base of transistor Q1 is driven by the not-Q output.

SHIFT REGISTERS

A flip-flop is able to strobe a single bit of digital data. When two or more flip-flops are organized to store multiple bits of data, they constitute a *register*. Most registers are merely specially-connected arrays of flip-flops.

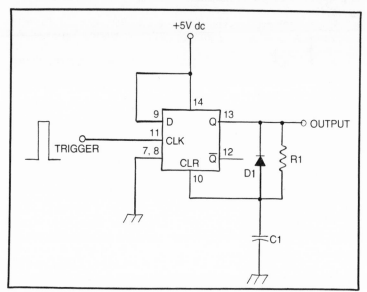

Fig. 1-29. CMOS 4013 type-D flip-flop as a monostable multivibrator circuit.

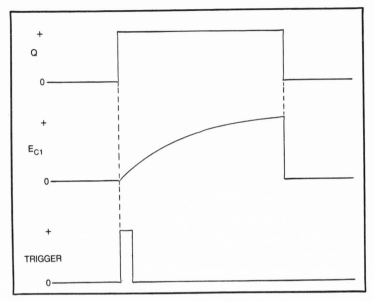

Fig. 1-30. Timing waveforms of monostable multivibrator.

There are several different circuit configurations that are called registers. They are classified by the method of which data input and output to and from the register. For example, *serial-in/serial-out* (SISO), *serial-in/parallel-out* (SIPO), *parallel-in/parallel-out* (PIPO), and *parallel-in/serial-out* (PISO).

Figure 1-32 represents both SISO and SIPO shift-registers. The only significant difference is the parallel output lines on the SIPO register are absent on the SISO register.

The SIPO shift-register consists of a cascade chain of type-D flip-flops that have their clock lines connected. Recall the rules for type-D flip-flops: data can be transferred from the input to the Q output only when the clock input is high. The input can change at will; the output remains the same—as long as the clock line is low. But, if the clock line goes high, then Q output follows the data input. The Q output retains the last valid data that is present before the clock drops low again.

This rule can be applied to the situation shown in Fig. 1-33 which shows the transmission of a single bit of data from left to right through a SISO shift-register.

At the occurrance of the first clock-pulse, the input line is high. This point is the data-input line flip-flop 1; so a high, which is applied to the data input of the second flip-flop, remains after the clock pulse disappears.

When the second clock-pulse arrives, flip-flop 2 sees a high on its data input, and flip-flop 1 sees a low on its data input. This situation causes a low at Q1 and a high at Q2.

The third clock pulse sees a low condition of the data inputs of flip-flop 1 and flip-flop 2, and a high at the input of flip-flop 3. The third clock-pulse, then, causes Q1 and Q2 to be low and Q3 to be high.

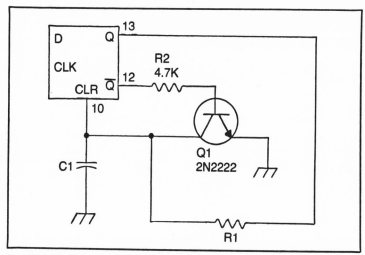

Fig. 1-31. Modifying the circuit for retriggerable operation.

Note that the SISO input remains low after the initial high during clock-pulse 1. This means that the single high condition is propagated through the entire SISO shift register—one stage at a time. The high bit shifts position one flip-flop to the right each time a clock pulse arrives.

If the data at the input changes, the bit pattern at that input is propagated through the shift register.

The shift register in Fig. 1-32 is a five-bit, or five-stage, register (any bit-length can be selected). On the sixth clock-pulse, therefore, the high is propagated out of the register; so all flip-flops are now low.

The SISO shift register can be made into a SIPO device by adding parallel output lines at Q1, Q2, Q3, Q4, and Q5.

One use for the SIPO register is serial-to-parallel binary-code conversion. For economic reasons digital data is usually transmitted as a serial

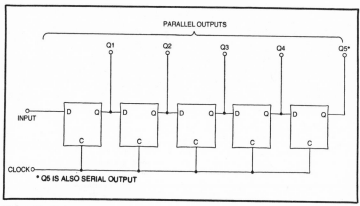

Fig. 1-32. Shift register.

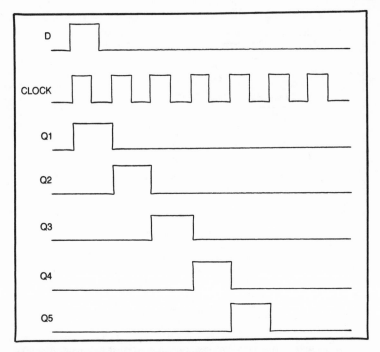

Fig. 1-33. Timing diagram for shift register.

stream of bits, i.e., the bits of the digital word are sent over a communications link. But, most computers and other digital instruments use a parallel form of data entry. Parallel data transfer is more expensive, but is considerably faster than serial transmission. If, for example, you have an eight-bit system, you need an eight-stage SIPO shift-register to convert the serial code to parallel form. The code is entered into the SIPO register one bit at a time. After eight clock-pulses the first bit appears at Q8 and the last bit at Q1.

Parallel-entry shift-registers are faster to load than serial-input shift-registers. This is because a single bit can be changed, if necessary. To change a single bit of data in the serial type requires you to ripple through the entire contents.

There are two basic forms of parallel data-entry: *parallel* and *jam.*

In parallel entry, shown in the partial schematic of Fig. 1-34, the register must first be cleared (i.e., all bits set to zero) by bringing the reset line momentarily low. The data that is applied to inputs bits 1-*n* can be loaded into the register by momentarily bringing the set line high.

The jam-entry circuit of Fig. 1-35 is able to load data from bits 1-*n* onto the other inputs. While this may not look superior at first glance, it is because IC shift-registers using this technique have internal inverter stages at the complementary inputs. These inverters have their inputs connected to the noncomplemented inputs; so the outside user never sees the complementing process.

A recirculating shift-register is shown in Fig. 1-36. Since the output of a serial shift-register allows the outside world to see only one bit at a time, you must empty the entire contents of the shift register in order to read these contents. Ordinarily that would destroy the data, because the input would be either high or low during the entire operation. A single read operation would fill the register with all ones or zeros. The recirculating shift register connects the output (serial output) back to the input; so a read operation automatically rewrites the data back into the shift register.

DIGITAL COUNTERS

A *digital counter* is a device or circuit that operates as a frequency divider. The most basic form of digital counter is the J-K flip-flop connected with the J and K inputs tied high (i.e., placed in the clocked mode). This produces one output pulse for every two input pulses. It is a binary, or divide-by-two, counter.

These fancy digital-frequency period-counters are nothing more than digital divide-by-ten counters connected so that the binary- coded output is converted to a decimal display.

There are two basic classes of digital counter circuits: serial and parallel. The serial counters are called *ripple counters* because a change in the input must ripple through all stages of the counter to its proper point. Parallel counters are also called synchronous counters.

In a ripple counter the data is transferred serially, which means that the output of one stage becomes the input of the next stage.

The basic element in most counters is the J-K flip-flop (Fig. 1-37). Note in the figure that the J and K inputs are permanently tied high; they remain active.

A timing diagram for this divide-by-two circuit is shown in Fig. 1-38. It shows the action of the circuit. Outputs of the J-K flip-flop change state on negative-going transitions of the clock pulse. In Fig. 1-38 the first negative-going transition causes the Q output to go high. Q remains high

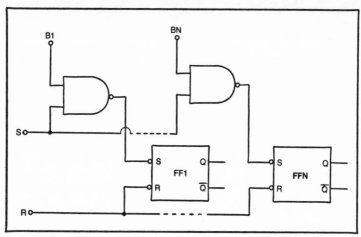

Fig. 1-34. Parallel entry shift register.

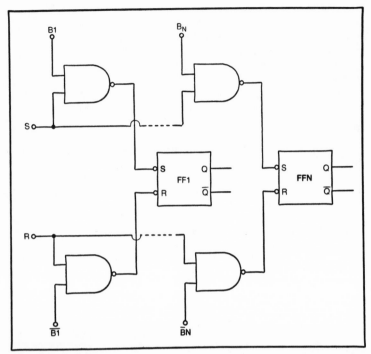

Fig. 1-35. Jam entry.

until the input sees another negative-going clock-pulse. At that time the output drops low. The action required to make a complete output requires two clock-pulses; so this J-K flip-flop is dividing the input frequency by two.

You can make a binary ripple-counter by cascading two or more stages, as shown in Fig. 1-39. This particular circuit uses four J-K flip-flops in cascade. Any number, however, can be used.

The major problem with this type of counter is that only those division ratios that are powers of two can be accommodated. In the four-stage circuit shown the possible division ratios are 2, 4, 8, and 16.

Frequency division is one major use for a counter circuit. In some electronic instruments, for example, you may want to prescale a frequency,

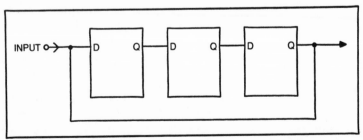

Fig. 1-36. Recirculating shift register.

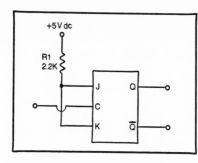

Fig. 1-37. J-K flip-flop as a binary divider.

i.e., divide it by some other frequency to a lower frequency that can be handled by a digital counter or other digital instrument.

This is only one application for the counter circuit. One of the most common applications is to count; i.e., the total number of pulses that pass. Consider again the circuit of Fig. 1-39 and the timing diagram of Fig. 1-40. Outputs A, B, C, and D are coded in binary, A being the least significant bit and the D the most significant. These are weighted in a 1-2-4-8 code system to represent decimal or hexadecimal digits. These figures are the normal weights of the binary number system.

Consider the timing diagram of Fig. 1-40. Note that all B output changes occur following the arrival of a pulse. After pulse 1 has passed, the QA line is high and all others are low. This means that the binary word on the output lines is 0001_2 (i.e., 1_{10}); one pulse has passed.

Following pulse 2 you expect 0010_2 (i.e., 2_{10}); because two pulses have passed. Note that QB is high and all others are low. The digital expression is 0010_2.

The counter in Fig. 1-39 is called a modulo-16 counter, a base-16 counter, or a hexadecimal counter.

The output of a hexadecimal counter can be decoded to drive a display device that indicates 0-9 (i.e., decimal) or 0-F (hexadecimal). A decimal readout is provided in most applications where people read the display.

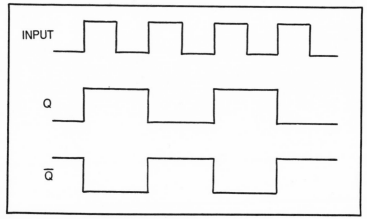

Fig. 1-38. Timing diagram for J-K flip-flop.

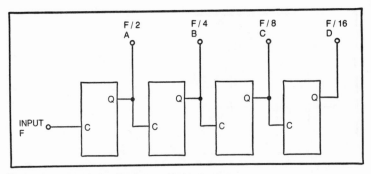

Fig. 1-39. Frequency divider (four stage) circuit.

Decimal Counters

A decimal counter operates in the base-10, or decimal, number system. The most significant bit of a decimal counter produces one output pulse for every ten input pulses. Decimal counters are also sometimes called decade counters. The decimal counter forms the basis for digital-event, period, and frequency-counter instruments. Thus, the hexadecimal counter in Fig. 1-39 is not suitable for decimal counting unless it is modified for base-10 operation.

Figure 1-41 shows a TTL hex-counter modified by adding a single TTL NAND-gate. Recall that a TTL J-K flip-flop uses inverted inputs for the clear and set functions. As long as the clear input remains high, the flip-flop functions normally. When the clear input is momentarily brought low, the Q output of the flip-flop goes low.

The decade counter in Fig. 1-41 is connected so that all four clear-inputs are tied together to form a common clear-line. This line is connected to the output of a TTL NAND-gate (i.e., one section of a 7400 device). Recall the rules of operation for the TTL NAND-gate: if either input goes low, the output goes high. But, if both inputs are high, the output goes low.

The idea behind the circuit of Fig. 1-41 is to clear the counter to 0000 following the tenth input pulse. Let's examine the timing diagram in Fig. 1-42 to see if the circuit does the correct thing. Up until the tenth pulse, this diagram is the same as the diagram for the base-16 counter.

The output of the NAND gate keeps the clear line high for all counts through ten. The inputs of this gate are connected to the B and D. The D line stays low, forcing clear high, until the eighth input pulse passes. At that time (i.e., T0 in Fig. 1-41), D goes high and bit B drops low; so the clear line remains high for the ninth pulse.

The clear line remains high until the end of the tenth pulse. At that point T2) both B and D are high; so the NAND-gate output drops low, clearing all four flip-flops (i.e., forcing them to the state where all four Q outputs are low). The counter is, therefore, reset to 0000.

The reset counter produces a 0000 code; so the B and D outputs are now low, forcing the clear line high again. The entire reset cycle occurs during period (T3– T2). This period has been expanded greatly for illustration in the figure, but actually takes only nanoseconds or microseconds.

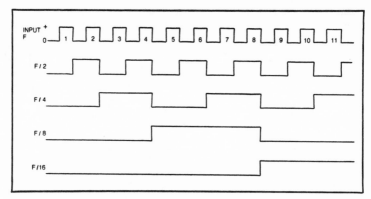

Fig. 1-40. Timing waveform.

The eleventh pulse increments the counter one time, so the output is 0001_2. The count sequence in decimal is 0-1-2-3-4-5-6-7-8-9-0-1, etc. The output code is a ten-digit version of four-bit binary (hexadecimal), called binary coded decimal (BCD).

Synchronous Counters

Ripple counters suffer from one major problem—speed. The counter elements are wired in cascade; so an input pulse must ripple through the entire chain before it affects the output. A synchronous counter feeds the

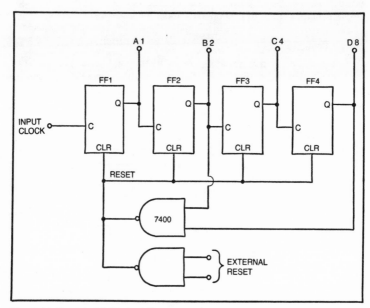

Fig. 1-41. Decade (divide-by-10) counter circuit.

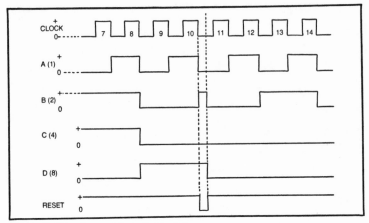

Fig. 1-42. Waveform of decade counter.

clock input to all flip-flops in parallel, and this results in a much faster operation.

Figure 1-43 shows a partial schematic for a synchronous binary counter. You can accomplish synchronous operation by using four flip-flops with clock inputs tied together and a pair of AND gates.

One AND gate is connected so that both Q1 and Q2 are high before flip-flop 3 is active. Similarly, Q2 and Q3 must be high before flip-flop 4 is made active. On a clock pulse any of the four flip-flops scheduled to change do so simultaneously. Synchronous counters attain faster speeds, although ripple counters seem to predominate most applications.

Preset Counters

A preset counter increments from a preset point instead of 0000. For example, suppose you want to count from 5_{10} (0101_2). Preset the counter to 0101 and increment from there.

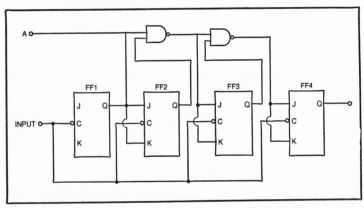

Fig. 1-43. Synchronous binary counter.

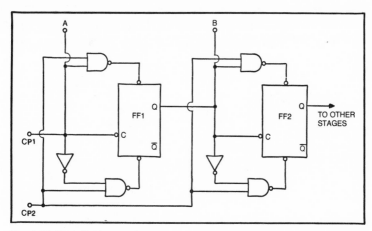

Fig. 1-44. Presettable counter.

Figure 1-44 shows a common method for achieving preset conditions, the jam input. Only two stages are shown here, but adding two more stages makes it a four-bit counter. Of course, any number of stages can be connected in cascade to form an n-bit preset-counter.

In Fig. 1-44, the preset count is applied to points A and B, and both bits are entered simultaneously when the line for clock pulse 2 is brought high. This line is sometimes called the enter or jam terminal.

Once the preset bit-pattern is entered, the counter increments with every transition of the clock line 1.

Down Counters

A down counter decrements, instead of incrementing, the count for each excursion of the input pulse. If the reset condition is 0000, then the next count is 0000−1, or 1111.

For the down counter use basically the same circuit as before, but toggle each flip-flop from the not-Q, rather than the Q, of the preceding flip-flop. An example of a four-bit binary down-counter is shown in Fig. 1-45. Note that the outputs are taken from the Q outputs of the flip-flops, but that toggling is from not-Q.

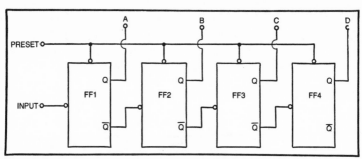

Fig. 1-45. Four-bit binary down counter (base-16).

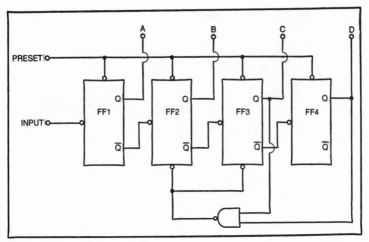

Fig. 1-46. Base-10 down counter.

The preset inputs of the flip-flops are connected to provide a means to preset the counter to its initial (i.e., 1111) state. This counter is also called a subtraction counter because each input-pulse causes the output to decrement by one bit.

A decade version of this circuit is shown in Fig. 1-46. As in the case of the regular decade counter, a NAND gate is added to the circuit to reset the counter following the tenth count. Detect the states where outputs C and D

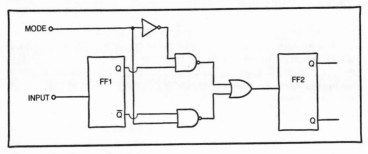

Fig. 1-47. Up/Down Counter.

are high, and then clear the two middle flip-flops. This action forces the output to 1001_2 (i.e., 9_{10}). The counter then decrements from 1001 in the decimal sequence 9-8-7-6-5-4-3-2-1-0-9, etc.

Up/Down Counters

Some counters operate in both up and down modes, depending upon both the logic level applied to a mode input. Figure 1-47 shows a representative circuit, in which the first two stages of a cascade counter are modified by the addition of several gates. If the mode input is high; the circuit is an up counter. If the mode input is low; the circuit operates as a down counter.

Chapter 2

Interfacing Digital IC Families

Although there have been several IC logic families available over the years, only two main families have been popular in microcomputer electronics: TTL and CMOS (and CMOS derivatives such as NMOS). The typical microcomputer might be a CMOS or NMOS device; all but a few have TTL-compatible output-lines and operate from the +5 V power-supply typical of TTL devices. In this chapter I discuss some techniques for interfacing different IC digital-logic families to each other.

The TTL logic family uses 0 V for low and +5 V for high. The CMOS family, on the other hand, might use the TTL levels but also can use anything between ±4.5 and ±18 volts for the high to low levels. Clearly, some means of interfacing is needed.

There are several families of TTL logic, and they are differentiated in their respective parts numbers. The L and LS devices (e.g., 74LS00 or 74L00) are lower-current versions of the regular TTL devices. Any CMOS output drives one L or LS TTL-gate. As long as the CMOS device is operated from only a ±5 V dc power-supply, you can get away with simply connecting the CMOS output to the L or LS TTL-input. The 4001A and 4002A (not the B versions!) also drive one regular TTL-input.

There are three CMOS devices that drive up to two (regular, L or LS TTL-gates. These are the 4049, 4050, and 4502 devices. The 4049 device is a hex inverter, while the 4050 is a noninverting hex buffer. The 4502 device is a Tri-state hex inverter, which means that the output lines float at a high impedance unless a *chip-enable* line is active. These devices are capable of directly interfacing CMOS outputs to TTL inputs. Figure 2-1 shows the typical circuit. Note that this only works if the 4049, 4050, or 4502 are operated from the +5 V power supply of the TTL circuits. The CMOS device that drives the 4049, 4050, and 4502 need not be a +5 V circuit; but should not be bipolar (e.g., it could be 0 to +12 V). If the 4050 is operated at any potential other than +5 V (applied to pin 1), the whole deal is off—the device won't interface with the TTL input to follow.

Figure 2-2 shows the connection of the 4049 (or 4050) device to interface up to two TTL-gates. If any larger number of TTL gates is

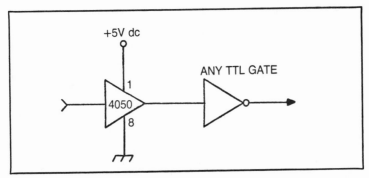

Fig. 2-1. Interfacing CMOS to TTL.

anticipated, as might be the case on a microcomputer bus, substitute a high-power bus-drive IC.

The 4050 device does not invert the input pulse. The 4049 and 4502 devices, however, are inverters and deliver a pulse to the TTL gate that is of opposite polarity from the main input pulse.

Figure 2-3 shows the connection required to interface a TTL output to a CMOS input. Remember that the TTL output line is a current sink (TTL inputs are current sources), while the CMOS input is the high-impedance gate of a MOSFET transistor. This means that you must provide a current source for the TTL output in order to interface with a CMOS input! In Fig. 2-3, a 2.2K ohm pull-up resistor to the +5 V line is used as the current source to keep the TTL output happy.

The CMOS device changes state only when the input voltage goes past the point that is equal to one-half the difference between the negative voltage and positive voltage power-supply limits. If a CMOS device is operated from 0 and a positive-voltage potential greater than +5 V, it is

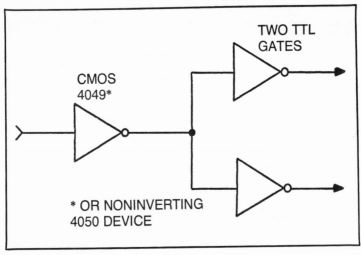

Fig. 2-2. CMOS-to-TTL.

40

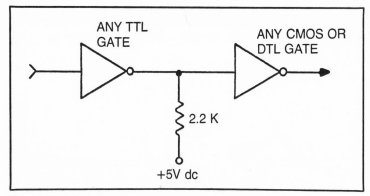

Fig. 2-3. TTL output to CMOS input.

possible that the TTL device (which delivers only +5 V) will never reach transition-voltage of the CMOS device. For example, if the CMOS device is operated from +12 V, the trip point is +6 V; so no TTL device drives the CMOS properly—unless it is an open-collector TTL with an output that is also operated from +12 V. Figure 2-4 shows a circuit that accomplishes this neat trick.

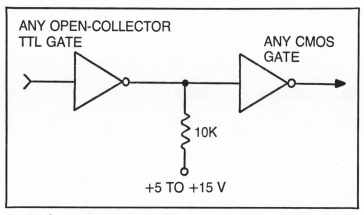

Fig. 2-4. Open-collector TTL to CMOS.

The open-collector TTL device is operated from +5 V (as any TTL device, is), but there is no collector load (internally) on the output transistor. You must provide a pull-up resistor from the output to the positive-voltage line. The typical TTL open-collector output operates at least to +15 V, while some operate to +30 V. To interface with a CMOS device that is operated from more than +8 V dc, use an open-collector TTL-gate with a 10K ohm pull-up resistor to the CMOS power supply (not the TTL supply!).

Chapter 3

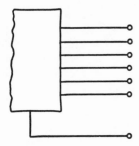

Control Signals

The control signals from a microprocessor chip either tell the outside world what the processor is doing or tell the processor something of what the outside world demands. Several such control signals are found on all microprocessors, and the status of these signals is of critical importance to the interface designer.

Z-80 CONTROL SIGNALS

The Z-80 microprocessor was designed to be at least somewhat compatible with the 8080A device. The software instructions of the Z-80 are inclusive of the 8080A instructions, so there is definitely software compatibility (except for timing loops in some cases). The Z-80 device, however, uses a different set of control signals, as defined below. (For the pin-outs see Fig. 3-1.)

$\overline{RD}$ — Indicates that the CPU (central processing unit) is reading something into the accumulator. This active-low output is used for both input operations and memory read operations. *Read.*

$\overline{WR}$ — This active-low output is the complement of the $\overline{RD}$ output and is used to indicate that the CPU is writing data to either a memory location or an output port. *Write.*

$\overline{IORQ}$ — This active-low output indicates that an input or output operation is taking place. This signal is used in conjunction with the $\overline{WR}$ and $\overline{RD}$ signals, as required by the type of operation. *Input/output request.*

$\overline{MREQ}$ — This active-low output tells the outside world that a memory read or memory write is taking place. It is used in conjunction with the WR and RD signals, as needed. *Memory request.*

$\overline{HALT}$ — This active-low output indicates that a halt instruction has been executed. A halt can only be terminated by receipt of an interrupt.

$\overline{\text{WAIT}}$	This active-low input causes the CPU to insert a specific number of clock periods before going on to the next instruction. This input is used by external peripherals or memory that is too slow to keep pace with the CPU. The external device drags the $\overline{\text{WAIT}}$ low in order to gain the needed breathing time.
$\overline{\text{INT}}$	This interrupt line is sampled by the CPU at the end of the execution of the current instruction. If $\overline{\text{INT}}$ is low, the CPU executes the interrupt program. This interrupt line can be masked by the condition of the CPU's interrupt flip-flop. *Interrupt request.*
$\overline{\text{NMI}}$	Similar to the $\overline{\text{INT}}$, except that $\overline{\text{NMI}}$ cannot be turned off and has priority over the $\overline{\text{INT}}$ interrupt. *Nonmaskable interrupt.*
$\overline{\text{BUSRQ}}$	This active-low input allows an external device (such as a direct-memory-access controller) to gain control of the data bus. *Bus request.*
$\overline{\text{BUSAK}}$	This active-low output tells the device that generated the $\overline{\text{BUSRQ}}$ that the request is granted and that the control of the bus is now in its hands. *Bus acknowledge.*
$\overline{\text{RESET}}$	This active-low input resets the microprocessor. This signal does not alter the contents of the registers, but is a hardware "jump to location 0000" instruction.

8080A CONTROL SIGNALS

The 8080A microprocessor is probably the oldest, complete, eight-bit microprocessor chip on the market. It was designed by Intel Corporation. The 8080A once sold for almost $200, but is now available for around $5. Although it is somewhat obsolete for new designs, it is still the mainstay of many older computers, including S-100 CPU boards that are being sold new. For the pin-outs see Fig. 3-2.

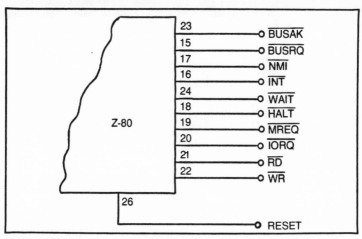

Fig. 3-1. Z80 control signal pin-outs.

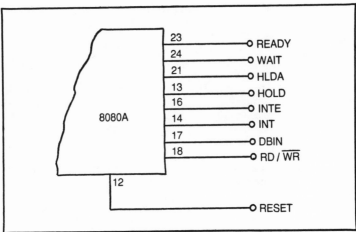

Fig. 3-2. 8080A control signal pin-outs.

RESET	This active-high (three clock-cycle) input causes a hardware jump to location 0000.
RD/WR	This input is high during a read operation and low during a write operation. *Read/write.*
DBIN	This is an active-high data strobe output. When DBIN is high, the external memory device or I/O port must place the data destined for the CPU accumulator on the data bus. *Data bus in.*
INT	This active-high interrupt requests input. *Interrupt.*
INTE	This active high output tells the world when the interrupt line is enabled. *Interrupt enable.*
HOLD	This active-high input causes the CPU to float the address and data bus pins of the 8080A so that an external device can gain control of the data and address buses. This is used in direct-memory-access operations.
HLDA	This active-high output lets the external world know when the CPU is in the hold state (i.e., address and data-bus pins inactive). *Hold acknowledge.*
READY	This active-high input inserts a few clock periods into the execution of an instruction. This line is used to let the slower peripherals catch up with the CPU.
WAIT	This output indicates when the CPU is in a wait state.

6502 CONTROL SIGNALS

The 6502 microprocessor has a simpler set of control signals (see Fig. 3-3) than either the 8080A or Z-80 machines. Architecturally, the 6502 device more nearly resembles the 6800 machine than either the 8080A or Z-80 devices. The 6502 was originated by MOS Technology of Norristown, PA, but is now also made by Rockwell International Corporation and Synertek.

44

R/$\overline{\text{W}}$	Since every machine cycle in the 6502 involves either a read or a write operation, this signal tells the outside world which is being performed. This line is high for read operations and low for write operations. *Read/write.*
SO	*Set overflow flag input.*
SYNC	This output tells the outside world that the instruction-fetch cycle is in existence.
$\overline{\text{IRQ}}$	*Interrupt request.*
$\overline{\text{NMI}}$	*Nonmaskable interrupt.*
$\overline{\text{RDY}}$	This is the single-cycle control. *Ready.*
$\overline{\text{RESET}}$	I.e., hardware "jump to location 0000" instruction.

6800 CONTROL SIGNALS

The 6800 microprocessor was Motorola's entry into the field. Like the Z-80, 6502 and 8080A machines, the 6800 has been with us for a long time. The control signal pin-outs are shown in Fig. 3-4. The signal meanings are as follows:

$\overline{\text{RESET}}$	This active-low input is essentially a hardware "jump to address in FFFE"—FFFF instruction.
RD/$\overline{\text{WR}}$	This three-state output indicates when read and write operations are taking place. This output is logically high for a read, and logically low for a write operation. *Read/write.*
VMA	This output terminal goes high whenever the 6800 CPU outputs a valid memory-location address onto the address bus. *Valid memory address.*
DBE	This pin is low to float the data bus, allowing direct memory access operations. *Data bus enable.*
BA	This signal goes high on two occassions: following a halt instruction and when the address and data buses have been floated (Tri-state).
	The pin tells the external device that requested control of the data bus that it can proceed. *Bus available.*

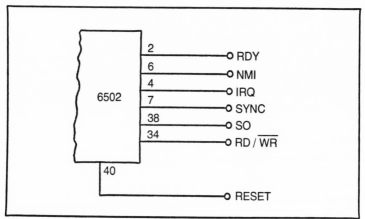

Fig. 3-3. 6502 control signal pin-outs.

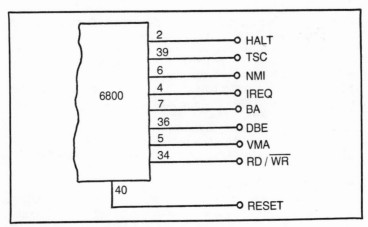

Fig. 3-4. 6800 control signal pin-outs.

$\overline{\text{IREQ}}$	*Interrupt request.*
NMI	This request has priority over IREQ and cannot be disabled by programming. *Nonmaskable interrupt request.*
TSC	This causes the address bus and R/W control lines to float at high impedance, being neither logically high nor logically low. *Tri-state control.*
$\overline{\text{HALT}}$	This active-low output tells the outside world that the CPU has executed a HALT instruction.

Chapter 4

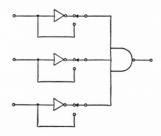

Address Decoder and Device Select Circuits

One factor that contributes to the power of the programmable digital-computer is that the CPU can communicate with a large array of input/output devices. There are also many memory locations and bus addresses that are common to the entire system. Control signals that are generated by the CPU tell the system which device or memory location is being selected and whether the operation is to read data from that location or to write data into it.

In this chapter, I discuss the circuits that are used to generate device-select pulses and to decode specific memory addresses or I/O port numbers. In the examples, I use Z-80 terminology and control-signal specifications. You can design circuits for other microprocessors by considering their respective control signals (see Chapter 3) and using information given in this chapter.

ADDRESSING IN MICROCOMPUTERS

Microcomputers must be able to uniquely identify specific locations in which to store data. Some of these locations are actual memory locations, while others are I/O ports. In the 6502 microprocessor, the I/O ports are treated as memory locations. Since the 6502 device has a 16-bit address-bus, it can uniquely address up to 2^{16}, or 65,536 different locations. Allocations of specific addresses to either memory or I/O is determined by the designer of the 6502-based computer.

The Z-80 microprocessor has a 16-bit address-bus; so it, too, can address up to 65,536 different memory locations. In both the 6502 and Z-80 devices each memory location stores a single eight bit (i.e., one byte).

The Z-80 differs from the 6502 in that it also provides eight-bit I/O-port addressing capability. During the execution of an I/O instruction, the address of the I/O port appears on the low-order byte of the two-byte address-bus. The contents of the accumulator register in the CPU are passed over the high-order byte of the address bus during this operation. Eight-bit I/O-port coding means 2^8, or 256, unique I/O-ports can be designated.

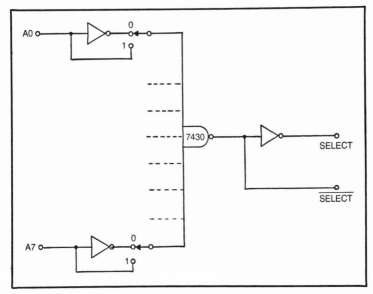

Fig. 4-1. Universal address decoder.

EIGHT-BIT DECODERS

An eight-bit address can uniquely designate either 256 memory locations, or, the same number of I/O ports. Many microcomputers use eight-bit address decoders for the following purposes:

- To uniquely decode memory locations 00 to FF (hex)
- To uniquely decode I/O ports 00 to FF (hex)
- With a second eight-bit decoder to uniquely decode memory locations 00 00 to FF FF (a full 64K bytes)
- With *bank select* decoders to select higher-order banks of 256 memory locations each

In order to design an address decoder, it is necessary to identify IC-logic devices that respond appropriately to the logic levels presented on the address bus. In most practical applications the devices selected include NAND gates, NOR gates, binary-word comparators (e.g., 7485), and inverters.

The decoder must be designed according to the memory or I/O devices that are being addressed. Most memory devices have active-low *chip enable terminals*. This designation means that the IC turns on (i.e., becomes active) when the chip-enable line is low, and is inactive when the chip-enable line is high. A 74100 TTL device used as an output port-register, on the other hand, is an active-high.

In practical microcomputers with 1024 or less memory locations, the memory chips have their own internal address decoders; so they are directly addressed from the address bus. No external address decoders are needed. The remaining three applications, however, require the generation of a decoded *select-signal*.

48

The first address decoder is shown in Fig. 4-1 and is one of the most popular circuits used. The 7430 IC is a TTL eight-input NAND-gate. Its output remains high as long as any one of the eight inputs is low. The output terminal of the 7430 goes low only if all eight inputs are high. The trick is to make the entire set of inputs high when the correct address is present on the lower eight-bits of the address bus. Of course, if the address is FF (hex) (11111111 in binary), you have no problem. Connecting one each of the 7430 inputs to one of the lower-order bits of the address bus automatically gives you the decoder. But, all other addresses require one or more inverters between the address bus lines and the inputs of the 7430.

If you want maximum flexibility, one inverter can be dedicated to each 7430 input. However, this is a terrible waste of inverters, because there is only one address which requires all the inverters: 00000000 (binary). All other addresses use fewer than eight inverters.

As a practical matter, most I/O printed-circuit-boards that are commercially available have only three or four inverters. You must carefully select I/O-port addresses so that no more than three or four zeros occur. It is rare that all 256-possible I/O-ports are required; so this is not the sacrifice that it might appear. In the example of Fig. 4-1 I show inverters only on the A0 and A7 lines, with those for the other lines implied. In actual practice most designers wire the inverters with small jumpers rather than formal switches; so they may be dedicated to any 7430 input that might be required.

By way of illustration, assign the address 11010011 (D3 in hex) to an I/O port. You see by inspection that all but three of the bits in this address are ones; so no inverters are needed for them. Only the zero bits (i.e., A2, A3, and A5) require inverters. The decoder is shown in Fig. 4-2B. Notice that the A0, A1, A4, A6, and A7 lines are connected directly to 7430 inputs, while the A1, A2, and A5 address lines are passed through inverters before being applied to the 7430 inputs. When the address 11010011 appears on the bus, all of the 7430 inputs see ones, and the 7430 can drop low. This creates a $\overline{\text{SELECT}}$ signal for use by the I/O circuitry. An optional inverter

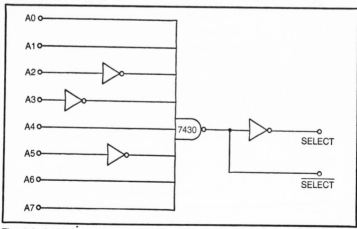

Fig. 4-2. Address decoder for 11010011.

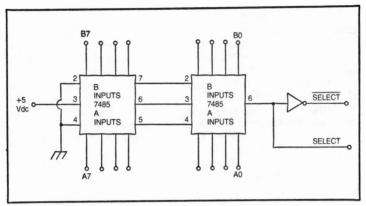

Fig. 4-3. Address decoder using 7485 four-bit binary comparators.

turns this signal upside down, creating a SELECT, for those cases where a positive-going transition is needed.

Another form of address decoder is shown in Fig. 4-3. This circuit is based on the TTL-type 7485-comparator IC. This device compares two four-bit words (A and B) and issues an output that indicates whether A is equal to, greater than, or less than B. Of these, you are interested in the A=B output (pin 6). The 7485 has cascading inputs that sense the status of the four lower-order bits. You need two 7485 devices connected in this cascade manner to use it to decode an eight-bit address bus.

Connect the bits of the address bus to the A inputs of the 7485s. The B inputs are used to program the device with the address of the port to be selected. In the previous case, I selected port D3 hex (i.e., 11010011 in binary and 211 in decimal) using a 7430. If you want to use the 7485s as shown in Fig. 4-3, program IC 1 with the binary word 0011 (i.e., 3 hex), and IC 2 with 1101 (i.e., D hex). When this address appears on the address bus, the A=B output of IC 1 goes high, forming a SELECT. An inverter is needed if a $\overline{\text{SELECT}}$ is desired instead.

You can also use any of the various 1-of-n decoder-ICs as address selectors. The 7442 is a 1-of-10 decoder, while the 74154 device is a 1-of-16 device. Each of these has a four-bit binary input to determine which output line (0-9, or 0-15) goes low. Figure 4-4 shows the use of the 7442 1-of-10 decoder. Two 7442 devices are needed. A NOR gate is connected so that one input of the NOR gate is driven by one of the outputs of each 7442.

As an example let's say you want to use the circuit in Fig. 4-4 to decode address 115 (decimal), which is 73 in hex. The binary code for seven is 0111, and the code for three is 0011. You want, then, to see binary code 01110011 on the A0-A7 lines. Connect the four-bit inputs of IC 1 to the lower-order four bits of the address line (A0-A3), and the high-order four bits (A4-A7) to the four-bit inputs of IC 2. One input of the NOR gate is then connected to the three output of IC 1, and the other input is connected to the seven output of IC 2. When the correct address appears, both of these outputs drop low, causing the output of the NOR gate to snap high. This signal then becomes your select signal. Again, an inverter is used to form a $\overline{\text{SELECT}}$.

ADDRESS-BLOCK DECODING

Most microcomputers use more than 1K of memory, yet many of the available memory chips are only 1024-byte (some being 256-byte). Although there are more modern devices capable of very large byte arrays, many users still prefer the older, smaller devices.

How does the memory device allocated to a location greater than the maximum address in each individual chip know when it is being addressed? The solution is to order the memory in 1K blocks and use some form of address decoding to tell which 1K block is designated.

Figure 4-5 shows a selection scheme used by several manufacturers of 8K memory banks. Each block of memory is an array of 1024 bytes; so every location can be addressed by bits A0-A9 of the address bus. The address pins for all devices are connected together to form the address-bus (A0-A9). You must, however, select which of the eight blocks is addressed at any given time. One way to do this is to use a data-selector IC. The 7442 device shown in Fig. 4-5 decodes binary to 1-of-10. It examines a four-bit binary (i.e., BCD) input word and issues an output condition that indicates the value tf that word. In this simplified example, I am limiting the memory size to 8K; so only the 1, 2, and 4 inputs of the 7442 are needed. Input 8 is grounded (i.em, set=0). The 7442 indicates the active output by going low, exactly the right condition for the RAM (random access memory) devices in the memory blocks. Table 4-1 shows the code that exists on the A10-A12 bits of the address bus for the various memory addresses in the range 0-8K.

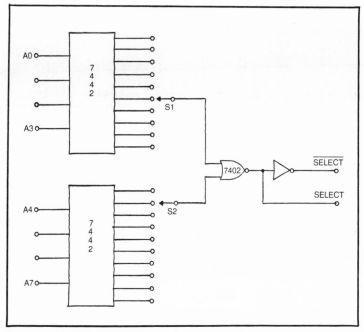

Fig. 4-4. Address decoder based on the 7442 TTL IC.

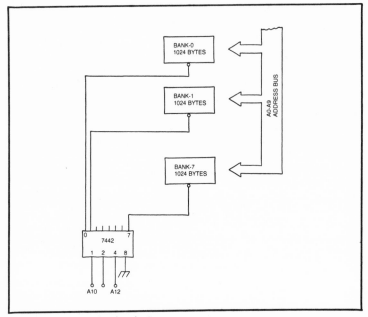

Fig. 4-5. 7442 as a bank select.

For an 8K memory the lower 10 bits of the address bus (A0-A9) select the desired location in the individual, and A10-A12 select which block of 1024 bytes contains the address.

In the example of Fig. 4-5, I limited the memory size to 8K. This keeps the circuit simple. But, how do you select memory in ranges higher than 8K? The answer is to use the 7442 input 8 as a *bank-select* control. Recall from Fig. 4-5 that this input was grounded. If it is high, none of the eight outputs of the 7442 go low. But if it is low, then the circuit works. Figure 4-6 shows a simplified selection scheme for all 64K, using eight-weighted input of the 7442 block selectors as a bank select terminal. Each bank of 8K contains its own block-select 7442; one additional 7442 is used to select the bank of 8K that becomes active. Table 4-2 shows the codes existing on address lines A-13-A15 for each 8K bank.

Figure 4-7 shows an alternate bank-selection circuit that is based on a three-input NAND gate (i.e., one section of a 7410 TTL IC device). The properties of a NAND gate are:

● If any input is low, the output is high.
● If all inputs are high, the output is low.

In this case all three of the inputs must be high for the output to drop low. If the output of the NAND gate is used to drive the eight input of the 7442, then the particular bank served by that 7442 is selected only when all three inputs are high.

How do you contrive the circuit to force all inputs high—only when the correct bit pattern is seen on lines A13-A15? The solution is the inverters and switches shown in Fig. 4-7. Each switch selects either the inverted

Table 4-1. Coding Table for Bits A10-A12.

MEMORY LOCATIONS	BLOCK NUMBER	7442 OUTPUT	7442 PIN	A13	A12	A11	A10
0 - 1K	0	0	1	0	0	0	0
1K - 2K	1	1	2	0	0	0	1
2K - 3K	2	2	3	0	0	1	0
3K - 4K	3	3	4	0	0	1	1
4K - 5K	4	4	5	0	1	0	0
5K - 6K	5	5	6	0	1	0	1
6K - 7K	6	6	7	0	1	1	0
7K - 8K	7	7	9	0	1	1	1

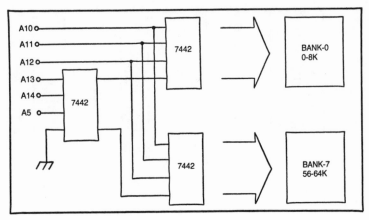

Fig. 4-6. 8K bank select.

(i.e., 0 position) or noninverted (i.e., 1 position) version of each address-bus signal. I set the three switches according to the bank-selection format, using the codes from Table 4-2. Each switch is set to the position corresponding to the digit expected at that input when the address-bus code is correct. For bank 0, for example, the code is 000. If S1-S3 are set to 0, the NAND gate sees the inverted address line signals. When 000 appears on A13-A15, the NAND gate sees 111. Since this is the condition required, the output drops low and turns on the selected bank.

Note that Intel manufactures a 1-of-8 decoder intended specifically for bank selection in the 8080A device. It should also work nicely with the Z-80 and other devices.

GENERATING PORT / DEVICE SELECT SIGNALS

Computers based on microprocessors that provide separate I/O functions (i.e., the Z-80) generally require a means to decode the port address and sense whether an input or output operation is to take place. The Z-80 microprocessor, for example, uses the following signals to define I/O operations: (a) an eight-bit address on the lower byte (A0-A7) of the 16-bit address-bus to specify the port number, (b) an active-low input/output request ($\overline{\text{IORQ}}$) line to indicate that an I/O operation is taking place, and (c) active-low read ($\overline{\text{RD}}$) and write ($\overline{\text{WR}}$) lines to indicate whether the request is an input or an output. (In these cases the bar indicates active-low states.)

Figure 4-8 shows a method for generating an active-high out or in signal in Z-80 microcomputers. This circuit is based on a single 7402 IC (quad two-input NOR-gate). Gates 3 and 4 are used to create the out and in signals and are controlled by the $\overline{\text{IORQ}}$ signal and signals from the read and write lines. Recall the rules governing NOR gate operation: a high on any input produces a low output, and it requires all inputs be low for the output to be high. When the $\overline{\text{IORQ}}$ line is inactive (i.e., high), the NOR gate outputs (gates 3 and 4) are forced low. If, however, $\overline{\text{IORQ}}$ becomes active (i.e., low), then the NOR gate outputs are unlatched and is high or low depending upon the state of the $\overline{\text{RD}}$ and $\overline{\text{WR}}$ lines.

Table 4-2. Bank-Select Coding.

MEMORY LOCATION	BANK NUMBER	7442 OUTPUT	7442 PIN LOW	A15	A14	A13
0 - 8K	0	0	1	0	0	0
8K - 16K	1	1	2	0	0	1
16K - 24K	2	2	3	0	1	0
24K - 32K	3	3	4	0	1	1
32K - 40K	4	4	5	1	0	0
40K - 48K	5	5	6	1	0	1
48 K - 56K	6	6	7	1	1	0
56K - 64K	7	7	9	1	1	1

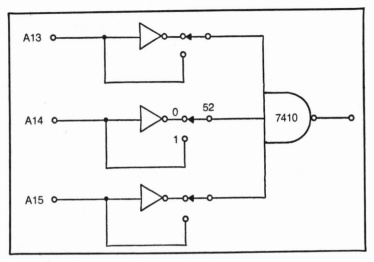

Fig. 4-7. Three-bit high-order address-decoder.

Input Operation

An input port operation is a read operation because data is transferred into the accumulator. When the Z-80 executes an input operation, therefore, the $\overline{IORQ}$ and $\overline{RD}$ go low. A low condition on $\overline{IORQ}$ unlocks gate 4 by bringing input A low. The $\overline{RD}$ line, and the $\overline{SELECT}$ line from the address decoder controls gate 2. When both of these lines are low, input B of gate 4 also goes low. You now find that both inputs of gate 4 are low; so the in line (gate 4 output) goes high.

Output Operation

An output operation is a write function because data is transferred from the accumultor to the outside world. When a Z-80 microprocessor executes an output operation, therefore, the $\overline{IORQ}$ and $\overline{WR}$ go low. A low condition on $\overline{IORQ}$ unlocks gate 3 by bringing input A low. The $\overline{WR}$ line and the $\overline{SELECT}$ line from the address decoder controls gate 1. When both of these lines are low, then input B of gate 3 also goes low. You now find both inputs of gate 3 low, so the out line goes high.

A select circuit based on the 7442 TTL IC is shown in Fig. 4-9. The 7442 ecodes TTL BCD to 1-of-10. It examines the four-bit binary coded decimal (BCD) input line and generates a unique active-low output that depends on the decimal equivalent of the input word. For example, when the binary word 0100 (4_{10}) appears on the inputs, output 4 (pin 5) goes low.

There are two methods shown in Fig. 4-9 for using the 7442 in this application. The main circuit is shown in solid lines, while the alternate circuit is shown in dotted lines.

The main circuit in Fig. 4-9 works by considering the $\overline{IORQ}$, $\overline{RD}$ and $\overline{WR}$ lines from the Z-80 as a three-bit binary word, and these lines are connected to the A, B, and C lines of the 7442, respectively. The D input line of the 7442 is wired permanently low. An input operation causes the

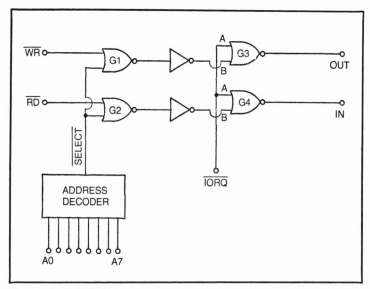

Fig. 4-8. 7402 IN/OUT device-select circuit.

$\overline{\text{IORQ}}$ and $\overline{\text{RD}}$ to be low; so the word applied to the 7441 is 0100, or decimal 2. This condition causes pin 3 to go low during the output operation.

Like the previous circuit, Fig. 4-9 is used with specific I/O ports; it must recognize the signal from the address decoder. The $\overline{\text{SELECT}}$ line goes low when the CPU selects its address; at all other times this line is high. The $\overline{\text{SELECT}}$ line is connected to both gate 1 and gate 2.

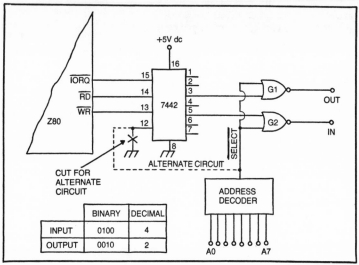

Fig. 4-9. 7442 used to generate in and out device-select signals.

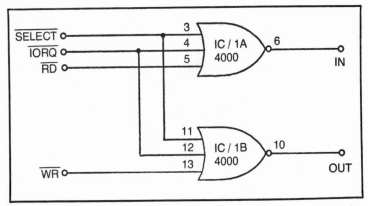

Fig. 4-10. CMOS three-input NOR gates used to generate IN and OUT device select signals.

When pin 3 of the 7442 goes low and the $\overline{\text{SELECT}}$ line is also low, then the output of gate 1 goes high, providing an output signal. This signal is used to tell the output-port circuitry to accept data on the bus.

An input signal is created by gate 2 under similar circumstances. The $\overline{\text{SELECT}}$ line goes low if the address for that port is indicated. Gate 2 knows that an input operation is demanded because pin 5 of the 7442 goes low in response to the binary code 0100 at its inputs.

In the alternate version of this circuit you can get rid of the two NOR gates by using the $\overline{\text{SELECT}}$ line from the address decoder to activate the D input of the 7442. This input wants to see a low condition before the in and out lines are activated (again, pins 5 and 3 are used). If another I/O port is being called up, the A, B, and C inputs still see the correct code from the Z-80 (010 and 100), but the D input sees a 1. The codes applied to the 7442 are 1010 and 1100; they do not activate any 7442 output line. When this port is selected, however, the 7442 input codes are either 0010 or 0100; so the appropriate input is activated.

Figure 4-10 shows a circuit that uses just two NOR gates to create the in and out signals. Three-input NOR gate sections of a CMOS 4000 IC are selected for this circuit. This circuit is simple and works with most microcomputer systems. It does not, however, work in high speeds (10 MHz and up) clock systems. These NOR gates require all three inputs low for the output to be high. The only time this situation occurs is during input operations for IC 1A, and output operations for IC 1B.

Thus far, all of the circuits presented are for specified I/O ports, i.e., an address decoder is included in the design. It is often desirable, however, to create system I/O-signals that are active for any input or output operation. In that case provide a simple address decoder at each port or on each printed circuit card within the microcomputer. This structure is popular in microcomputers that allow for future expansion through the addition of plug-in I/O cards. In a Z-80 based system, you can create the system by adapting the circuit of Fig. 4-10. Either ground the 4000 device inputs used for the $\overline{\text{SELECT}}$ signal, or use two-input NOR gates such as the 7402 device.

Chapter 5

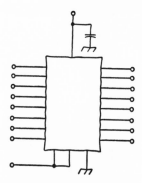

I/O Interfacing

In the last chapter I discussed the selection of I /O Ports. Now I will discuss the data.

I /O PORTS

Input and output ports (collectively known as I/O ports) are used to transfer data to and from the world outside of the computer. An input port is used to transfer data from the outside world into the CPU (central processing unit), while the output port is used to transfer data to the outside world from the CPU.

Data transferred in an I/O port operation must typically go through the CPU accumulator register. This limitation differentiates I/O operations from these operations that transfer data directly between the CPU register and memory locations, or, those that read and write data directly from the outside world to memory locations. This latter operation is known as *direct memory-access*, or DMA.

Some microprocessors provide for separate I/O ports, while others use a memory mapped system for the I/O ports. In the latter type of system, the I/O ports are treated as memory locations by the CPU. An input operation is then treated as a memory-read operation from the location assigned by the designer as a port. Of course, each memory location specified as an I/O port is one less location that is available for data.

The easiest I/O to design is the ordinary *parallel port* that transfers all bits to or from the data bus simultaneously.

The *serial port* is designed to transfer the data one bit at a time. Serial I/O ports are a little more difficult to design than parallel ports, but permit the most efficient transfer of data over a communications link. To transmit eight bits of data in parallel form requires eight separate telephone lines or radio channels—obviously too costly for most applications!

There are various ways to design serial I/O ports and several standards that could possibly apply. In this chapter I consider the most common methods.

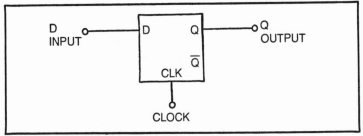

Fig. 5-1. Type-D flip-flop.

PARALLEL-OUTPUT PORT-DESIGN

Although many microcomputers use special-purpose ICs for I/O ports, it is often less costly to use ordinary ICs from the regular digital-logic families in these applications.

A type-D flip-flop can be used to store one bit of data; so an array of eight type-D flip-flops can be used to hold one byte of data. Figure 5-1 shows the symbol for the type-D flip-flop. Data applied to the D input is transferred to the Q output only when the clock line is high. If the clock line remains high, the data on the Q output follows the data on the D input. If, however, the clock line is low, then the data on the Q output remains the same; i.e., the flip-flop holds the last valid D-input data that was present before the clock dropped low. The flip-flop then ignores all further changes of the D-input data.

There are a number of type-D flip-flops available in the major digital logic IC families. Certain devices called data latches contain four or eight type-D flip-flops in arrays that share a common clock line. An example is the 74100 device shown as an output port register in Fig. 5-2.

The 74100 is a dual four-bit data-latch, and it contains a pair of type-D flip-flop arrays—each containing four flip-flops. If the two clock-lines (pins 12 and 23) are tied together, the 74100 operates as an eight-bit register. The eight D-inputs are connected to the data bus, while the eight Q-outputs are used as the output bits. This type of circuit forms a latched output because the data remains fixed on the output lines after the execution of an output instruction is completed.

The common clock-line from the 74100 is connected to the out signal from the port-select circuit (see Chapter 4). The data on the data bus is transferred to the output side of the 74100 register whenever the out signal line goes high.

PARALLEL-INPUT PORT-DESIGN

Ordinary IC devices can also be used in the design of input ports. There is, however, a design constraint that limits the selection to those which provide three-state output lines.

The microcomputer data-bus serves several functions, including data transfers to and from many memory locations and I/O ports. If any one device causes a permanent high or low condition on any line of the data bus, there will be massive errors in the data! All devices connected to the data bus must, therefore, be three-state.

A three-state device becomes effectively disconnected from the output terminal when it is not active. All digital ICs are at least two-state, i.e., the output terminal sees either a low impedance to ground (low condition), or a low impedance to +5 V dc (high condition). The three-state has a third state, in which the output terminal sees a high impedance to both ground and +5 V dc anytime the *chip enable* (CE or $\overline{CE}$) terminal is inactive. There are only a few devices from the regular TTL lines that meet this requirement, an example is the 74125 device.

The 74125 is a four-bit TTL that contains four noninverting-buffers that each has its own active-low chip enable ($\overline{CE}$) line. When $\overline{CE}$ is low, the buffer acts like any TTL buffer; so the output data directly follows the input data. However, when the $\overline{CE}$ line is high, the buffer output line goes to a high impedance, and the device is effectively disconnected from the output line.

Figure 5-3 shows a pair of 74125 devices used to form an eight-bit input-port. (Since an input should not provide latching, you cannot use the 74100 device.) All four $\overline{CE}$ lines in both 74125 devices are tied together to form a master $\overline{CE}$ line that turns the port on and off in response to the IN signal.

The $\overline{IN}$ line is normally held high until an input operation takes place from that port. At that time the IN line drops low, turning on the 74125s. This action connects the bits of the input ports to the data bus as long as IN is low; so input data appears briefly on the data bus.

BIDIRECTIONAL PARALLEL-I/O PORT-DESIGN

The job of designing and interfacing I/O ports is made easier by the use of certain special purpose integrated circuit I/O devices. Some of these are

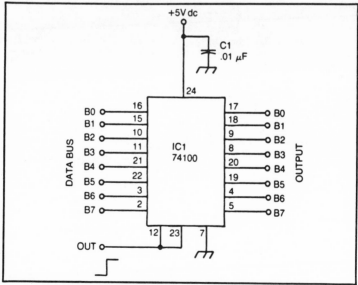

Fig. 5-2. 74100 data register.

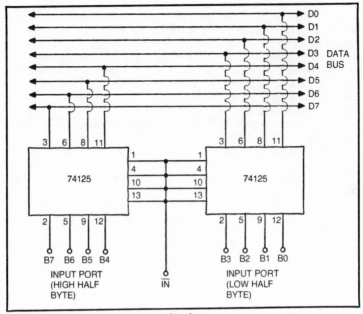

Fig. 5-3. 74125 input interfacing to data bus.

general enough that they can be used with a wide variety of microprocessor chips.

The 8216, 8226 and 8212 devices are examples produced by Intel for use with the 8080A microprocessor chip, but are also frequently adapted for use with other microprocessor chips.

The 8216 and 8226 devices are almost identical to each other, except that the 8216 contains noninverting line-drivers, while the 8226 contains inverting line-drivers. Both are four-bit devices; so two are needed to drive an eight-bit data-bus.

Figure 5-4 shows the logic diagram for the 8216 device. This same diagram is also used for the 8226, except that the line-driver buffers are inverters. Lines DB0 through DB3 are connected to four bits of the data bus. The four input port lines are labeled DI0 through DI3, while four output port lines are designated DO0 through DO3.

The $\overline{\text{DIEN}}$ line controls the data direction. If this line is low, the input lines are connected to the data bus. Alternately, if $\overline{\text{DIEN}}$ is high, the output port is connected to the data bus.

The lines connected to the data bus have three-state outputs; they can be made to float at high impedance when not needed. The *chip select* ($\overline{\text{CS}}$) is an active-low terminal that controls the three-state output. If $\overline{\text{CS}}$ is high, then the outputs have a high impedance and do not load the bus. However, when $\overline{\text{CS}}$ is low, the output lines become active.

Only the $\overline{\text{DIEN}}$ line of the 8216 and 8226 devices affects the input function. To make an output port active, though, requires a high on $\overline{\text{DIEN}}$ and a low on $\overline{\text{CS}}$.

62

The actual circuit configuration depends upon the use of the chip (input or output) and the microprocessor used. In a Z-80 system, for example, you could connect $\overline{CS}$ to $\overline{IORQ}$ and $\overline{DIEN}$ to $\overline{RD}$ (which is low for input operations and high for output operations).

The Intel 8212 device is shown in Fig. 5-5. This chip is an eight-bit directional I/O-port that was designed to be compatible with the 8080A microprocessor. It also has been used with many other microprocessor

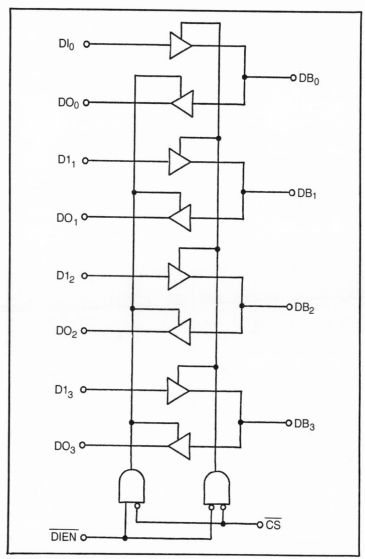

Fig. 5-4. 8216 bidirectional four-bit Tri-state register.

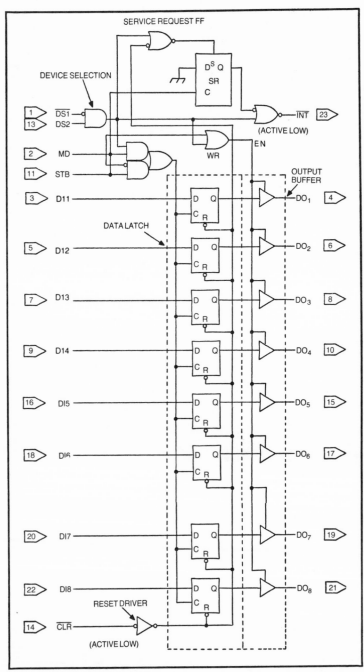

Fig. 5-5. 8212 eight-bit register.

chips. The 8212 also differs from the previous example in that it is (a) unidirectional (two are needed for a complete I/O), and (b) it contains latches to retain the last valid data. The latter feature is necessary for most microcomputer applications. An example showing a pair of 8212 devices in a bidirectional I/O port circuit is given in Fig. 5-6.

SERIAL I/O-PORTS

Parallel I/O-ports prove to be expensive when data must be communicated over a long distance to another device. Unless the communications link is only a few feet in length, serial communication is usually cheaper. Transmission of eight data-bits in parallel, for example, requires at least eight lines, and usually a ninth line is needed as a common or ground. The excessive cost of radio and telephone links should be obvious. In contrast, a serial communications link requires only one channel: local wire, telephone lines, or a radio channel.

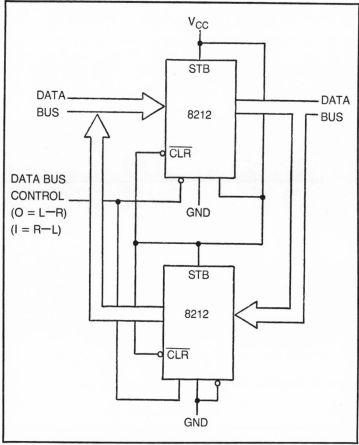

Fig. 5-6. Application of 8212 eight-bit register.

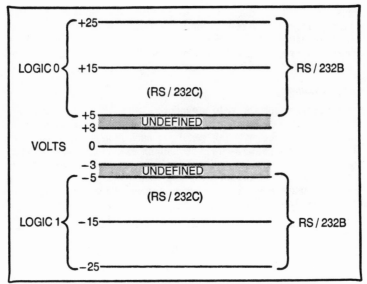

Fig. 5-7. RS-232 definitions.

A serial input-port can be built in a similar manner, but using a serial-in/parallel-out (SIPO) shift register. Remember, Tri-state outputs must be available to prevent loading of the data bus when the port is inactive.

In addition, there are numerous peripherals, such as teletypewriters, that use serial inputs or provide serial outputs.

Serial data ports are slower than parallel ports because the data can be transmitted only one bit at a time. The bit length is also greater because certain *format bits* must be added, i.e., a start bit, a parity bit, plus one or more stop bits.

SOFTWARE SERIAL-I/O-PORTS

Some designers use software to force a single bit of a parallel I/O port to function as if it were a serial port. In one simple method, the output word is loaded into the accumulator, then the shift instructions are used to output the word bit by bit.

Another, more formal, technique is to write a software program to perform the logic functions of a *universal asynchronous receiver/transmitter,* or UART (see Chapter 7). Such programs are often designated teletypewriter or printer-driver routines.

TTL/CMOS HARDWARE METHODS

The basic circuit needed to make a serial output port is the parallel-in/serial-out (PISO) shift register. Data from the accumulator is written to the parallel inputs of the shift register as if the register were either a memory location or a parallel output-port. A program is then executed that clocks the flip-flop left-to-right, causing the shift register to output the data in serial format. Various clocking schemes are used, including successively generating an out signal, or writing to a specific (unused) memory location. In both cases a device or location-select pulse must be provided.

RS-232 INTERFACING

The Electronic Industries Association (EIA) standard *RS-232* pertains to a standardized serial-data-transmission scheme. The idea is to use the same connector (i.e., the DB-25 family), wired in the same manner all of the time, and to use the same voltage levels. Supposedly, you can connect any two devices that provide RS-232 I/O without any problem (it usually works).

Modems (cathode-ray tube) terminals, printers, teletypewriters, and other devices are fitted with RS-232 connectors. Some computers provide RS-232 I/O, and this feature can be added by using a set of Motorola ICs called RS-232 drivers/receivers. An RS-232 driver IC accepts TTL outputs from a computer or other device, and produces RS-232 voltage levels at its output. The RS-232 receiver does just the opposite. It takes RS-232 levels from the communications interface and produces TTL outputs.

Unfortunately, the RS-232 is a very old standard, and it predates even the TTL standard. That is why it uses such odd voltage levels for logical-1 and logical-0.

Besides voltage levels, the standard also fixes the load impedances and the output impedances of the drivers.

There are actually two RS-232 standards: the older RS-232B and the current RS-232C (see Fig. 5-7). In the older version, RS-232B, logical-1 is any potential in the -5 to -25 V range, and logical-0 is anything between

Table 5-1. RS-232 Connector (DB-25) Pin-outs.

PIN NO.	RS 232 NAME	FUNCTION
1	AA	Chassis ground
2	BA	Data from terminal
3	BB	Data received from modem
4	CA	Request to send
5	CB	Clear to send
6	CC	Data set ready
7	AB	Signal ground
8	CF	Carrier detection
9	undef	
10	undef	
11	undef	
12	undef	
13	undef	
14	undef	
15	DB	Transmitter bit clock, internal
16	undef	
17	DD	Received bit clock
18	undef	
19	undef	
20	CD	Data terminal ready
21	undef	
22	CE	Ring indicator
23	undef	
24	DA	Transmitted bit clock, external
25	undef	

+5 and +25 V. The voltages in the range −3 to +3 are a transition state, while +3 to +5 and −3 to −5 are undefined.

The speedier RS-232C standard narrows the limits to ±15 V. In addition, the standard fixes the load resistance to the range 3000-7000 ohms, and the driver output-impedance is low. The driver must provide a slow rate of 30 volts per microsecond. The Motorola MC1488-driver and MC1489-receiver ICs meet these specifications.

The standard wiring for the 25-pin DBM-25 connector used in RS-232 ports is shown in Table 5-1.

CURRENT-LOOP PORTS

The *current-loop port* was designed specifically for use with teletypewriters, but has been adopted over the years to a variety of communications problems in digital instruments. The original 60 (and later 20) milliampere (mA) current-loop systems were intended for Baudot encoded Teletype machines, and were used to energize the solenoids in the printer. But the same idea has also been adopted for use with a variety of printers other than teletypewriters and is also found in certain other instruments that must communicate with computers. The 60 mA version of the current loop is obsolete, but is included here because it is often necessary to design into older, existing systems.

Chapter 6

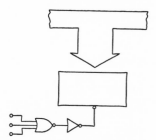

Memory Interfacing

The memory of the microcomputer is an array of storage locations for data and program instructions. The typical 8 bit microprocessor chip has a 16 bit address-bus and can address up to 2^{16} (i.e., 65, 536) different memory locations.

There is quite an array of possible memory devices in a microcomputer. You might have a mixture of random-access memory (RAM); *read-only memory* (ROM; or certain *memory-mapped* devices (i.e., devices treated as memory locations), such as I/O ports (6502 machines), digital-to-analog converters, analog-to-digital converters, and so forth.

In this chapter, I use the terminology of the Z-80 microprocessor, but you may refer to Chapter 3 in order to learn the types of control signals that are available for some of the other popular microprocessor chips.

You must be cognizant of the basic control signals that apply to memory operations, e.g., $\overline{MREQ}$, $\overline{WR}$, and $\overline{RD}$ in the Z-80. These signals are memory request, write, and read, respectively. The memory request signal drops low whenever the CPU is executing either a memory-read or memory-write operation. It tells the system that the data on the bus is memory data. If a memory-write operation is taking place, then the write ($\overline{WR}$) signal also goes low. If, on the other hand, it is a memory read, then the read ($\overline{RD}$) signal goes low. All memory operations, therefore, generate a low on two control pins of the Z-80: $\overline{MREQ}$/WR for memory-write operations and $\overline{MREQ}$/RD for memory-read operations.

Most integrated-circuit memory-devices have at least one chip-enable (CE) pin, and some have two chip-enable pins (labeled CE 1 and CE 2). There also can be a read/write (W/R) pin to instruct the device whether the desired operation is a memory-read or memory-write.

One of the simplest cases is shown in Fig. 6-1. Here you see 1024 bytes of ROM interfaced directly to the Z-80. In this case I assigned the ROM to the lower 1K of the memory-address range. The locations available, then, are 00 00 (hex) to 03 FF (hex). Since I am dealing with the lower 1K, I need only the lower-order byte of the address bus, A0-A7, plus the two least-significant-bits (LSB) of the upper-order byte (A8 and A9).

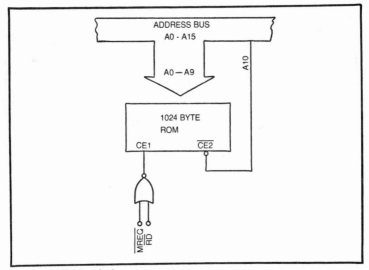

Fig. 6-1. ROM interfacing.

Two chip-enable (CE) terminals are available. Use one of them (CE 2) to make sure that the ROM responds only to address in the lower 1K of memory. Address-bus bit-A10 always remains low when the CPU is addressing a location in the lower 1K, but goes high when an address greater than 03 FF (hex) is selected. The ROM, therefore, is enabled only when the address on the address bus is less than 03 FF (hex).

The second chip-enable pin (CE 1) is used to turn on the ROM only when the memory-read operation is taking place. This CE pin wants to see a high to turn on the ROM. Recall that a NOR gate outputs a high only when both inputs are low. You can, therefore, create a device-select command for CE 1 by applying the $\overline{MREQ}$ and $\overline{RD}$ control signals from the CPU to the inputs of a NOR gate. CE 1 goes high only when a memory-read operation takes place.

At least two of the more popular ROM chips require only a single chip-enable command. In the example shown in Fig. 6-2, the chip enable is an active-low input (it is designated $\overline{CE}$). This terminal is brought low whenever you want to read the contents of one of the locations in the chip.

The example shown in Fig. 6-2 is a 256-byte ROM, with a single $\overline{CE}$ terminal. You must, therefore, construct external circuitry that brings the chip-enable terminal low when you want to perform the read operation.

The simplest way is to use a three-input NOR gate and an inverter. The output of the NOR gate goes high only when all three of the inputs are low. Connect the $\overline{MREQ}$, $\overline{RD}$, and bit A8 of the address bus to the respective inputs of the NOR gate. When the conditions are met, the output of the gate snaps high and is inverted to become the $\overline{CE}$ signal required by the EPROM (erasable-programmable ROM) chip.

An alternate method is shown in Fig. 6-3. Here use two inverters and a pair of NOR gates to form the CE signal. The idea is to cause CE to go low when the three conditions are met. To do this, both inputs of NOR-gate 2

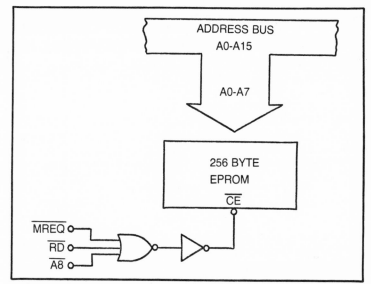

Fig. 6-2. RAM interfacing circuit.

must go low simultaneously. One of the inputs is connected to bit A8 of the address bus, while the other is connected to the inverted output of NOR-gate 1. The inputs of gate 1 are, in turn, connected to the $\overline{MREQ}$ and $\overline{RD}$ signals.

A situation that is a little more complicated is shown in Fig. 6-4. Here I am interfacing static RAM devices that have a chip-enable and a $\overline{R/W}$ terminal. This latter terminal causes the device to read data out when low, and allows writing data in when high. Connect the $\overline{R/W}$ terminal to the $\overline{RD}$ signal of the Z-80 CPU.

The chip enable in this example wants to see a high in order to turn on the device. You can connect the CE to the output of a NOR gate. The $\overline{MREQ}$ and $\overline{A8}$ signals are connected to the two inputs of the NOR gate. If both of these signals go low simultaneously, and the $\overline{RD}$ is also low, a memory-read operation takes place from the location addressed by A0-A7. Alternately, if the $\overline{MREQ}$ and A7 signals are low, and the $\overline{RD}$ signal is high, then a memory-write operation takes place.

Note in Fig. 6-4 that two chips are used to form a 256-byte static-RAM. Most memories require more than a single chip in order to form a complete byte-array. In this case each memory chip contains a 256 × 4-bit array; so

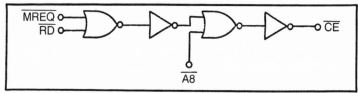

Fig. 6-3. Chip-enable device for RAM interfacing.

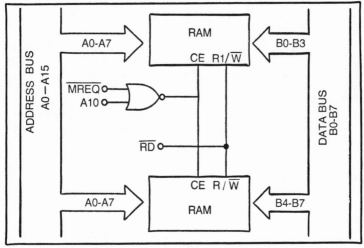

Fig. 6-4. RAM interfacing.

two connected form a 256 × 8-bit array (i.e., 256 bytes of memory). The popular 2102 is listed as a 1024 × 1-bit device. Connecting eight of these devices into an array results in a 1024-byte memory.

DYNAMIC MEMORY

Dynamic RAM does not hold its data for an indefinite length of time unless a *refresh* operation is performed. The refresh operation is a function of the CPU in most cases, but some non-CPU examples exist. Although the use of static RAM eliminates this problem, it is only at the cost of a higher power-consumption. The Z-80A device provides for refresh of the dynamic memory by adding a refresh segment to the first machine cycle (instruction fetch).

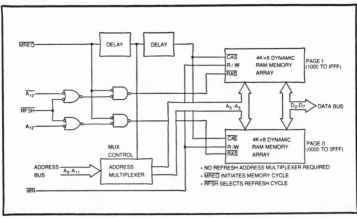

Fig. 6-5. Dynamic RAM interfacing.

During clock periods T3 and T4 of the first machine cycle, used by the Z-80 for the decoding of the instructions fetched in the earlier T-periods, a refresh ($\overline{\text{RFSH}}$) signal is generated. (A machine cycle is almost the same as a T-period, except it also includes the time that is necessary for information to be transferred back to the device that originated the cycle, e.g., when a bus request signal is sent, the machine cycle is complete when a ready signal is returned. Each of thes actions requires one T state, and together make one machine cycle.) The $\overline{\text{RFSH}}$ terminal (pin 28) of the Z-80 goes low during this period. Note that this signal must be used in conjunction with the $\overline{\text{MREQ}}$ (memory request) signal, because the $\overline{\text{RFSH}}$ is guaranteed to be stable only when the $\overline{\text{MREQ}}$ is active.

During the refresh period the lower portion of the address of a refresh location is placed on the lower seven bits (A0-A6) of the address bus (A7 is 0). The data on A0-A6 is from the R register in the Z-80, which is incremented after each instruction fetch. The upper eight-bits of the address

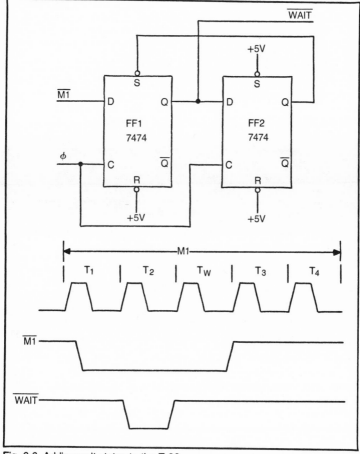

Fig. 6-6. Adding wait states to the Z-80.

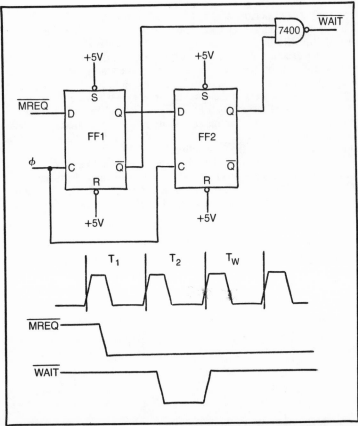

Fig. 6-7. Adding wait state for memory to the Z-80.

bus carry the contents of the I register. Figure 6-5 shows an example of an 8K dynamic RAM interfaced to a Z-80. In this particular case 4K × 8-bit dynamic RAMs are used. If no other RAM is used, you can use bit A12 of the address bus as a chip-select line.

ADDING WAIT STATES

All solid-state memory chips require a certain minimum period of time to write data into, or read data from, any given location. Many such devices are graded (and priced!) according to memory speed. The popular 2102 device, a 1K × 1-bit IC, is available in 250-nanosecond, 400-nanosecond, and 500-nanosecond versions. Of course, the cost per chip rises with the speed. (The higher the speed, the lower the access time in nanoseconds.)

Since the Z-80 can operate at speeds up to 4 MHz, sometimes the first machine-cycle (M1) is over before the data have settled to or from memory.

The problem can be overcome by adding the circuitry shown in Fig. 6-6. Both of these circuits generate a $\overline{WAIT}$ input (pin 24 of the Z-80) equal to the period of one clock pulse.

The circuit in Fig. 6-6 uses both sections of a TTL 7474 dual type-D flip-flop. The 7474 is a positive edge-triggered device, meaning that data on the D input is transferred to the Q output only during the positive-going transitions of the clock pulse.

Immediately after the onset of clock pulse of T1, the $\overline{\text{M1}}$ (machine-cycle 1) line goes low, forcing the D input of flip-flop 1 low. When clock pulse T2 snaps high, then, this low is transferred to the Q output of flip-flop 1. This signal becomes the $\overline{\text{WAIT}}$ signal for the CPU, and inserts one additional clock period (TW) into the first machine-cycle.

At the onset of clock period TW flip-flop 2 sees a low (i.e., the $\overline{\text{WAIT}}$ signal) on its D input. This low is transferred to the Q output of flip-flop 2. The Q_2 terminal (flip-flop 2) is connected to the set input of flip-flop 1; so this condition forces the Q_1 (flip-flop 1) high again, thereby terminating the action.

A similar circuit, shown in Fig. 6-7, is used to add a wait state to any machine cycle. When the first clock pulse (T1) arrives, the $\overline{\text{MREQ}}$ line goes low, forcing the D input of flip-flop 1 low. At the onset of clock pulse T2, then, this low is transferred to the Q output of flip-flop 1. At this time Q_1 is high and $\overline{Q_2}$ is high, so the output of the NAND gate drops low. (Both NAND inputs must be high for the output to be low.) This causes the $\overline{\text{WAIT}}$ input of the CPU to become active. But at the onset of TW, the added clock period, the low on Q_1 is transferred to Q_2. This forces one input of the NAND gate high, thereby canceling the WAIT signal.

MEMORY-MAPPED DEVICES

Some peripheral devices used with microcomputers can be more efficiently employed if they are treated as memory locations instead of I/O

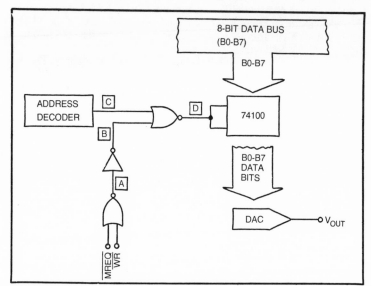

Fig. 6-8. Memory-mapped digital-to-analog converter.

devices. An example might be a *digital-to-analog converter* (DAC), which is a device that creates an analog output-voltage (or current) that is proportional to a binary digital-word applied to its input.

Figure 6-8 shows how an eight-bit digital-to-analog converter can be interfaced with a Z-80 as if the converter were a memory location. The digital-to-analog requires stable input data, but the data on the bus are transitory. Therefore, you need a data latch between the eight-bit data-bus and inputs to the digital-to-analog converter.

There are a number of interface chips that perform this job, but most of these special-purpose devices are costly. A low-cost solution, which works just as well, is to use a 74100 TTL dual quad-latch. The two four-bit sections of the 74100 become an eight-bit latch when the strobe terminals are tied together.

The 74100 latch transfers the information on the data bus to the digital-to-analog converter when the strobe line is high. The 74100 outputs, connected to the converter inputs, retain these data when the strobe line again goes low. The idea is to make the 74100 strobe-line high during the period when the desired converter input-data are present on the data bus.

Three requirements must be met before the data on the bus can be input to the digital-to-analog converter: (1) The write signal ($\overline{WR}$) must be active (2) the memory request ($\overline{MREQ}$) must be active, and (3) the correct address (the address of the location assigned to the digital-to-analog converter) must be present on the address bus.

The first two requirements are examined by a single NOR gate. When both WR and MREQ are low (i.e., active) they produce a memory write operation. This causes point A to go high and point B to go low. You do not want the digital-to-analog converter to respond, however, unless point C is low at the same time. When point C is low, you know that the address for the digital-to-analog converter is being sent over the address bus.

When all three requirements are met, the strobe input of the 74100 (point D) goes high. This allows transfer of data from the data bus into the digital-to-analog converter.

Most microcomputers have less than the full 64K of memory. This is the reason why most memory-mapped devices tend to be allocated addresses in the upper 32K memory. This, incidentally, allows you to use bit A15 of the address bus to discriminate between the various addresses.

Chapter 7

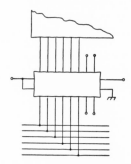

UART

The universal asynchronous receiver/transmitter, or UART, is a special digital-IC that contains independent data-transmitter and receiver sections. The transmitter accepts n-bit parallel-format data and transmits it in serial form. The receiver, on the other hand, accepts serial-format input-data and reassembles it into parallel format. The UART makes the task of designing serial I/O ports in parallel-format computers easier.

Asynchronous transmission is preferred over synchronous transmission because it is not necessary to precisely track the clocks at each end. The clocks must be operating at very nearly the same frequency, but they need not be locked together. This eliminates the added circuit or extra communications channel needed to synchronize the two clocks. The tolerance of the clock rates in asynchronous transmission is said to be 0.01 percent, but this is easily obtained if modern ICs and crystal-control are used.

The UART is a single large-scale integration chip that performs all of the data transmission functions on the digital side. Bit length, parity, and the overall length of the stop bits can be programmed into the UART.

The block diagram of a common UART IC is shown in Fig. 7-1. This particular device is the TR1602A/B by Western Digital. Note that the pin-outs for the UART are almost universally standardized and are based on the now obsolete AY-1013. Most UARTs are capable of all three communications modes: *simplex*, *half-duplex* and *full-duplex*. This feature is due to the fact that 111 of the transmitter and receiver control pins are independent of each other.

The UART is capable of being user-programmed to determine transmitted word-length, baud rate, parity type (odd/even, receiver-verification/transmitter-generation), parity-inhibit and stop-bit length (1, 1.5, or 2 clock periods). The UART also provides six different status flags: *transmission completed, buffer-register transfer completed, received data-available, parity error, framing error,* and *overrun error.*

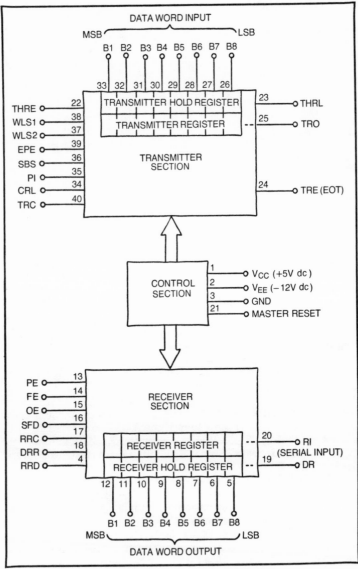

Fig. 7-1. UART block diagram.

The maximum clock speed is between 320 kHz and 800 kHz, depending upon the particular type selected. Note that the clock rate actually used in any given application is dependent upon the baud rate. The clock frequency is always 16 times the data baud-rate.

The receiver output lines are three-state, which means there is a high impedance to both ground and positive voltage when the outputs are inactive. This allows the outputs of the receiver section to be connected directly to a data bus without extra circuitry.

The transmitter section uses an eight-bit input register. This feature makes it capable of accepting an eight-bit parallel word from a source such as a keyboard, computer output port, data bus, etc. It assembles these bits and then transmits them at the designated time, adding any demanded parity or stop bits.

The receiver data-format is a logical mirror image of the transmitter section. It inputs serial data-bits; strips off the start, stop, and parity bits (if used); and then assembles the binary word in parallel form. In addition, it tests the data for validity by comparison of the parity bits and stop bits.

The standard UART data format is shown in Fig. 7-2. The data line (transmitter serial-output or receiver serial-input normally sits at a logical high level unless data is being transmitted or received. The start bit (B0) is always low, so the high-to-low transition is what the UART senses for the starting of a word or transmission. Bits B1-B8 are the data bits loaded into the transmitter register from the outside world. Although Fig. 7-2 shows all eight bits, you can program the device for fewer if needed. Lengths of 5, 6, 7, or 8 bits are allowed. Bits are dropped in shorter formats from the B1 side of the chain.

Figure 7-3 shows typical receiver and transmitter configurations for the UART. The transmitter section is shown in Fig. 7-3A, while Fig. 7-3B shows the circuitry for a receiver section. If the serial output of the transmitter is connected to the serial input of the receiver, a closed loop exists; and the output word from the receiver matches the transmitted word. In most cases the UART is used to drive some external communications channel, such as an audio-frequency shift-keyer, for transmission over some standard communications media.

The UART can be connected as in Fig. 7-3, with separate transmit and receive lines, but that method is not the most optimal and requires separate I/O-ports for the connection. You can also connect the UART directly to the data bus of a microcomputer!

Figure 7-4 shows the basic connections for the standard UART to an eight-bit data-bus. The receiver-output-register lines are Tri-state; so they can be connected directly to the lines of the bus. The transmitter-register lines also have a high impedance; so they also can be connected to the data bus. You can enable the transmit-hold register by bringing the line low momentarily when output data is present on the line. This is done by

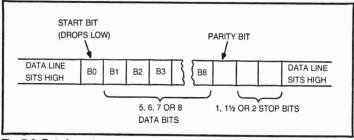

Fig. 7-2. Data format.

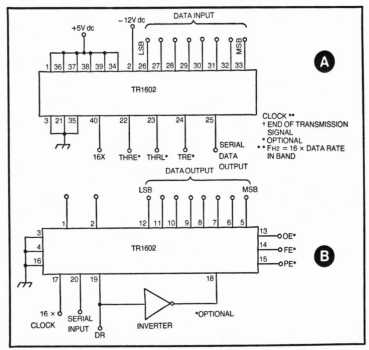

Fig. 7-3. Transmitter circuit (A) and receiver circuit (B).

connecting the transmit-hold register-line to an output-device select-line. Circuits to generate in and out pulses are discussed in Chapter 4.

The receiver register is dumped to the data bus when the IN2 line is dropped low. The IN2 line is connected to the RRD and DRR lines.

The IN1 line is an active-low control-line that connects the status flags to the data bus when low. Keeping this line prevents the status flags from entering the data bus. The status flag lines are set to high impedance (i.e., three-state) when the first input line is high.

In the circuit of Fig. 7-4, the programming lines (CRL, PI, SBS, WLS1, WLS2, and EPE) are set permanently high through a pull-up resistor. You can program the UART any way that you wish by setting specific lines high or low (see Table 7-1). Sometimes, however, you might not wish to have a preprogrammed UART; you might want to operate UART programming under software control. You can adapt the UART to this mode of operation, which is common among UARTs that are designed for use with specific microprocessor chips, by using a 74100 data-latch as an output port-register. Ths six control lines of the UART (pins 34-39) are connected to the outputs of the 74100. The inputs of the 74100 are connected to lines B0-B5 of the data bus. To set the UART load the CPU accumulator with a binary word that contains the correct bit pattern for the programming desired. For example, if you want to program the UART with the hardwires in Fig. 7-4, you need to load the accumulator with the binary word xx111111 (x indicates "don't care"). You can load the accumulator with either FF

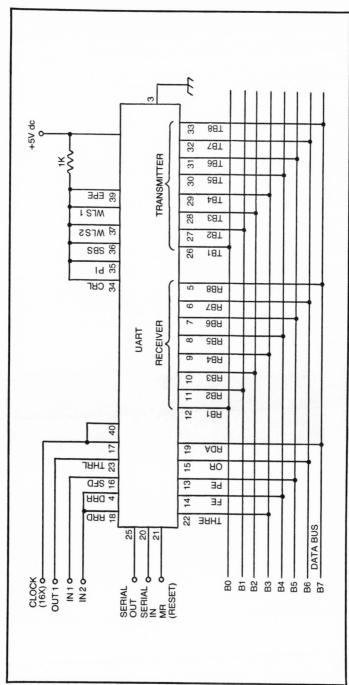

Fig. 7-4. Direct interface to the data bus.

Table 7-1. UART-Pin Functions.

Pin No.	Mnemonic	Function
1	Vcc	+5 volts DC power supply.
2	Vee	-12 volts DC power supply.
3	GND	Ground.
4	RRD	Receiver Register Disconnect. A high on this pin disconnects (i.e., places at high impedance) the receiver data output pins (5 through 12). A low on this pin connects the receiver data output lines to output pins 5 through 12.
5	RB8	LSB
6	RB7	
7	RB6	
8	RB5	Receiver data output lines
9	RB4	
10	RB3	
11	RB2	
12	RB1	MSB
13	PE	Parity error. A high on this pin indicates that the parity of the received data does not match the parity programmed at pin 39.
14	FE	Framing Error. A high on this line indicates that no valid stop bits were received
15	OE	Overrun Error. A high on this pin indicates that an overrun condition has occurred, which is defined as not having the DR flag (pin 19) reset before the next character is received by the internal receiver holding register.
16	SFD	Status Flag Disconnect. A high on this pin will disconnect (i.e., set to high impedance) the PE, FE, OE, DR, and THRE status flags. This feature allows the status flags from several UARTs to be bus-connected together.
17	RRC	16 × Receiver Clock. A clock signal is applied to this pin, and should have a frequency that is 16 times the desired baud rate (i.e., for 110 baud standard it is 16 × 110 baud, or 1760 hertz).
18	DRR	Data Receive Reset. Bringing this line low resets the data received (DR, pin 19) flag.
19	DR	Data Received. A high on this pin indicates that the entire character is received, and is in the receiver holding register.
20	RI	Receiver Serial Input. All serial input data bits are applied to this pin. Pin 20 must be forced high when no data is being received.
21	MR	Master Reset. A short pulse (i.e., a strobe pulse) applied to this pin will reset (i.e., force low) both receiver and transmitter registers, as well as the FE, OE, PE, and DRR flags. It also sets the TRO, THRE, and TRE flags (i.e, makes them high).
22	THRE	Transmitter Holding Register Empty. A high on this pin means that the data in the transmitter input buffer has been transferred to the transmitter register, and allows a new character to be loaded.
23	THRL	Transmitter Holding Register Load. A low applied to this pin enters the word applied to TB1 through TB8 (pins 26 through 33, respectively) into the transmitter holding register (THR). A positive-going level applied to this pin transfers the contents of the THR into the transmit register (TR), unless the TR is currently sending the previous word. When the transmission is finished the THR→TR transfer will take place automatically even if the pin 25 level transition is completed.
24	TRE	Transmit Register Empty. Remains high unless a transmission is taking place, in which case the TRE pin drops low.
25	TRO	Transmitter (Serial) Output. All data and control bits in the transmit register are output on this line. The TRO terminal stays high when no transmission is taking place, so the beginning of a transmission is always indicated by the first negative-going transition of the TRO terminal.
26	TB8	LSB
27	TB7	
28	TB6	
29	TB5	Transmitter input word.
30	TB4	
31	TB3	
32	TB2	
33	TB1	MSB

82

Table 7-1. UART-Pin Functions (continued from page 82).

34	CRL	Control Register Load. Can be either wired permanently high, or be strobed with a positive-going pulse. It loads the programmed instructions (i.e., WLS1, WLS2, EPE, PI, and SBS) into the internal control register. Hard wiring of this terminal is preferred if these parameter never change, while switch or program control is preferred if the parameters do occassionally change.
35	PI	Parity inhibit. A high on this pin disables parity generation/verification functions, and forces PE (pin 13) to a low logic condition.
36	SBS	Stop Bit(s) Select. Programs the number of stop bits that are added to the data word output. A high on SBS causes the UART to send two stop bits if the word length format is 6, 7, or 8 bits, and 1.5 stop bits if the 5-bit teletypewriter format is selected (on pins 37-38). A low on SBS causes the UART to generate only one stop bit.
37 38	WLS1 WLS2 }	Word Length Select. Selects character length, exclusive of parity bits, according to the rules given in the chart below: Word Length WLS1 WLS2 5 bits low low 6 bits high low 7 bits low high 8 bits high high
39	EPE	Even Parity Enable. A high applied to this line selects even parity, while a low applied to this line selects odd parity.
40	TRC	16 × Transmit Clock. Apply a clock signal with a frequency that is equal to 16 times the desired baud rate. If the transmitter and receiver sections operate at the same speed (usually the case), then strap together TRC and RRC terminals so that the same clock serves both sections.

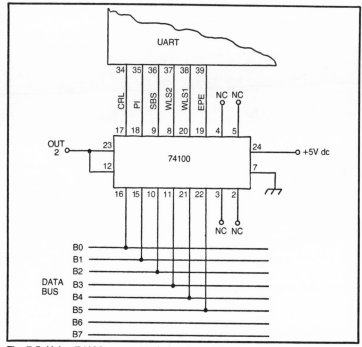

Fig. 7-5. Using 74100 as a control-signals register.

(hex) or 3F (hex) to accomplish the job! Then output the word stored in the accumulator to output-port 2 (i.e., make the OUT2 line high). Of course, any combination can be programmed into the 74100, and the UART responds accordingly. The output lines of the 74100 are latched; they remain at the word programmed.

Chapter 8

Interfacing Keyboards, Push-buttons, and Sensors

There are a variety of input devices that can be used to interface with a human operator. Some of these devices are formal keyboards and produce an ASCII or hexadecimal word at their output when a key is pressed. Other devices are mere push-buttons and are used on the front panels of instruments that incorporate microcomputers. In still other cases, the interface is some sort of sensor. Although some of these are not strictly human interfaces, their principles are none the less important for the microprocessor interfacer.

DIGITAL CAR-RADIO TUNER

Although radio is beyond the scope of this book, it is instructive to examine one model produced by Delco Electronics for General Motors automobiles. This car radio uses a digitally controlled phase-locked loop-tuner for the AM and FM bands.

The phase-locked loop is a special-purpose circuit that compares the frequency of the superheterodyne local-oscillator with a fixed-reference frequency of 10 kHz. This reference is crystal controlled; so the stability of a properly locked local-oscillator in a phase-locked loop system is that of the crystal oscillator. The frequency of the local oscillator is divided down to 10 kHz by a programmable divide-by n counter. The n-code applied to this counter is used to determine what frequency is being received.

In the Delco design, a microprocessor-like chip is used to control the phase-locked loop according to the conditions scanned on the input lines. Figure 8-1 shows the relevant digital-control circuitry from this GMC radio. The programmer is the DM-68 device. There are five output lines, and three input lines, on the DM-68 IC.

The DM-68 device is trained to respond to certain commands that allow functions such as *manual tune, select, store, seek, scan,* and *recall.* The manual-tuning mode allows the operator to select a station manually using a knob on the front panel of the radio. The recall mode affects the digital display seen by the user. Ordinarily, the radio frequency is displayed

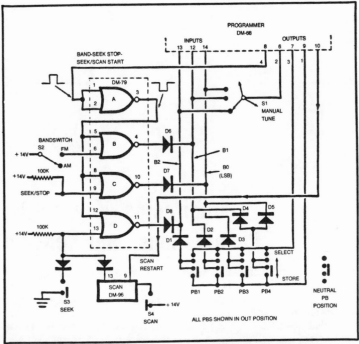

Fig. 8-1. Control circuits of the Delco all-digital AM/FM radio receivers.

only under two circumstances, and then only for a few seconds: when the power is initially applied and when a new station is selected by any of the methods allowed. At other times, the data from the internal digital clock, also a feature of the radio, is displayed on the digital readout.

The Select and store modes refer to different operating modes of the push-buttons on the front panel. In the store mode, the DM-68 stores in a specific internal register the n-code for the station being received at that time. When the same push-button is pressed later on, in the select mode, the radio immediately goes to the stations whose n-code had been stored. There are four select/store push-buttons on the Delco radio. They are pushed in to select, and pulled-out to store.

SEEK AND SCAN FUNCTIONS

Seek and scan are similar functions. Both are automatic tuning modes. In the seek mode, the tuner advances to the next higher frequency station and stop. If the user wants to preview another station, a new seek command must be initiated for the radio to go on. In the scan mode, however, the radio increments to the next higher station and stops for only five seconds. It then increments again, unless the scan command has been intentionally can-celled by the user. This mode allows the user to preview all of the stations in an area before selecting the one that is best suited.

The gating circuit that selects the different modes of operation for the DM-68 is shown in Fig. 8-1. There are two data buses associated with the

DM-68: a three-bit input command-bus and a four-bit timing, or output, bus. The output lines are active-high, meaning that they normally sit low and snap high only when that line is active. These four lines go high in sequence at an 80-Hz rate. Each output line causes the DM-68 to examine or poll a different facet of the tuning protocol. Each of the four cycles controls one of the four tuning modes. See Fig. 8-2.

The DM-68 knows what to do next by monitoring the data on the input buses during each of the four cycles. Timing is taken care of internally; so no additional external synchronization circuits are needed.

Cycle 1 controls the operation of the front-panel push-buttons in the store mode. If one of the front-panel push-buttons is pulled out during cycle 1, the n-code applied to the synthesizer at that instant is stored in the internal DM-68 register corresponding to that button. The DM-68 examines the input bus during cycle 1. If a station is to be stored on, say, push-button 2, one merely pulls out push-button 2 on the front panel. When output 1 goes high (indicating cycle 1), a high is passed through isolation diode D2 to bit 1 of the input bus. The DM-68 input bus, then, sees the binary code 010 during cycle 1, which it interprets to store the present n-code in the register of push-button 2. The store codes for the other push-buttons are 100 for 1, 001 for 3, and 011 for 4.

Cycle 2 controls manual tuning. This radio differs from other automobile radios in that it lacks a permeability-tuning mechanism (PTM); hence, the manual tuning-shaft must operate some device or circuit that generates a binary code. In the Delco circuit, they have selected a specially-designed three-prong switch (S1) that has a wiper always connected to one or the other input lines. When output line 2 goes high, the DM-68 examines the input bus to determine if the data word is the same as it was on the immediately previous cycle 2. If no change has occurred, then no action is taken. If the new data word is different from the old data word,

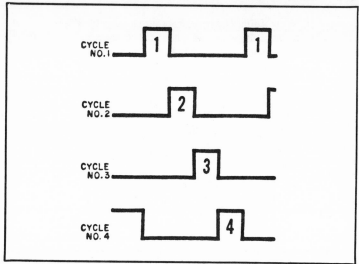

Fig. 8-2. Timing diagram.

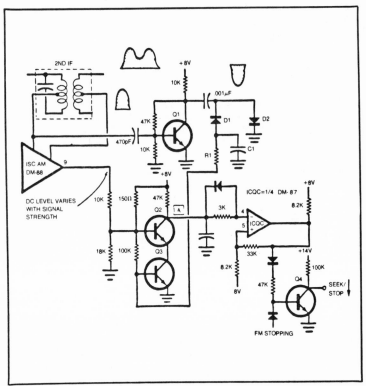

Fig. 8-3. AM stop-circuit.

however, the DM-68 either increments or decrements the n-code depending upon the direction of the manual tuning-code change. This is controlled by the direction that the tuning knob was turned.

Cycle 3 is the opposite or complement of cycle 1. It selects the stations stored if one of the push-buttons is pressed. Again, using push-button 2 as the example, if push-button 2 is pressed, the code on the input bus during cycle 3 is 010. This tells the DM-68 to output the n-code stored in register 010.

Cycle 4 controls the bandswitching and all of the signal-seeker or automatic-tuning functions. This cycle is controlled by a CMOS 4002 NOR gate IC. Section A of the NOR gate inverts the high-pulse of DM-68 cycle 4 to form a low and applies the low to one input on each of the remaining three 4002 gates. This enables the gates only during cycle 4 and keeps them off during the other three cycles. When the inverted cycle 4 pulse goes low, it enables NOR gate sections B, C, and D.

Different n-codes are required for AM and FM tuning. Bandswitch S2 makes the remaining input of gate B high for AM operation and low for FM operation. The DM-68 tells which has been selected by looking at input line B1 during cycle 4. If B1 is low, FM is selected. If B1 is high, AM is selected. The n-codes are adjusted accordingly.

Seek and scan modes are controlled by gate D. The input (pin 13) of this section is normally high. If it goes low, the DM-68 initiates seeking action. The scan circuit also causes pin 13 to drop low, but it contains a five-second resistance-capacitance timer to produce the scanning and stopping action described earlier. The DM-68 initiates a seek or scan operation if B2 is high during cycle 4.

Seeker stopping is controlled by gate C. This input (pin 9) of the gate is normally held high, but drops low if the stop circuits indicate that a station is tuned in. The DM-68 recognizes this command by a high on B0 during cycle 4.

The AM and FM stop circuits are shown in Figs. 8-3 and 8-4, respectively. In both cases Q4 is the seek the stop switch that is connected to NOR gate C (Fig. 8-1). The collector terminal of Q4 goes to ground when a stop command is issued. It remains high at all other times.

SWITCHES

There are quite a number of switches and devices that perform switch-like functions (e.g., optoisolators). These devices are often interfaced with microprocessors for various purposes. Of course, the ordinary toggle or push-button mechanical switches are among these devices. You might also find a *reed switch,* especially in certain security-electronics areas or in process-control applications. The operation of a reed switch depends upon a magnetic field (see Fig. 8-5). The reed switch is also called a vacuum switch because it is enclosed in an evacuated glass-tube. When there is no magnetic field present, the switch contacts are open. When a magnetic field is present, the switch contacts are closed. The magnet might be an electromagnet coil that is coaxial with the reed switch (as in vacuum relays), or it might be a permanent magnet (as in door and window alarm-switches used in security electronics).

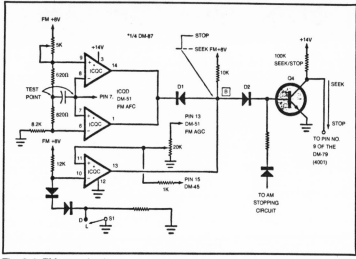

Fig. 8-4. FM stop-circuit.

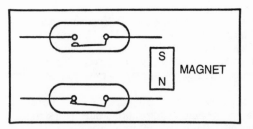

Fig. 8-5. Reed relay.

Another form of switch is the optoisolator. These devices are used in cases where some isolation is needed between circuits. They are also configured, as in Fig. 8-6, to operate as switches. The optical path between the light emitting diode (LED) and the phototransistor (Q1) is interrupted by a gap. If there is an object in the path, the transistor is blinded and produces a high at B0 of the computer input. But, if there is no object in the path, the light from the LED shines on Q1 and turns it on. The collector of Q1 is then grounded; so the level at B0 is low.

An example of the use of the optoisolator as a switch is shown in Fig. 8-7. In this case, we are looking at the end of travel indicator on a printer. The optoisolator (such as Fig. 8-6) is positioned at the lefthand side of the print-head travel. A *tang* on the print head mechanism is designed to blind the transistor when the print head is at the left margin (Fig. 8-7).

A similar idea is shown in Fig. 8-8, except that most of these use an LED and a photoresistor cell (R2). The circuit is shown in Fig. 8-9. The LED is connected to the +5 V; so it is permanently turned on. The photo resistor is also connected to the +5 V through a 100K ohm resistor. When the path is empty, allowing the LED to fall on the photoresistor, the resistance is low, which keeps the voltage applied to the TTL *Schmitt-trigger* low. However, when the paper is in the path, the photoresistor is no

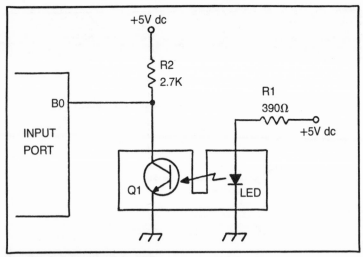

Fig. 8-6. Optically coupled switch.

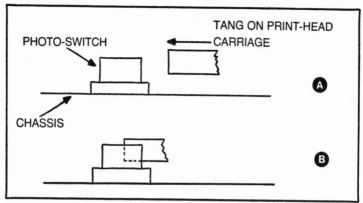

Fig. 8-7. Position sensor (LED).

longer illuminated; so its resistance is high. This increases the voltage applied to the Schmitt trigger above its threshold value, causing the output to drop low.

In the application shown in Fig. 8-9, the LED and photoresistor are placed on opposite sides of the paper path at the printer platen. When there is no paper in the machine the output of the Schmitt trigger is low, telling the microprocessor that controls the process to stop sending data.

INTERFACING SWITCHES

You can correct switches directly to the input port of a microcomputer. When there is no port available, you can also connect the switch to the data bus. This is not always easy to do! If the switch is left in the low condition, then the data-bus line is permanently shorted to ground! You must, therefore, connect the switch to the data-bus line through a three-state device.

The concept of a three-state device is shown in Fig. 8-10. All digital devices are at least two-state. When the output is low, there is a low

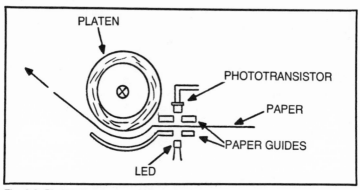

Fig. 8-8. Photocell sensor application—paper detector.

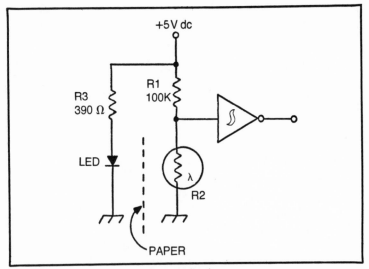

Fig. 8-9. Circuit for photocell sensor application.

impedance from the output terminal to ground. Similarly, when the output is high, there is a low impedance to +5 V. In the third state, there is a high impedance, effectively an open circuit, between the output terminal of the device and either +5 V or ground. This is shown in Fig. 8-10.

When the chip enable turns the device on, switch S2 is closed, connecting the output terminal to the IC's circuitry. Switch S1 connects to either +5 V or ground, depending on the state of the input signal. When the chip-enable signal turns off the chip, however, switch S2 opens, allowing the output terminal to float free.

There are several devices that are used for switch interfacing, and all of them have tri-state outputs. Typical devices are the 8216, 8226 (both by Intel), 74125, 74126, 74LS244, and 74LS245.

A typical switch interface is shown in Fig. 8-11. The switch could be an optoisolator or photoresistor (as shown earlier), or it might be a real switch as shown in Fig. 8-6B. The switch is connected so that it produces a high when open and a low when closed. When the switch is open the resistor (R1) applies +5 V to the IC input. However, when switch S1 is closed, the input of the IC is shorted to ground; it is low.

The computer must be programmed to ground the chip-enable line $\overline{(CE)}$ when an input is required. In the example shown, the output of the three-state buffer is connected to line B0 of the data bus. Since the buffer is noninverting, a low appears on B0 when the switch is closed and a high when the switch is open. Keep in mind that this means that the low condition indicates that the switch is being pressed.

The program to service this switch must periodically come back to the switch and sample B0. Since the input can occur at any time in some cases, this scanning must be performed at a high rate. In most cases, a 100-Hz scan-rate is sufficient. The $\overline{CE}$ line is connected to the output of a device select (see Chapter 4) circuit. You can connect it as either an I/O port or a

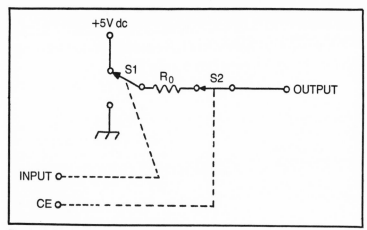

Fig. 8-10. Model of the Tri-state circuit.

memory location. Let's suppose it is a I/O port and CE is connected to bit B0 (assigned port 1). The circuit works as follows:

● Write a 00000000 to port 1. This turns on $\overline{\text{CE}}$.

● If S1 is closed, then B0 of the data bus is low; so the computer sees xxxxxxxx0 ("x" meaning either state is all right). If, on the other hand, the switch is open, the computer sees xxxxxxx1 on the data bus.

● Mask the word stored in the accumulator (i.e., the word previously on the data bus during the input operation) by anding it with 00000001. If the B0 bit is low, the result stored in the accumulator is zero. If, however, the B0 line

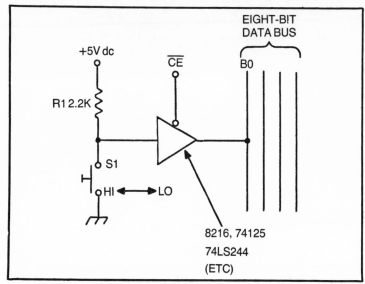

Fig. 8-11. Tri-state driver to interface push-button to data-bus.

was high, the result left in the accumulator after the AND instruction is 00000001. The branch and compare (BNE and BEQ) instructions in 6502 language) can be used to test the Z flag for the zero condition. The program can then branch on zero for the subroutine that services the push-button.
●The switch interface is disabled by writing 11111111 to the CE output-port.

There is no reason why you cannot interface as many switches as there are lines on the data bus and service them with the same operation. Of course, the program to service such an arrangement is more complex than that for a single push-button. You must program into the system some priority so that the most important push-button (if any) is recognized first.

Figure 8-12 shows the use of the three-state buffer to interface four switches. The 8216 (inverting) and 8226 (noninverting) devices can be used in this application. You can also use the 74125 and 74126 devices. If eight switches are to be accommodated, then, use the 74LS244 and 74LS245 devices. All four buffers are served by a single chip-enable line in the 82xx Intel devices, but in the 74125/6 devices there are four separate CE lines that must be connected to form a single CE line. In the 74LS244/5 devices, there are two CE lines (pins 1 and 19) that must be joined in a like manner.

A single device-select pulse turns on all four (or eight) switch buffers. The word that is transmitted to the data bus (and into the computer accumulator) depends upon which switches are open or closed. If all switches are open, the word on the data bus is xxxx1111. Similarly, if they are all closed, the word is xxxx0000. Other combinations of open and closed switches produce binary words from xxxx0000 to xxxx1111. In programming this computer, you must (1) prioritize the switches so that more important switches are serviced first and (2) prevent contradictory actions.

In the example of Fig. 8-12 you have a burglar-alarm controller. The sensors are switches that open when someone messes with the windows or tries to enter a door. They can also be the outputs of devices such as infrared or ultrasonic sensors. The computer, which can be used for environmental control and other purposes, scans the bank of alarm switches at a periodic rate. Given the nature of the alarm, a slow scan rate, say 1 Hz, should be sufficient—it is unlikely that any burglar can open a window or door and do damage in milliseconds!

KEYBOARD INTERFACING

The keyboard is a constant feature of most practical microcomputers. There are at least two configurations in common use: hexadecimal and ASCII. The hexadecimal keyboard is a 16-key device that outputs a hexadecimal binary word when a key is pressed. For example, when the "6" button is pressed, the binary word appearing on the output is 0110. The ASCII keyboard is a little more complex, and produces an ASCII character in binary form when a key is pressed. Of course, one has to be aware that there is a difference between the number six and the character 6. When the ASCII key marked 6 is pressed, the seven-bit binary number appearing on the output is 0110110. We must be aware of the difference between characters and numbers.

The ASCII code is a seven bit code; so fits nicely into the format of the typical microcomputer. This arrangement leaves an eighth bit available for the strobe, a signal that tells the outside world that the data on the output of the keyboard is valid. Since the ASCII code uses seven bits, you can represent up to 128 different characters or control functions ($2^7 = 128$). In most microcomputers, use the lower seven-bits (B0-B6) of the input port for the ASCII data from the keyboard, and the most significant bit (B7) for the strobe pulse.

Figure 8-13 shows the circuit for one of the most popular forms of ASCII keyboard. This keyboard uses a special integrated circuit (3600). This device is called a scanning keyboard encoder and operates from resistance-capacitance clock. Resistor R1 and capacitor C6 form the timing elements for the keyboard. The seven output lines are connected to bits B1-B7 of the microcomputer input-port.

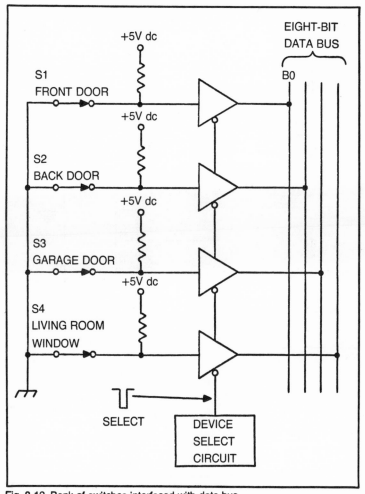

Fig. 8-12. Bank of switches interfaced with data bus.

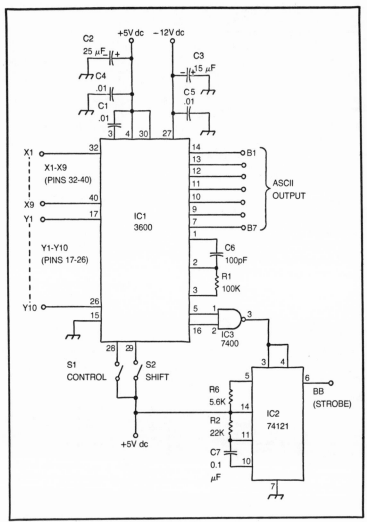

Fig. 8-13. Keyboard circuit.

The strobe bit is generated by a TTL monostable-multivibrator (74121). This circuit produces one output pulse with a duration of approximately 1.5 microseconds. This speed is a little too slow for some microcomputers; more on this later.

The selection of the ASCII characters that are output is determined by which button is pressed. The keyboard buttons are connected to short-circuit the lines of an X-Y matrix. On the 3600 encoder IC there are nine X lines (X1-X9), and ten Y lines (Y1-Y10). This particular form of encoder requires push-button switches that actually connect the lines together, while others use capacitance keys or other techniques.

The control (CNTRL or CRTL) key and the shift key are single-pole/single-throw switches that apply +5 V to an appropriate input of the 3600.

There are two forms of strobe output seen on microcomputer keyboards: one-shot and constant. The one-shot type consists of a short-duration pulse that tickles the microcomputer to let it know when the data is valid. This type of pulse is shown in 8-14B. The other form is the constant method, and is shown in Fig. 8-14A. You must be aware of the type of strobe used in your microcomputer. Some digital-computer software depends on the type of pulse used on the strobe line. One program, for example, wants to see a short duration strobe pulse (Fig. 8-14B) and triggers response to the strobe on the negative-going falling-edge of the strobe pulse. The constant method is most often used on low cost hobbyest keyboards.

Doping Out the Keyboard

Microcomputerists often obtain keyboards from a variety of sources, and not all sources are too good about delivering proper information with their product. Sometimes the keyboards are commercial or industrial surplus and can have some odd tendencies; if you can identify the original manufacturer, you may be able to contact the in-house expert and to obtain information.

Unfortunately, there is no universally accepted method or standard for keyboard design. The keyboard that you obtain may have any of several different designs used.

Shooting in the Dark

First try to get whatever printed technical-data is available. If none comes with the keyboard, call the manufacturer. I make it a habit to always ask to speak to one of the repair technicians, or, the service department manager. These people usually have access to the schematics and, often, don't mind sending copies.

You might also find the circuit for the keyboard in the service manual for an instrument or computer that used the keyboard. In my case I used a

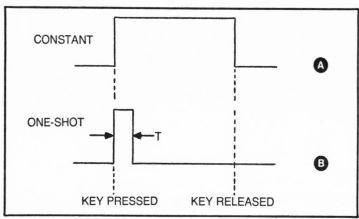

Fig. 8-14 (A) Continuous strobe and (B) one-shot strobe.

Texas Instruments Silent 700 keyboard for a couple of years. The TI service manual on that product contains the schematic; so I copied it for my own use.

The very first thing that you need to know is the pin-outs of the keyboard connector. Most keyboards use a printed circuit card-edge connector or a 14-pin DIP socket. If the schematic is available, use it to locate the various pins. Otherwise, you may be faced with the chore of manually doping out the circuit. This job is not too fearsome if the keyboard uses the standard chip circuits to generate the ASCII code—otherwise it can be a ruddy bore! Figure 8-13 and a low current ohmmeter make the job a lot easier for many keyboards.

The next thing to determine is whether or not the keyboard is TTL compatible. Some are not, especially those from older machines. Most keyboards, however, are TTL compatible, so you have little to fret over. If the data bits come up with a voltage between 2.5 and 5 V then it is TTL.

If it is not TTL compatible, or if you use one of those computers that needs a CMOS-compatible keyboard, then some interfacing on a bit-for-bit level is needed. More on that in a moment.

The third thing you needed to know is what the strobe looks like. Find out the duration of the strobe pulse (using and oscilloscope) and the polarity. It is also necessary to know whether the strobe signal is one-shot or continuous. If the strobe is of the wrong polarity, which usually means that you got one that sits high normally and then drops during the strobe period, an ordinary TTL or CMOS-inverter (as needed) will correct it.

If the strobe pulse is too short, or if it is of the wrong type (i.e., one-shot versus continuous), then certain remedies are available and will be given shortly.

The last thing that you must determine is whether the data output of the keyboard is latched or unlatched. The latched type retains the last valid data that existed, i.e., the last character, until a new character is commanded. Other keyboards are unlatched; so they either (1) have continuous invalid data (trash) on the output lines except during a key closure, or (2) return all output lines to ground during periods between key closures.

The type of keyboard that you have often determines whether or not the software works properly. On many computers the program loops continuously as long as the data on all lines is zero, and tries to input data whenever the input port sees anything except 00000000! If your keyboard is not the type that returns all output lines to ground between key closures, then the program will keep trying to input garbage data. Also, if your program uses a relatively slow loop (which to that computer might be fast if the clock rate is slow!), the duration of the strobe pulse may be too short! In this case the computer seems to miss some key closures! The cause of this annoying phenomenon is that the program is seeking a high on the strobe line, but the 1-microsecond strobe-pulse disappears before the program loop for the keyboard routine gets around to looking for it.

Solving Keyboard Problems

Figure 8-15 shows simple solutions to the problems of compatibility. If the strobe is a negative-going pulse and your computer wants to see a positive-going pulse, use a simple TTL inverter, as in Fig. 8-15A. The strobe line will strobe on the other side of the inverter. This same is true if the other lines are complemented, i.e., turned over. You can use other inverters to flip that data as well.

But before you solder-tack a 14-pin DIP IC onto the circuit board in order to get a single inverter, make sure that there are no unused sections of ICs on the keyboard already. You can use sections of the NAND gate (i.e., 7400) and NOR (7402) gates for the same purpose. Also, if you are planning to write your own monitor program, then it is a simple matter to have the program look for a low instead of a high to indicate valid data.

The circuits in Fig. 8-15B and 8-15C are used to make the keyboard outputs compatible with TTL or CMOS inputs, respectively. If the keyboard seems to have CMOS outputs (i.e., output levels greater than +5 V), use the circuit of Fig. 8-15B. This circuit uses a CMOS 4050 device (hex buffer) which accepts CMOS levels at the input. It produces TTL-compatible output levels, provided that only +5 V dc is used to supply power to the IC. If the chip power-supply potential is greater, all bets are off.

In Fig. 8-15 you have the method for making the TTL-keyboard compatible with the input of a CMOS system. The inverter is a 7406, and two sections are used to keep from flipping the data (note: the second inverter is not strictly necessary if you are going to write your own keyboard-service subroutine. Merely complement anything that comes in from the keyboard before it is stored anyplace). The 7406 device is an inverter with an open-collector output; so it requires a pull-up resistor between the output terminal and the positive voltage. The input section of the circuit uses a pull-up resistor to the +5 V dc power supply (TTL level). Note that the TTL power supply is +5 V, while the CMOS power supply can be anything from +5 to +18 V. Again, use any chip sections available on the board before tacking a new chip.

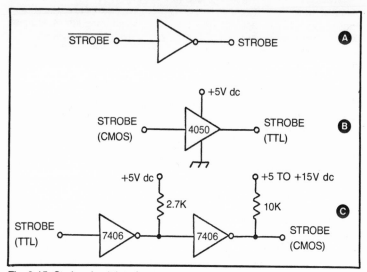

Fig. 8-15. Strobe circuit interfaces.

PULSE STRETCHER

The problem of too-short duration on the keyboard strobe-pulse can be overcome by using one of two different strategies. The method shown in Fig. 8-16 is probably the simplest and uses a 74121-TTL monostable-multivibrator as a pulse stretcher.

The name pulse stretcher is actually a little misleading—in fact it is downright wrong. The circuit does not stretch anything; it is a monostable multivibrator that generates a new pulse with a longer duration. If you look at the circuit as a black box and note that the short-duration strobe-pulse is applied to the input and a long duration pulse appears after at the output; you might conclude that the circuit inside of the black box has stretched the pulse. The duration of the output pulse from the 74121 device is approximately 0.7 R × C. Select values for resistance 1 and capacitance 1 that allow the strobe pulse to be high long enough for the microcomputer that you are using to recognize it.

Most microcomputer keyboard routines are machine language programs that perform a loop looking for a high condition on the strobe line. The programming guide for the microprocessor used in the computer gives the number of machine cycles required by the program, while the clock frequency tells you the time required per cycle (T=1/F). If the clock is 1 MHz, for example, then the duration of each clock period is 1/1,000,000, or, 1 micro-second. Similarly, if the clock is 2 MHz, then the period of the clock cycles is 0.5 micro-second, and so on. You can then multiply the number of clock cycles required to execute the keyboard-input program-loop by the period of the clock and arrive at some idea of the minimum time required for the strobe pulse to be recognized.

The seven ASCII lines from the keyboard are connected directly to bits B1 through B7 of a microcomputer input-port. The strobe bit is first inverted (unless it is negative-going) in a TTL inverter (e.g., 7404). The output of the inverter is applied to the trigger input of the 74121. The output lines of the 74121 are applied to bit B8 of the computer input port. In most cases a strobe-pulse duration of several microseconds is sufficient.

Two alternate versions of the same idea are shown in Fig. 8-17. In these methods, a type-D flip-flop is used as a 1-bit memory to remember that the strobe pulse existed.

Let's review briefly the rules for the 7474 type-D flip-flop. A type-D flip-flop passes the data on the D input to the Q output only when the clock line is high. In this circuit, the D input is wired permanently high. The Q output goes high and remains high when the clock line is high. The 7474 also has an active-low clear line. All clear terminals have the effect of causing the Q to go low, and the not-Q (Q) to go high. It is this terminal that gives us the ability to reset the flip-flop.

The seven bits from the ASCII output of the keyboard are connected to bits B1 through B7 of an input port. The Q output of the 7474 flip-flop is connected to either (a) bit B8 of the same input port that handles the ASCII data or (b) bit B8 of another port. The other bits of this second input-port are connected permanently low. The program to input data poles input-port 2 for the binary number 10000000 and recognizes the number 00000000 as meaning that the data on input-port 1 is invalid. When it sees 10000000, the data on port 1 is known to be valid; so the program must branch to input the data on port 1. This seems a waste, but is popular. If this method is used, set bit B8 of the first input port permanently low by grounding the appropriate pins.

After the program inputs the data from port 1 it must clear the 7474, or the program will never again see a valid new-data condition. There are several possible ways to do this job. If there is an output-port available, write a loop that sends a high to one of the output bits and use that bit to control the 7474 clear input line. This bit is normally kept high and is momentarily brought low to reset the flip-flop. The other method shown in Fig. 8-17 connects the clear line of the 7474 to the out line of an address decoder circuit.

You now know how to handle inverted strobe-pulses, and too-short strobe pulses. How do you handle the problem of the continuous strobe-level (as opposed to strobe pulse), especially when your software package wants to see a brief pulse? See Fig. 8-18.

The idea in Fig. 8-18 is to invert and then differentiate the output strobe level. The output of the keyboard strobe-line snaps high when the output data is valid. This level is inverted by the 7404; so the input of the resistance-capacitance *differentiator* is a negative-going translation. The purpose of a differentiator is to produce an output voltage that is proportional to the rate of change of the input signal and with a polarity that indicates whether the change is positive-going or negative-going. In this case, since the change is very rapid, negative-going, level shift, the output of the differentiator is a high-amplitude negative-voltage spike. This spike momentarily causes the level on pin 3 of the 74121 to drop from its normal high condition to a low condition, thereby triggering the monostable.

USING THE 555

The 555-IC timer-chip is often a good choice in this application because it is relatively easy to trigger and can be operated at TTL voltage

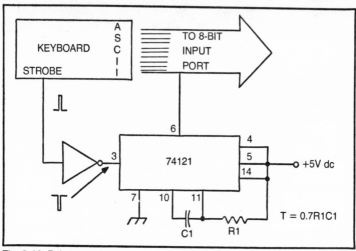

Fig. 8-16. Pulse stretcher.

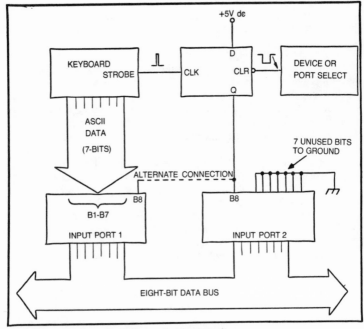

Fig. 8-17. Strobe methods for too-fast keyboards.

levels. I recommend using an output buffer from the 555, however, because this device sometimes has a little trouble driving some TTL loads. I like to follow the 555 with either 7404 or a CMOS 4050 (or 4049) device. Note that the 7404 and 4049 devices invert the pulse; so two stages are required.

The last problem that you see on some keyboards is the matter of unlatched output-lines. You can create a latched output using the circuit of Fig. 8-19. The 74100 is a TTL dual quad-latch and handles all eight bits. The ASCII output-lines are connected to inputs of the 74100, while the 74100 outputs are connected to the lower seven bits of the input port that serves the keyboard. The strobe line from the keyboard is connected to the strobe inputs of the 74100. when the data on the output lines of the keyboard is valid, the strobe pulse clocks this data over to the outputs of the 74100. There the data is held until another strobe occurs, the next time a character is selected.

What if you don't have a convenient input port? This is the situation if all of the I/O ports are filled, if you don't even have an I/O board for your microcomputer (it happens!), if you are using a single-board computer, or if you are homebrewing on a piece of perfboard.

What do you do now? Why, make an input port, of course!

Figure 8-20 shows a typical microcomputer input-port based on the Intel 8212 device. With appropriate circuit modifications, you can also use the 74LS244 or a pair of either Intel 8216 or 74125. There are eight bits on the 8212 device, and these are connected to the seven output lines that pulse the strobe line of the keyboard. The output lines of the 8212 are

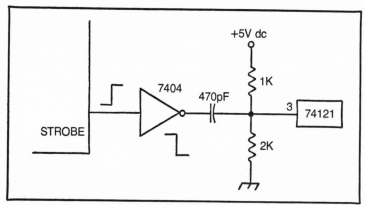

Fig. 8-18. Converting continuous strobe to one-shot strobe.

connected to the data-bus lines of the microcomputer. It is very important that the correct IC be selected for this type of application; not all work satisfactorily. The 8212 (and the other ICs mentioned above) uses three-state output lines. The output lines float at a high impedance that is neither high nor low logically. This arrangement allows the 8212 to float harmlessly across the lines of the data bus when it is not active. Otherwise, the input-port IC would load the data bus lines and cause problems.

The 8212 has a terminal that turns on the output lines when it (pin 1) is brought low. This line is connected to the IN device-select (an address decoder) signal of the microcomputer. This line drops low only when the microcomputer executes a read (i.e., input) operation from that particular input port. Recall that you required a device-select pulse in Fig. 8-17. The same sort of circuit (see Chapter 4) generates either IN or OUT device-select pulses. A sample circuit is shown in Fig. 8-21.

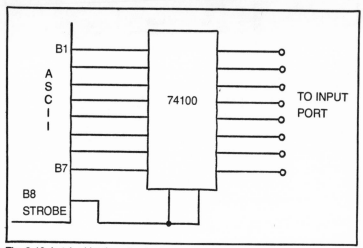

Fig. 8-19. Latched keyboard output.

In Fig. 8-21 I use the terminology of the Z-80 microprocessor chip because it is so popular. For other chips consult the manufacturer's literature on specific control signals.

In the Z-80 device there are three control signals that are needed for I/O operations: input/output request ($\overline{IORQ}$), read ($\overline{RD}$), and write ($\overline{WR}$). The IORQ is used in all input and output operations, while the $\overline{WR}$ is used only for output operations, and the $\overline{RD}$ for only input operations (these designations are given from the CPU's point of view, not that of the outside world). When the microprocessor chip executes an output operation the $\overline{IORQ}$ and $\overline{WR}$ lines drop low. Similarly, when the computer is executing an input operation, the $\overline{IORQ}$ and $\overline{RD}$ lines drop low. These conditions must be decoded by the circuit of Fig. 8-21.

There is also one further requirement. You cannot simply execute an I/O operation of either type; it must be directed someplace. That place is an I/O port with a specific number. In the Z-80 device the address of the port required in the program is passed down the lower eight bits of the address line (i.e. A0-A7). Since this address is eight bits in length, you can designate up to 2^8, or 256, different address locations. You must, therefore, also provide an address decoder in your device-select circuit.

Figure 8-21 contains all of the necessary elements to make an I/O port work. The heart of the device select circuit is the 7442 BCD to 1-of-10 decoder. This IC was originally designed to drive Nixie[R] tube displays. It has ten output lines that drop low according to the four-bit BCD word applied to the 7442 input lines. When the BCD word for one of the ten output lines is received, that output line drops low. For example, the BCD word 0010 has a decimal value of 2. When 0010 is applied to the ABCD lines of the 7442, the 2 output (pin 3) drops low.

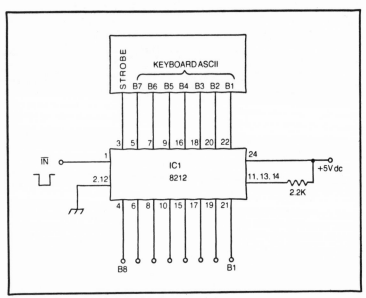

Fig. 8-20. Direct interface to data bus.

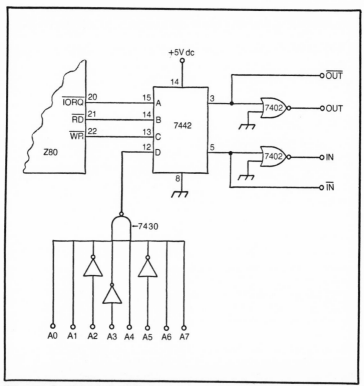

Fig. 8-21. Device select circuit.

The circuit in Fig. 8-21 uses an address-decoder section that is made from a single 7430 eight-input NAND-gate. When all eight inputs of the 7430 are high, the output drops low. This means that the D input of the 7442 is low when the correct address is present on the lower eight bits of the address bus. You must make all lines of the address bus look high in this circuit when the correct address is present. In the case of Fig. 8-21, the correct address is 11010011; so bits A2, A3, and A5 are low when the correct address is present. This means that you need inverter sections (7404) on these inputs to the 7430. Therefore, when the address is 11010011, the 7430 sees 11111111.

When the program calls for a read (i.e., input) operation from port 211_{10} (which is 11010011_2), the output of the address decoder is low, as are the $\overline{IORQ}$ and $\overline{RD}$ lines of the Z-80. The $\overline{WR}$ line is high. In the way that this circuit is designed there is a BCD word 01002_2 (4_{10}) on the input of the 7442. The output-line 4 of the 7442 (pin 5) is connected to one input of the IN NOR gate (7402 device). This line goes low, causing the 7402 output marked IN to become active high. If an active-LOW in signal is needed, instead, use pin 5 of the 7442 directly.

A similar action occurs when the microprocessor chip executes write i.e., output) operation, except that the WR goes low instead of the RD.

Chapter 9

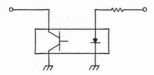

Interfacing Printers
and Teletypewriters

Printers and teletypewriters provide hard copy for computer output. Some systems have only LED readouts or CRT video output. While these computers do everything that computers are supposed to do, there is no record of it after the power is turned off. The printer provides such an output.

There are a number of different types of printers available. The lowest cost printers use either an impact or thermal dot-matrix to print characters. These printers are the ones that produce the funny looking letters made of dots. For most purposes this is the only type of printer that is required. Letter grade printers, however, are needed when high quality printing is needed. The DECWRiters[R] and the Model 43 Teletype[R] machines are examples of dot-matrix printers.

The model 33 (and earlier models) Teletype[R] machines provide a higher quality of printed page. These models use a print cylinder to impact print characters on the page. The Model 33 is available on the surplus market and is encoded in ASCII (so it is compatible with most microcomputers). The teletypewriter uses a 20 mA current-loop (60 mA for earlier models) to operate the solenoids that actuate the print cylinder to make an impression. I will discuss the current loop interface shortly.

Certain earlier model teletypewriters are encoded in Baudot (a five-bit code) and are not directly compatible with ASCII-encoded modern computers. You can, however, provide either software or hardware Baudot-to-ASCII converters. One method is to use a table in memory (ROM for hardware) that contains the Baudot equivalents of the ASCII characters used by the computer. The ASCII, then, can be used to form the address of the memory location that contains the Baudot equivalent of that character.

For example, you can locate the loop-up table for the Baudot equivalents in page two (i.e., locations 0200 to 02FF hex). Let's consider the character A. In ASCII code the character A is represented by 41 (hex), which is 01000001 in binary. In the Baudot code, however, the character A is represented by 03 (hex), which is 00000011 in binary. Of course, since

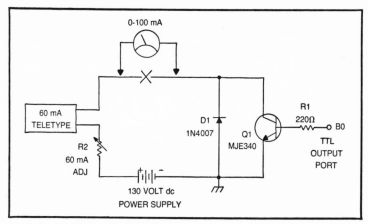

Fig. 9-1. Circuit to connect 60-mA teletypewriter to computer.

Baudot is a five-bit code, only the five lower-order bits are used (00011). If you want to convert ASCII to Baudot for the character A, use the ASCII character 41H as the pointer to the location that contains the Baudot representation 03H. In page two, then, location 0241 is loaded with 03H. When 41 (ASCII A) is loaded into an index register and added to 0200 in an indexed-addressing scheme to form 0241H, then the contents of 0241H (i.e., 03H) can be loaded into the accumulator for output to the teletypewriter.

You can also use certain models of IBM Selectric I/O typewriters certain non-IBM printers that are based on the Selectric mechanism to form a high quality letter-grade printer.

Also available on the market are daisy-wheel printers. These printers are also letter grade, and examples are the Diablo[R] and NEC Spinwriter[R].

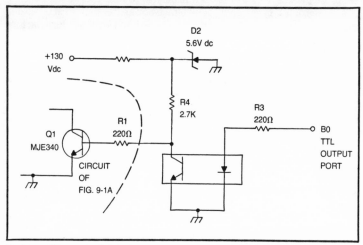

Fig. 9-2. Circuit with photoisolation.

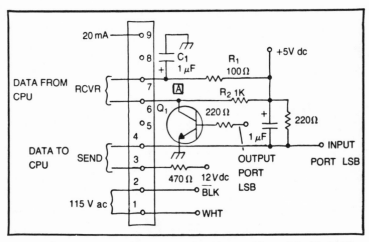

Fig. 9-3. Connecting a microcomputer to 20-mA current-loop of the Model 33.

Many commercially-available printers are available in either RS-232 (see Chapter 5) or current-loop systems.

The older teletypewriter machines use a 60-mA current-loop to operate the solenoids that select the correct character.

Figure 9-1 shows the most basic circuit for a 60-mA machine. An external 130 V dc power-supply is needed. The current-loop circuit consists of the dc supply, resistor R2, the teletypewriter machine, and chip-enable path of transistor Q1.

Diode D1 is used as a spike suppressor. The solenoid coils produce a spike-like pulse (i.e., high amplitude, short duration) every time the current-flow in one of the coils is interrupted. Diode D1 is connected to suppress these spikes and is used mainly to protect transistor Q1.

Transistor Q1 can be any high-voltage power-transistor that is capable of handling a 60-mA collector-current. Q1 acts as a switch to turn the loop on and off.

If a high appears on the LSB of the selected output port, Q1 is forward-biased. Its chip-enable path conducts current, closing the loop.

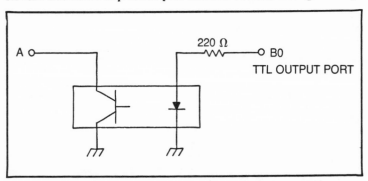

Fig. 9-4. Using the optoisolator.

When the LSB of the output port is low, Q1 is reverse-biased. Under this condition its chip-enable path is turned off; so the loop is open.

It is best to adjust resistor R2 to obtain a loop current of 60 mA. Place a high on the LSB of the selected port and press one of the teletypewriter keys. A millammeter placed at the point indicated in Fig. 9-1 shows the current. Adjust the resistor (R2) for a flow of 60 mA.

It is probably best if all high-voltage circuits are isolated from your computer's output. Otherwise, a fault in transistor Q1 can cause damage to the output port circuits. An appropriate circuit for this is shown in Fig. 9-2. The secret is to use an optoisolator device. On the computer side of the device is an LED, while on the teletypewriter side is an optotransistor. The transistor is turned off unless the LED is turned on. The collector of the optoisolator transistor is connected to the point in the previous circuit that connected to the computer. This collector is also connected to a 5.6 V dc power-supply that is derived from the +130 V dc power-supply used in the current loop. On the computer side the LED is connected through a current-limiting resistor (R5) to the LSB of the selected port.

When the LSB of the output port is high, the LED is turned on. This turns on the transistor in the optoisolator, shorting-out the bias to the current-loop transistor. This action turns off the loop. Similarly, the low in the LSB of the port turns off the transistor; so Q1 is turned on, closing the loop. The action in this circuit is inverted; so it is necessary to complement the Z-80 accumulator before outputting data. Alternately, you can use one other transistor inverter, between the isolator and Q1, to invert the output of the isolator.

Figure 9-3 shows a circuit that is used to interface the Model 33 teletypewriter to a Z-80 output port. Looking from the front panel, there is a terminal strip on the right-rear side of the Model 33. This terminal strip, shown schematically in Fig. 9-4, contains the send/receive connections for the teletypewriter.

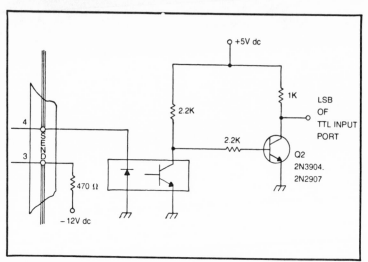

Fig. 9-5. Connecting the transmit section of the keyboard.

The receive side of the machine (terminals 6 and 7) contains the loop, so that the solenoids can be pulled in.

The send side is merely a set of contact closures. In my own experience, this circuit has produced some problems. If the loop is turned on after the microcomputer is loaded and ready to work, a random pulse seems to change a few (important) bits in a few memory locations. The problem is partially relieved by using +5 V and −12 V power-supplies that are completely divorced from the computer power supply. But, I like the approach shown in Figs. 9-4 and 9-5. Use R1, R2, and C1 (from Fig. 9-3), but replace Q1 with the transistor from the optoisolator (connect the collector to point A). The LED is connected, again through a current-limiting resistor, to the LSB of the selected output-port.

You can use the −12 V supply to drive the LED or the +5 V supply (in which case, the polarity is reversed). The isolator transistor (Q1) drives an inverter stage (Q2). When the LED is turned on, Q2 is turned off; so the LSB of the selected input-port is high. But, if the LED is off, Q2 is turned on, dropping the LSB of the input port to zero.

Chapter 10

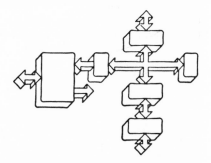

Single-Board Computers

Single-board computers are, quite literally, those computers in which all functions are on a single printed-circuit board. Some of these computers are intended as trainers and minidevelopment systems. Others are intended to be used as the control element in an instrument or process controller, or as the heart of a digital computer. The typical single-board computer has a microprocessor IC as the CPU, some read-only memory (ROM) to hold the program, random-access memory (RAM) to hold data, and at least one input/output (I/O) port. In some machines the entire system is based on a single-chip computer, such as the 8048 device. In others there are several different chips involved. A popular configuration, for example, is the 6502/6522 arrangement. The 6502 is a microprocessor integrated-circuit, while the 6522 is billed as a *versatile interface-adapter* (VIA). The 6522 contains two ports (A & B) that can be configured as either input or output, on a bit-for-bit basis.

It is common practice to use one of the more complex single-board computers to develop software and interface packages, and then one of the less complex ones for the actual product. For example, you can use a Rockwell AIM-65 to design a product based on the 6502/6522 concept. When the program is written and debugged, and when the interface hardware is designed and tested, you no longer need the keyboard, display, and printer of the AIM-65. At that point you can opt for something like the John Bell Engineering 6502-controller PCB (printed-circuit board), which lacks the amenities of the AIM-65. The program object-code can be burned into a 2708 PROM, and the PROM installed in the Bell Engineering computer.

The first single-board computer to attract a lot of attention was the KIM-1, by MOS Technology (inventers of the 6502 family of devices). The KIM-1 is considered a trainer and is an excellent starting point for the microprocessor beginner. It has a hexadecimal keyboard for entering instructions plus several other keys that allow you to examine and change memory locations and otherwise manipulate the computer. The KIM-1 is cheap enough that some people, after using them as a minidevelopment system, install the KIM-1 in the product! At last look, the KIM-1 was selling for less than $200; so it is a low-cost way into the computer hobby.

The SYM-1 is a machine by Synertek, the second source for the 6502, and is functionally very similar to the KIM-1 machine. It is also a trainer and minidevelopment system. Like the KIM-1, the SYM-1 contains the necessary circuitry and monitor programming to permit storage of programming on audio cassette tapes, and output to a 20 mA teletypewriter. Any teletypewriter or printer that accepts ASCII code and uses a 20 mA current-loop for control is a good candidate for this application. The Heath H14 printer and the Teletype[R] models 33 and 43 are good selections.

The Rockwell AIM-65 is a step up from the KIM-1 and SYM-1 machines. The AIM-65 is almost compatible with these other machines, but is more versatile. Like the KIM and SYM machines, it has a bus connector and an interfacing connector (left rear of board, as viewed from front) to permit expansion and interfacing, respectively. The AIM-65 is available in two versions: one that has 1K memory and another that has 4K. There are also three software packages available for the AIM-65 in the form of ROMs. The machine comes with a monitor ROM, and both assembler and BASIC ROMS are available as options.

The nice thing about the AIM-65 is that it has a 54-key keyboard that produces ASCII code, a 20-column printer, and a 20-column 5 × 7 dot matrix display. The LED display scrolls left-to-right for the first 20 characters, and then right-to-left for the next 40 characters. After 60 characters the display buffer must be cleared for additional characters. These features make the AIM-65 a lot more useful as a bench engineer's development system than some of the other machines.

A more recent entry into the 6502 single-board computer market is Ohio Scientific's Superboard II. This computer promises to be everything that the AIM-65 is, and more.

The 6502-based single-board computers seem to have dominated the market, probably because of the early influence of the KIM-1 machine. The one Z-80 board that I am aware of is SD Systems' Z-80 Starter Kit. The Heath-Zenith Company makes a microprocessor-trainer based on the 6800, and Netronics makes both an 8085 (Explorer) and an RCA 1802 (ELF II) single board kit.

Chapter 11

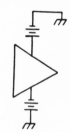

Operational Amplifiers

The principal device used in analog subsystem-circuits is the *operational amplifier* (op amp). The op amp is one of the most basic of all electronic building-clocks. The amplifier might be found as an input amplifier or buffer between the analog voltage and the input of the analog-to-digital converter. In still other cases, the operational amplifier might be used to scale the output of a voltage DAC (digital-to-analog converter). The operational amplifier might also convert the current output of some DACs to a voltage output. The operational amplifier is also used as the principal component of active electronic-filters.

The original operational amplifiers were discrete units built from vacuum tubes. Later versions were essentially discrete transistorized-versions of the original designs. Such amplifiers were quite large by modern integrated-circuit standards, but they did work quite well. The term operational amplifier came about because the original op amps were conceived to perform mathematical operations in analog computers. Today many analog instruments still have op amps performing mathematical operations. These instruments are essentially little more than analog computers with a dedicated program. However, the main use of operational-amplifier devices in modern data-converter applications is in preamplifiers (analog-to-digital converters) or postamplifiers. They may also provide some *signal processing*, as in integration or logarithmic amplification. The nature of analog circuitry, however, is such that you should endeavor to perform most signal-processing functions, other than amplification, in software rather than hardware. The only place where analog signal-processing should be used in computer data-crunching systems is where the software overhead for such processing is prohibitive.

The basic circuit symbol for an operational amplifier is shown in Fig. 11-1. It is the basic triangle symbol used for amplifiers in general. Note that there are two inputs shown. This is not strictly necessary; only the inverting (−) input is really necessary. The differential inputs are so useful, however, that all operational amplifiers have two inputs. The inverting

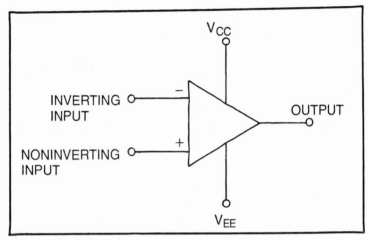

Fig. 11-1. Operational amplifier.

input (negative) produces an output voltage that has the reverse polarity of the input signal voltage; i.e., there is a 180-degree phase inversion between input and output. The noninverting input (+) produces an output that is in phase with the input signal. The phase reversal seen by the noninverting input is 360 degrees. The gain of the operational amplifier is quite high—at least 10,000 and many up to over 1,000,000! But each input, inverting and noninverting, sees the same open-loop voltage gain, A_{VOL}. This means that the two inputs produce equal, but opposite-polarity, effects on the output signal.

Notice also that there are two power supply terminals on the operational amplifier. All true op amps have two power supplies. These are not a hot and ground, but two independent (bipolar) power-supplies. The V_{CC} supply is positive with respect to ground, while the V_{EE} power supply is negative with respect to ground. There is no ground terminal on the operational amplifier. The output signal, however, is taken between the output terminal and the power-supply ground. The proper power-supply configuration for an operational amplifier is shown in Fig. 11-2. The connections to the op amp are shown in Fig. 11-2, while the basic functional power supply is shown in Fig. 11-3. The batteries shown are merely representative, and in most cases are actually electronically regulated dc power-supplies. More often than not, the V_{CC} and V_{EE} power-supplies have equal values. Although, there is a slight hitch in the specifications of some units; each supply has a certain maximum voltage rating. However, the differential voltage-rating ($V_{CC} - V_{EE}$) must be less than a certain limit. This limit is less than two times the voltage specified as the maximum for either supply. For example, the 741 device usually has a specified maximum supply voltage for either V_{CC} or V_{EE} of 18 V; i.e., $V_{CC} = +18$ V and $V_{EE} = -18$ V. But, the same device has a differential supply-voltage of only 30 V. Note that $+18$ V $-(-18V) = +36$ V, which is greater than the maximum. In the case of the 741, therefore, be a little careful in selecting the power-supply potentials. For example, if V_{CC} is selected to be the maximum (i.e., 18V),

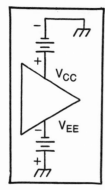

Fig. 11-2. Power supply connections.

then the V_{EE} supply must be $30 - 18$ V, or 12 V. In that case $V_{CC} = 18$ V, and $V_{EE} = 12$ V.

IDEAL OPERATIONAL-AMPLIFIERS

The *transfer function* of any electronic circuit is defined as the output function divided by the input function. For a voltage amplifier, then, the transfer function can be calculated by $E_{OUT}/E_{IN} = A_V$. This is a way of expressing the gain (A_V) of the circuit. You can calculate the transfer function of any operational-amplifier circuit if you go back to basic principles, i.e., the properties of the operational amplifier, Ohms's law, and Kirchhoff's current-law. ($I = E/R$ is Ohm's Law, Kirchhoff's Law states that the current of all points going into a circuit is equal to the current of all points coming out.)

The properties of the operational amplifier are:

- Infinite input impedance ($Z_{IN} = <$).
- Zero output impedance ($Z_{OUT} = 0$).
- Infinite open-loop voltage gain ($A_{VOL} = <$).
- Zero internal noise generation.
- Infinite bandwidth.
- Differential inputs must be treated exactly the same.

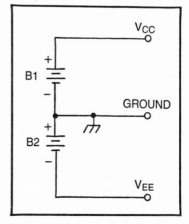

Fig. 11-3. Typical power supply.

115

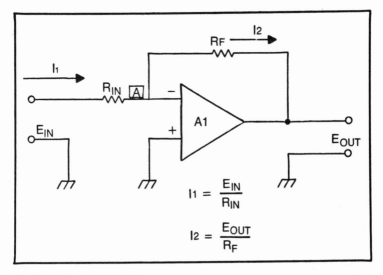

$$I1 = \frac{E_{IN}}{R_{IN}}$$

$$I2 = \frac{E_{OUT}}{R_F}$$

Fig. 11-4. Inverting follower.

The last property means that anything that happens to one input also happens to the other. In other words, if you apply a voltage to one input, you must treat the other input as if the same voltage were also applied to it. This is not some matter that works on paper only! If you apply a voltage to, say, the inverting input, and then measure the potential at the noninverting input, you will find that both are at the same voltage.

There is one implication of the first property on the list that can be used in the creation of the transfer function for the various circuits. If the input impedance is infinite, the input current is zero. Remember that $Z_{IN} = E_{IN}/I_{IN}$. The only way that Z_{IN} can be infinite, then, is for I_{IN} to be zero. In general, therefore, the inputs of an ideal operation-amplifier neither sink nor source current! Now let's see how these principles can be applied to deriving a transfer equation.

INVERTING FOLLOWERS

Figure 11-3 shows one of the simplest operational-amplifier circuits. It is the *inverting follower*, or inverter, circuit. The noninverting input is grounded; so it is at a potential of 0 V. Because of the last property outlined, therefore, you must treat the inverting input as if it were also grounded. This concept is sometimes called a virtual ground, for the lack of a better word. Point A in Fig. 11-4 is, therefore, grounded for all practical purposes. In the analysis of the circuit, assume a ground is at point A.

Kirchhoff's current-law tells you that the sum of all currents into and out of a junction must be zero. Because the first property 1 tells you that the inverting input of the operational amplifier neither sinks nor sources current, you must conclude that I1 + I2 = 0, so:

$$I1 = -I2$$

From Ohm's law, you know the following about current I1 and I2:

116

$$I1 = \frac{E_{IN}}{R_{IN}}$$

and

$$I2 = \frac{E_{OUT}}{R_F}$$

If you substitute the two equations into the earlier one, you find:

$$\frac{E_{IN}}{R_{IN}} = \frac{-E_{OUT}}{R_F}$$

This expression relates the input and output voltages to certain resistor values. Solve the transfer equation and you conclude that the gain is R_F/R_{IN}:

$$A_V = \frac{E_{OUT}}{E_{IN}} = \frac{-R_F}{R_{IN}}$$

This equation is the proper transfer equation for the inverting-follower operational-amplifier circuit of Fig. 11-4. This is not, however, the usual form in which the equation is presented. In most cases, you see the versions below:

$$E_{OUT} = -A_V E_{IN}$$

or

$$E_{OUT} = \frac{R_F E_{IN}}{R_{IN}}$$

One of the beauties of the operational amplifier is that the voltage gain can be programmed with only two resistors, R_F and R_{IN}. Figures 11-5 through 11-8 show several applications for the operational amplifier. The pin-outs shown are sometimes called industry standard, but are basically for the 741 device. In Fig. 11-5 the power supply terminals have been

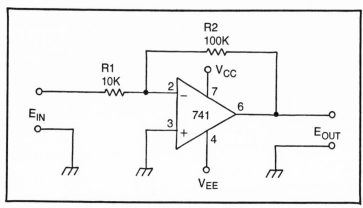

Fig. 11-5. Gain-of-ten inverting-follower.

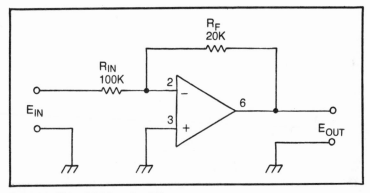

Fig. 11-6. Gain-of-0.2 inverting-follower.

shown so that there is a reference for that device and any others based on the industry-standard pin-outs. But in the later circuits, standard practice of deleting the power-supply terminals in order to simplify the drawing is followed.

The circuit shown in Fig. 11-5 is a gain-of-10 inverting amplifier. The ratio of the resistors sets the gain, which is:

$$A_V = -R2/R1$$
$$= -(100K)/(10K)$$
$$= -10$$

If an input voltage, E_{IN}, is applied, then the output voltage is $10E_{IN}$. The maximum allowable output-voltage depends upon the operational amplifier used. For most manufacturers' 741 devices, the maximum output is about 3.5 V less than the power-supply potential. For some modern devices, such as the RCA CA3140, the maximum output-voltage may be as much as 0.5 V less than the power-supply rail.

You may also obtain less than *unity* in operational amplifiers. The transfer function is R_F/R_{IN}, and no limits are placed on this function. If you want to make an amplifier with less than unity gain, it is merely necessary to make R_F less than R_{IN}. The circuit in Fig. 11-6 is such an amplifier. The gain of this circuit is:

$$A_V = -R_F/R_{IN}$$
$$= -(20K)/(100K)$$
$$= -1/5 = -0.2$$

This type of amplifier circuit is sometimes seen in cases where an analog-to-digital converter is being interfaced with an instrument or other voltage source that has a range greater than the converter's input range. You might, for example, have a 0-20 V signal and a 0-+2.5 V analog-to-digital converter. In that case set the ratio R_F/R_{IN} to 2.5/20 or 1/8(0.125).

You might also elect to provide gain-trimming for the operational amplifier. If a precise gain is needed, it might not be wise to trust the tender mercies of the resistor tolerances to set the gain. In such cases you want R_F to be a circuit such as shown in Fig. 11-7 resistors R1 and R2. If R2 has a total value that is approximately 10 percent of the total (R1+R2), you can

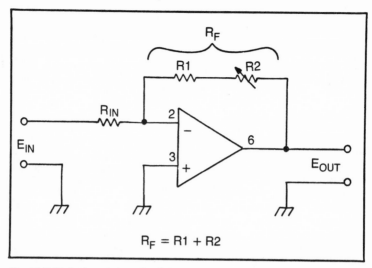

Fig. 11-7. Variable-gain inverting-follower.

trim the value of the gain quite neatly. This is especially true if the potentiometer is a 10-turn trimmer.

It is sometimes desirable to make the overall gain of an amplifier quite high. However, certain problems with real operational amplifiers limit the gain obtainable from a single stage. In these cases, you can make a cascade amplifier, if appropriate, such as shown in Fig. 11-8. The total gain of the circuit is the product of the individual gains:

$$A_V = \frac{R2}{R1} \times \frac{R4}{R3}$$

$$= R2R4/R1R3$$

This circuit can also be used to provide a phase inversion of the output, so that the total phase shift will be 360 degrees (2 × 180 degrees). This means that the output signal, E_{OUT}, is in phase with E_{IN} (360° = 0°).

The input impedance of the inverting follower is usually quite low.

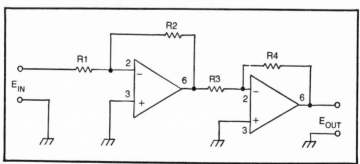

Fig. 11-8. Two-stage noninverting-amplifier based on inverting-followers.

119

Because the inverting junction is essentially grounded, the input impedance seen by the signal is R_{IN}. If R_{IN} is low, then the input impedance is also low. You could try to force R_{IN} to high, but this limits available gain. There is a practical value to the maximum value that can be assigned to R_F. These problems are overcome by using the noninverting follower of the next section.

NONINVERTING FOLLOWERS

The input impedance problems of the inverting follower can be overcome with one of the circuits shown in Figs. 11-9 and 11-10. These are noninverting followers. The feedback is still applied to the inverting input because *degenerative* feedback is desired. Applying the feedback to the noninverting input results in regenerative feedback, and the circuit is likely to oscillate. The signal, however, is applied to the noninverting input. Recall that first property: infinite input impedance means that the signal source sees an infinite input impedance. In real operational-amplifiers infinite might be a little optimistic; it exists only in idealized, paper, operational amplifiers. The approximations of infinity, however, can be quite exciting! Even poor, rejected, 741s go over 500K ohms, and most are in the megohm range. Some of the newer op amps, such as the RCA CA3130, CA3140, and CA3160 models, use MOSFET transistors in the front end of the op-amp circuit. These devices approximate infinite impedance with 1.5 *terraohms* (that's 1.5×10^{12} ohms).

It seems that the input impedance problem has been solved, but what do we have? The transfer function is analyzed in the same manner as for the inverter. You know that I1=I2, but you must also take the last property into account once again. In this circuit, however, the noninverting input is at a potential of E_{IN}, so treat the inverting input (point A in Fig. 11-9) as if it were also at potential E_{IN}. You already know:

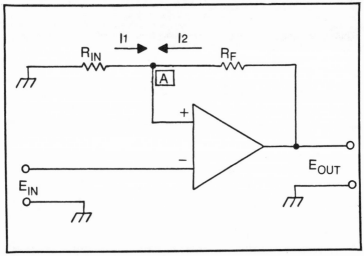

Fig. 11-9. Noninverting follower with gain.

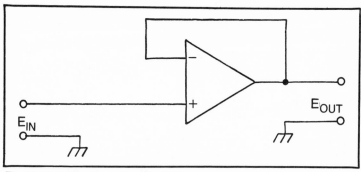

Fig. 11-10. Unity-gain noninverting-follower.

$$I1 = I2$$

$$I1 = \frac{E_{IN}}{R_{IN}}$$

$$I1 = \frac{E_{OUT} - E_{IN}}{R_F}$$

By substituting the last two equations into the first:

$$\frac{E_{IN}}{R_{IN}} = \frac{E_{OUT} - E_{IN}}{R_F}$$

Solving for E_{OUT}:

$$\frac{R_F E_{IN}}{R_{IN}} = E_{OUT} - E_{IN}$$

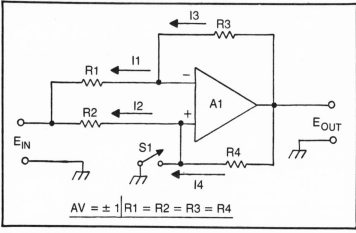

Fig. 11-11. Gain of ± 1 amplifier.

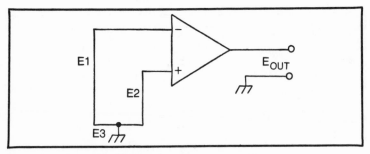

Fig. 11-12. Input voltages affecting a differential amplifier.

And by rearranging:

$$E_{OUT} = \frac{R_F E_{IN}}{R_{IN}} + E_{IN}$$

$$= E_{IN} \left[\frac{R_F}{R_{IN}} + 1 \right]$$

The last equation is the normal transfer-equation for the circuit in Fig. 11-9: the noninverting follower with gain. For very high gain application, the equation can be reduced to the same as the inverting follower, but with a + sign. At lower gains, the +1 factor must be taken into consideration.

Figure 11-10 shows a special case of the noninverting follower in which the entire output signal is applied to the input. This reduces the gain to unity. This can be proven using ordinary feedback theory (which has not been used in this chapter), if you desire. The use of the noninverting follower is in buffer service and in impedance-transformation between two circuits. A buffer is merely an isolation amplifier. It keeps load variations from affecting the driving circuit. In data converters unity-gain followers are often seen in this application. Many analog-to-digital converter circuits have changing input-impedance over the analog input-signal voltage range. Many DACs require a high-impedance load in order to operate correctly, yet are scaled to the correct voltage. In those cases, the unity-gain noninverting-follower is the answer.

The noninverting-follower circuits can be cascaded in the same manner as inverting amplifiers. Once again, the total gain is the product of the gains of all stages in cascade.

POSITIVE-NEGATIVE AMPLIFIER-CIRCUIT

It is sometimes appropriate to place a polarity switch in an amplifier circuit so that the signal can be flipped over. In some applications a circuit such as Fig. 11-10 can be used to accomplish this purpose. When switch 1 is closed, the circuit operates as a unity gain ($R_F/R_{IN} = R3/R1 = 1$), inverting follower. When switch S1 is open, though, the circuit operates as a unity-gain noninverting-follower (not the same as in Fig. 11-10, but unity gain nonetheless).

In most actual applications, it is wise to make S1 an electronic switch. The circuit can then sense the polarity of the input signal and open or close

S1 as needed to make the signal proper for the data converter to follow. All resistors in this circuit have the same value. Resistance values in the 1-10K ohm are usually recommended.

DIFFERENTIAL AMPLIFIERS

The inputs of an operational amplifier are *differential*; i.e., the negative and positive inputs have equal but opposite effect on the output signal. There are actually three types of signal voltage to which the op amp responds: *single-ended* input-voltages, differential input-voltages, and *common-mode* input-voltages. A single-ended input-voltage is the voltage appearing between ground and one input. A differential-input signal is one that appears between the two input terminals. A common-mode input-voltage is one that appears equally on both inputs.

These signals are shown in Fig. 11-12. Voltages E1 and E2 are single-ended voltages, while voltage E3 is common mode. The differential voltage is the difference between the two single-ended input voltages; i.e., $E_D = E2 - E1$. The operational amplifier is designed to reject the common-mode signal and amplify the differential signal. The ability of the amplifier to reject the common mode signal is expressed in the common-mode rejection-ratio (CMRR). Most garden-variety, low-cost, op amps will boast common-mode rejection-ratios of around 60 dB, while premium models have CMRR figures as high as 120 dB.

The common-mode rejection-capability of the differential amplifier (diff amp) makes it primary for many instrumentation applications. Whenever there is a strong, outside, interfering signal, the CMRR of the diff amp might eliminate the interference. Consider the case where an amplifier must be connected to its signal source through wires. These wires must be shielded in a single-ended circuit. Even then, some degree of 60-Hz interference from nearby power lines might be found. In the differential amplifier, however, the interfering field affects both inputs equally; so the signal cancels out the input. Remember the equal-but-opposite

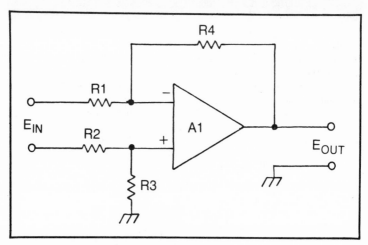

Fig. 11-13. Simple dc differential amplifier.

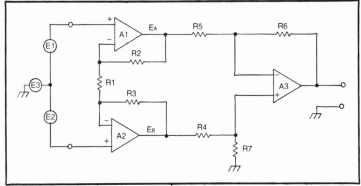

Fig. 11-14. Instrumentation amplifier.

polarity-effect on the output signal. The signals from a common-mode source tend to cancel algebraically in the output.

Figure 11-13 shows the simple dc differential-amplifier using just one operational amplifier. Resistors 1 and 2 are input resistors, one to each input terminal of the op amp. It is necessary that R1=R2. Similarly, feedback resistor-4 must equal grounded resistor-3. The voltage gain of this circuit is:

$$A_V \;=\; \frac{R4}{R1} \;=\; \frac{R3}{R2}$$

R1 = R2, and R3 = R4.

In actual practice resistor 3 in Fig. 11-13 is a potentiomer or a combination of a potentiometer and a fixed resistor. In most circuits it is sufficient to make the resistance of the potentiometer about 15 percent of the total. The use of the potentiometer for R3 makes a common-mode adjust-control. The usual procedure for adjustment of CMRR is:

●Short the two input-terminals (E_{IN} side of R1/R2) together.
●Apply a sine wave signal of several volts amplitude to the shorted input-terminals.
●Examine the output signal on an oscilloscope or with an ac voltmeter.
●Adjust R3 until the output signal is minimum. This signal may well drop very close to zero, although it may be several volts initially. It may, therefore, be necessary to readjust the sensitivity of the output-indicator progressively downward as the adjustment proceeds towards completion.

The simple circuit of Fig. 11-13 suffers from the same problem as the inverting follower—limited input-impedance range. The solution to this problem is the use of the instrumentation-amplifier circuit of Fig. 11-14. This circuit uses two input-amplifiers in the noninverting-follower configuration to drive a differential-output stage. The voltage gain of this circuit is given by:

$$E_{OUT} = \left[\frac{2R2}{R1} + 1\right] \times \left[\frac{R6}{R5}\right] \times \left[E_{IN}\right]$$

R4 = R5, R6 = R7, and R2 = R3.

It is interesting to note that making R2 = R3 does not affect the common-mode rejection-ratio, although it produces a serious gain-error that is predicted by the last equation.

OPERATIONAL-AMPLIFIER PROBLEMS

When you analyzed various operational-amplifier circuits, you assumed that the op amps were ideal devices. Real operational amplifiers, however, only approximate the ideal parameters given earlier in the chapter. They have some problems that can affect circuit operation, and these must be dealt with properly.

One of the problems is that the input impedance is not infinite. There is a finite input impedance in real op amps. This means that a certain input current flows either to or from the junction. This current is an input-offset current and is due to the bias currents needed to operate the input transistors. With some bipolar input devices this current can be substantial, yet some MOSFET and superbeta (i.e., Darlington) input op-amps have input currents measured in picoamperes.

The input-bias current causes an offset voltage to appear at the inverting input. The current flows through the feedback and input resistors and causes this voltage drop. The voltage caused by the current is equivalent to the voltage created if the current is flowing in a resistance equal to the parallel combination of R_F and R_{IN}.

One low-cost solution to this problem is shown in Fig. 11-15. A compensation resistor is connected between the noninverting input and ground. The same level of bias-current flows in both inputs. If the resistor compensation has a value equal to the parallel combination of R_F and R_{IN}, the voltage applied to the noninverting input is equal to that applied to the inverting input. This makes the differential offset-voltage approximately zero and the output offset is thereby nulled.

Several other forms of offset problem result in an output voltage that is not due to the input signal. Figures 11-16 through 11-19 show methods for nulling all classes of offset voltage. In Fig. 11-16 a pair of special offset-null terminals found on some operational amplifiers is used. The ends of the potentiometer are connected to the offset null terminals, while the wiper is connected to the V_{EE} negative power supply. The potentiometer is adjusted until the output-offset potential, regardless of its cause, is nulled to zero.

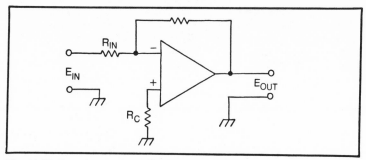

Fig. 11-15. Use of a compensation resistor to reduce the effects of input-bias currents on output offset-voltage.

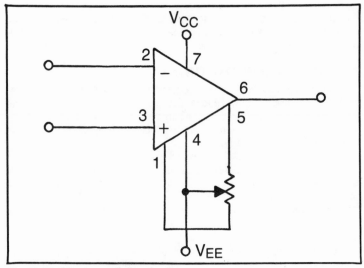

Fig. 11-16. Offset cancellation circuit.

A more universal circuit is shown in Fig. 11-17. In this case a third current is summed with the input and feedback currents in order to cancel the effects of the output offset. This current is fed to the summing junction (point X) through resistor 2. The level and polarity of the current are set by adjusting potentiometer R1. The output voltage created by this offset null-adjustment circuit is:

$$E_o' = \frac{R_F E_N}{R2}$$

where E_o' is the component of the output voltage created by the null circuit and should not exceed the unnulled offset voltage (i.e., E_{OUT} when $E_N = E_{IN}$ = 0), R_F is the feedback resistor, R2 is the resistance to the potentiometer wiper, and E_N is the voltage at the wiper of the potentiometer.

This equation is based on the assumption that the value of R1 is small compared with the value of R2. In many cases the value of R1 will be 0.1 to 0.2 of the R2 value; R2 will have a value in the 10-100K ohm range.

It sometimes happens that a fine degree of control over current I3 is needed. This occurs when the offset voltage is small and becomes especially acute when the voltage gain of stages to follow is very high. A small offset, say 10 mV (millivolts), might not be much in some cases, but what happens if that stage is followed by stages with an overall gain of × 1000 or more? Then the 10-mV offset of one early stage in the cascade chain becomes a 10-mV input-signal, amplified 1000 times. This means a 10,000 mV (or 10 Volt) offset at the output of the chain. The circuits in Figs. 11-18 and 11-19 are designed to increase the resolution of the offset null-circuit of Fig. 11-17. The version in Fig. 11-18 is designed with the potentiometer connected in series with two resistors. The resistance of the potentiometer should be approximately 10 percent of the total resistance. The two end-resistors have equal values in most circuits using this technique.

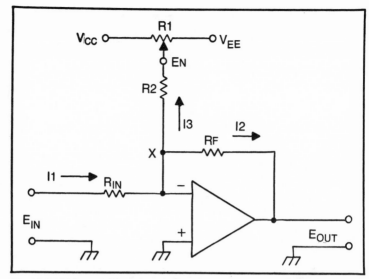

Fig. 11-17. Universal offset-cancellation circuit.

The alternate circuit is shown in Fig. 11-19. This version uses a pair of *zener diodes* to keep the potential at the ends of the potentiometer low compared with V_{CC} and V_{EE}. Very-high-resolution control over the offsets can be created by using a 1.2-2.45 V *band-gap* zener diode at this point.

Both circuits can be fined tuned by the correct selection of the series resistor (R2 in Fig. 11-17) and one of the circuits in Figs. 11-18 and 11-19.

SPECIAL OPERATIONAL-AMPLIFIER CIRCUITS

Most data acquisition systems use operational amplifiers in one capacity or another. In most cases, however, the operational amplifier is merely a

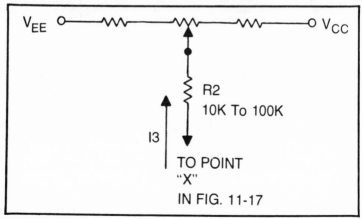

Fig. 11-18. High-resolution offset null-circuit.

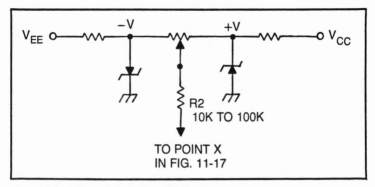

Fig. 11-19. High-resolution offset null-circuit.

voltage amplifier or a current-to-voltage converter (i.e., an inverting amplifier with the input resistor shorted out). In a few cases, however, it might be necessary to provide some amount of signal processing in the analog circuitry that follows the digital-to-analog converter or proceeds the analog-to-digital converter. In this section some of these circuits are considered.

Comparators

A *voltage comparator* circuit is a differential operational-amplifier with no feedback. The gain on the circuit, therefore, is essentially the open-loop gain of the operational amplifier. With real devices, the gain is not the infinity of the ideal case, but approaches 10^6 routinely. Even the least-expensive rejects sold by the dozen boast gains of 10^4 to 10^5. Figure 11-20 shows a typical op-amp voltage-comparator. One input is connected to one of the voltages, while the other input receives the alternate voltage. The output transfer-function is shown in Fig. 11-21. When the two voltages are equal (E1=E2), the output voltage is zero. But, if E1 is less than E2, the output is the maximum positive voltage. On the other hand, if E1 is greater than E2, the output is the maximum negative voltage. The voltage comparator, issues an output that indicates which voltage is higher or if the voltages are equal.

There is usually a small amount of hysteresis in comparators, however. This means that there is a small band of voltage difference, about

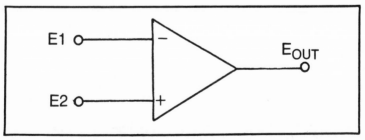

Fig. 11-20. Operational amplifier as comparator.

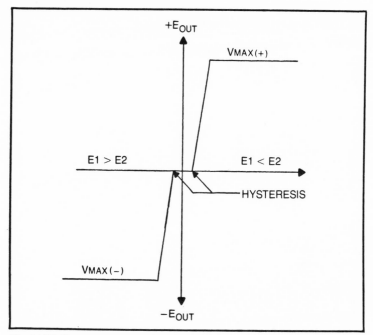

Fig. 11-21. Comparator-transfer function.

zero, in which E1=E2, but the output remains zero. This hysteresis is in the millivolt range.

The current comparator of Fig. 11-22 is usually faster than the voltage version. The noninverting input is grounded. The currents are applied to the noninverting input. If they are equal, the output is zero. The output reflects which of the two possible inequalities exist. Some analog-to-digital converter circuits use current-output digital-to-analog converters. In these circuits the analog input voltage is converted to a current (as in Fig. 11-22) by passing it through a series resistor.

Integrators

An *integrator* is an electronic circuit that produces an output proportional to the time average of the input waveform. The simplest form of

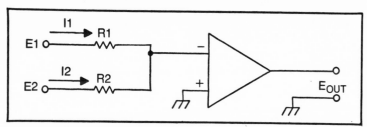

Fig. 11-22. Current-mode comparator.

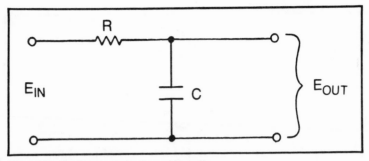

Fig. 11-23. Resistance-capacitance integrator.

integrator is the resistance-capacitance network of Fig. 11-23. The charge accumulated in the capacitor is proportional to the time average of the input potential. The active integrator of Fig. 11-24, however, is more commonly used.

The same method of analysis can be used to find the transfer equation for this circuit, as in the other circuits.

$$I1 = -I2$$

$$I1 = \frac{E_{IN}}{R}$$

$$I2 = C \frac{dE_{OUT}}{dt}$$

By substituting the last two equations into the first

$$\frac{E_{IN}}{R} = -C \frac{dE_{OUT}}{dt}$$

You can solve the problem by integrating both sides of this equation:

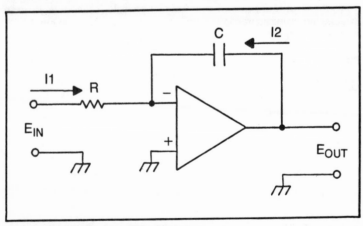

Fig. 11-24. Operational-amplifier integrator.

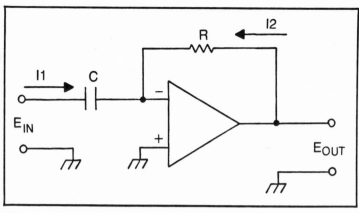

Fig. 11-25. Operational-amplifier differentiator.

$$\int \frac{E_{IN}}{R} \, dt = \int -C \; \frac{dE_{OUT}}{dt} \, dt$$

$$\int \frac{E_{IN}}{R} \, dt = -CE_0$$

Rearranging the first of the two equations:

$$E_{OUT} = \frac{-1}{RC} \int E_{IN} dt$$

The integrator *gain* is given by the expression, 1/RC. Consider what this means. If the resistor is 100K ohms and the capacitor is 0.01 μF (microfarad), the gain is:

$$A = -1R/C$$
$$= -1/(10^5 \text{ ohms}) \, (10^{-8}F)$$
$$= -1/10^{-3} = 1000$$

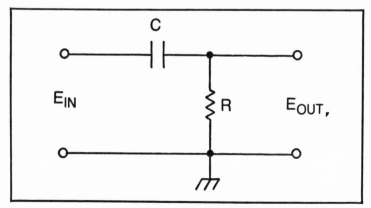

Fig. 11-26. Resistance-capacitance differentiator.

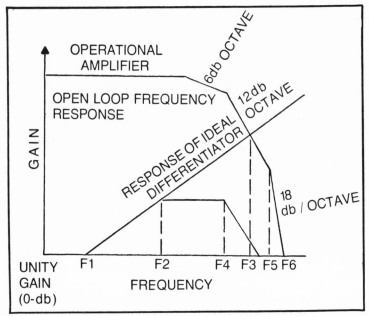

Fig. 11-27. Differentiator frequency-response plot.

The gain of the integrator is then 1000. If the input voltage is 10 mV, then the output rises at a fast rate to the supply voltage (a 10 mV input produces a 10,000 mV output).

Now consider what happens when the RC time constant is changed to $R = 10^5$ ohms and $C = 100$ pF. The gain becomes 100,000. This integrator charges rapidly to the supply rail just on the bias current of the operational amplifier!

Differentiators

A *differentiator* outputs a signal that is proportional to the time rate of change of the input signal; i.e., the derivative of the input signal. Figure 11-25 shows the usual resistance-capacitance integrator-circuit, while Fig. 11-26 shows the active differentiator based on the operational amplifier. Again, use the same method of analysis:

$$I1 = -I2$$

$$I1 = \frac{C \, dE_{IN}}{dt}$$

$$I2 = \frac{E_{OUT}}{R}$$

By substituting the last two equations in the first:

$$\frac{C \, dE_{IN}}{dt} = \frac{-E_{OUT}}{R}$$

132

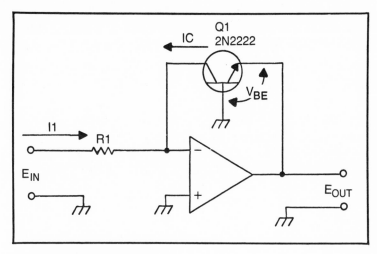

Fig. 11-28. Logarithmic amplifier.

Rearranging this equation to solve for E_{OUT}:

$$E_{OUT} = -RC \ \frac{dE_{IN}}{dt}$$

The differentiator is basically a high-pass filter and is often used as such. To make a correct differentiator, however, the time constant of the RC network in the differentiator circuit must be short compared with the period of the input waveform. On the other hand, the integrator wants to see a time constant that is long relative to the input waveform. Figure 11-27 shows the frequency-response plot of an operational-amplifier differentiator that is compensated to produce a low-noise output.

Log-Antilog Amplifiers

An amplifier with a logarithmic transfer function is shown in Fig. 11-28. The collector current of the transistor in the feedback loop has a logarithmic relationship to the base-emitter potential, V_{BE}:

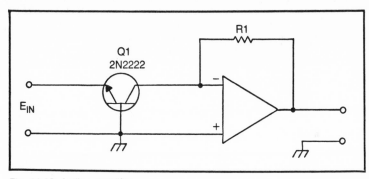

Fig. 11-29. Antilog amplifier.

$$V_{BE} = \frac{kT}{q} \ LN\left[\frac{I_C}{I_S}\right]$$

where V_{BE} is the base-emitter potential, k is Boltzmann's constant (1.38 × 10⁻²³ joules/°K), and T is the temperature in degrees Kelvin, q is the electronic charge (1.6 × 10⁻¹⁹ coulombs), I_C is the collector current in amperes, and I_S is the reverse-saturation current in amperes. At room temperature (300°K), the term kT/q is equal to 26 mV/°K, so this equation can be rewritten in the form:

$$V_{BE} = 26 \ mV \ Ln(I_C/I_S)$$

When analyzing the circuit in Fig. 11-28, the transfer equation

$$E_{OUT} = 26 \ mV \ Ln \left[\frac{E_{IN}}{I_S R1}\right]$$

where both I_S and R1 are constants.

If the equation is changed to allow for base-10 logarithms, the transfer function is:

$$E_{OUT} = 60 \ mV \ Ln \left[\frac{E_{IN}}{I_S R1}\right]$$

Reversing the positions and roles of R1 and Q1 forms an antilog amplifier, an example of which is shown in Fig. 11-29. Neither the log nor antilog-amplifier shown here works unless the ambient temperature is held constant. Otherwise, you must modify the circuits to temperature compenstate them with additional circuitry.

Chapter 12

Basics of Data Conversion

At one time all data converters were made from discrete electronic components. The manufacturer or builder designed the circuit right down to the finest detail. It was assembled just like all other electronic circuits, usually on some sort of chassis or wire-board arrangement. But, today, that is almost unheard of from the user's point of view. The three main forms of data-converter-construction parallel the other forms of electronic circuit construction: *monolithic ICs, hybrid,* and *semidiscrete function modules.*

Most readers are familiar with integrated circuit technology. Transistors, resistors, and certain other circuit-elements are formed on a substrate made of silicon. This silicon chip is then mounted and packaged inside a metal can or dual in-line package (DIP). See Fig. 12-1. To the external world the IC device appears simple, and most users are aware only of the basic block-diagram of the device and the pin-outs protocol. In reality, though, the device can be quite complex. The silicon substrate holds the transistors, resistors, and other circuit elements formed using some high-technology metallurgy; the interconnecting wires are photographically deposited onto the surface. Various layers can be used to form multidepth highly-complex devices.

A number of device manufacturers now offer hybrid devices that are sophisticated microminiature printed-boards. The printed circuit is actually a ceramic substrate, and the wires are actually gold tracks deposited onto the surface. There may be many layers of ceramic, each very thin, and each containing its own tracks of wiring. Interlevel connections are made in the form of very fine gold *angel hair* wire.

The hybrid device uses IC chips (see Fig. 12-2) mounted on the ceramic substrate. There may also be other types of electronic components, such as tiny chip-capacitors that appear to the naked eye like little more than a small black speck. The hybrid device package is then sealed with epoxy or some other potting compound.

Two basic package forms are used, and some of them appear very much like large DIP ICs. There is a ceramic package. The substrate is built

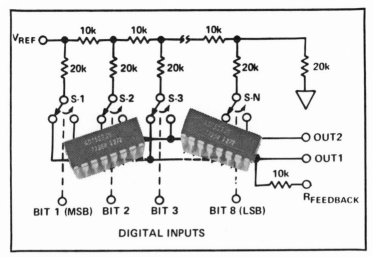

Fig. 12-1. Integrated circuit DAC.

into the hollow inside, and the assembly is potted. The package is sealed with a ceramic top cemented in place. Some of these appear very much like monolithic ICs and may well be mistaken for such a device.

The other type of construction commonly seen is the metal can. The metal can is usually hermetically sealed. It is often the case that a manufacturer offers two versions of the same device. The commercial-specifications version is housed in the ceramic package, while the premium military specification model is housed in the metal can. Of course, the military-specification version is more costly. Although monolithic ICs have improved, it has been true that hybrid devices had more precision. The maker could fine tune the product in hybrid form more easily.

At one time there would be no argument that the function-module form of data converter produced the most precise results. An example of a

Fig. 12-2. Hybrid DAC.

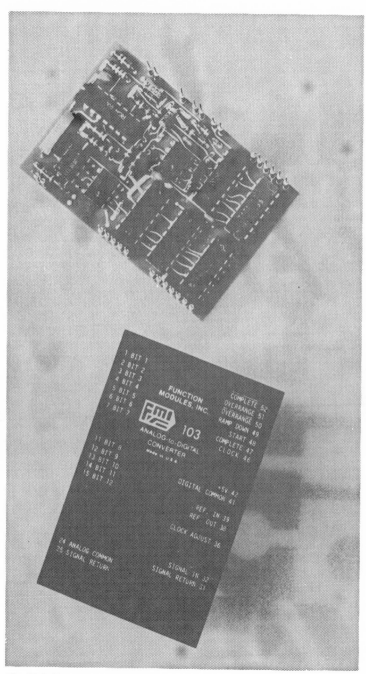

Fig. 12-3. Function module DAC.

function module is shown in Fig. 12-3. These devices can be of discrete construction, semidiscrete construction, or even hybrid form. They generally have internal adjustments (sometimes available to the outside world) that allow the circuit to be fine tuned to optimum accuracy. In general, the most expensive data converters—and the most precise—are of the function-module type.

The function-module circuit can be built onto the ceramic substrate or on a printed-circuit board of rather ordinary composition. Often, there is nothing at all exotic about its internal construction. After the circuit is built, tested, and fine tuned, it is sealed inside a plastic container. Some function modules are potted in epoxy, while others are left unpotted and sealed by gluing the top to the bottom substrate.

Most function modules are multipin devices, with some having as many as 100 pins. Their manufacturers often sell matching sockets, or a user can solder them directly to a printed circuit board. Some require no external trimming, while others require the user to add some external circuitry of his own.

Before going any further in the discussion of data converters, some of the signals that you will encounter need defining. This allows you to see the function and limitations of various types of circuits more clearly.

Figures 12-4 through 12-6 show the three types of basic signal that you will encounter. There are several subclasses that become important in certain instances, but these are the most representative.

The basic analog signal is shown in Fig. 12-4. Notice one fact about this signal, if none other: it can take on any value in either range or domain. While there can be limits imposed on the permissible end-points of both range and domain, the signal can take on any value within that set of limits. You might, for example, label the domain in units of time, with zero being the turn-on point or some arbitrarily selected point at which you become interested in the signal. The units to the right of zero, then, are the time units from the beginning of your interest. The range is some voltage region. In some cases, the low-end limit is zero volts, while in others it is some

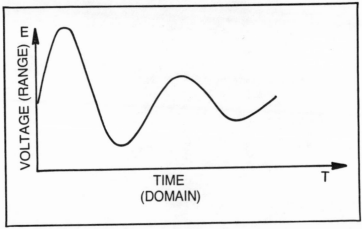

Fig. 12-4. Analog signal.

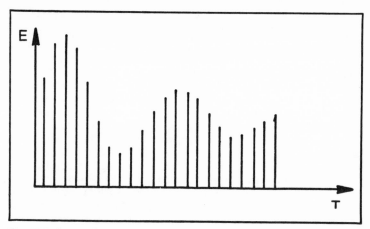

Fig. 12-5. Sampled signal.

negative value set by design considerations. You might find that the signal has any value within the limits of the range.

Analog signals can be either voltages or currents. Both types are used in this book. In many cases when one type of signal is discussed, it is implied that the opposite signal obeys the same rules.

If an analog signal is allowed to exist only at certain discrete instants in time, then the signal is the version shown of Fig. 12-5. The voltage or current can take on any value within the range, but the domain is considered at only specific points. In the case of most electronics applications, the domain is time, so the value of the signal is known precisely only at certain instants in time. This might be measured once every millisecond; there would be 1000 samples per second.

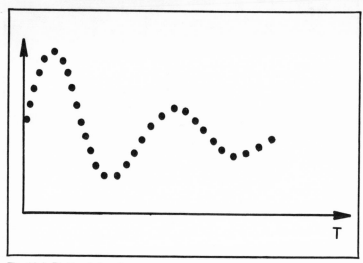

Fig. 12-6. Digitized signal.

Sampled signals are not without difficulty. There are certain rules regarding the rate at which the signal is sampled. If you fail to sample the signal often enough, you lose the overall waveshape. Any continuous signal can be represented mathematically by a Fourier series. This is a series of figures that expresses the function (signal) as a summation of sine and cosine terms. There is a fundamental, plus some number of odd, even, or odd-even harmonics of the fundamental frequency. Coefficents of each term gives the amplitude. All such functions can be expressed by a Fourier series. The sine (or cosine) wave is expressed by only one term; so it has no dc component or harmonics. In other words it is a pure single-frequency waveform. All other waveforms contain some harmonics. If these harmonics are lost, it is impossible to reproduce the signal properly.

The sampling rate of the data converter must be set to at least twice the highest frequency component present in the waveform being sampled. If, for example, a passband of 0.5-100 Hz is needed for proper reproduction of a waveform, the analog-to-digital converter (ADC) must provide a sampling rate of at least 2×100 Hz, or 200 Hz (200 samples per second). This specification, incidentally, is minimal, not optimal. In actual practice much faster sampling rates are often found. One computer-based instrument samples at a rate of 1000 samples per second.

A sampled signal can be produced by a *sample and hold* circuit. These circuits typically close a switch to admit the signal and then open it again after the signal is measured. In most cases, the instantaneous value of the signal is stored in a capacitor. ADC converters can also produce a signal that looks sampled. It is, however, truly a *digitized* signal.

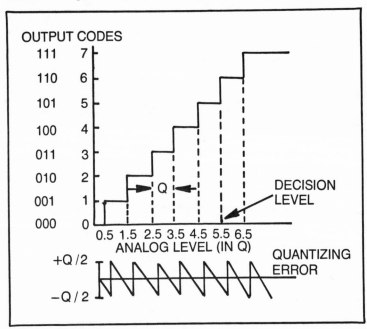

Fig. 12-7. Quantizing error.

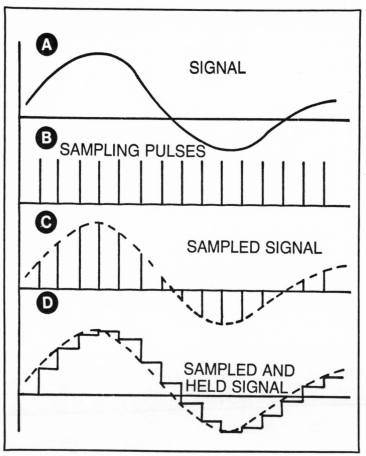

Fig. 12-8. A) Analog signal, (B) sampling pulses, (C) sampled signal, (D) sampled and held signal.

The sampled signal can take any value within the limits imposed upon the range, but can take only certain discrete values in the domain. A truly digitized signal, on the other hand, must exist only in certain discrete values in both the range and the domain. For example, a digitized voltage, such as shown in Fig. 12-6, can take only certain values (five shown) and is known only at certain discrete instants of time. The ADC produces a signal of this type, although the values are not voltages, but binary words that represent the voltage at some given time. Voltage levels between the allowed levels are in error, but will be given whatever values are nearest the actual values.

When a continuous signal, such as an analog voltage or current, is converted into a signal that can take only discrete values, the signal is *quantized.* Figure 12-7 shows a quantizer transfer function. Note that an ADC converter is basically a quantizer. The analog input signal is plotted along the horizontal axis, while the permissible digital-output codes are plotted along the vertical axis.

An error is inherent in the quantization process. Notice that the analog signal can take on any value between 0 and 7 V. But the three-bit quantized output can only accommodate the specific values 0, 1, 2, 3, 4, 5, 6, and 7. If the value is, say 2.56, then it lies between two of the permissible output numbers (2 and 3). In this particular example, the output shows the binary code 111, indicating a decimal 3. If you denote the quantizing error by Q, then the error is $\pm \frac{1}{2}Q$ at worst case, falling to zero only at those points where the analog input voltage exactly corresponds to the binary output number, or at 0, 1, 2, 3, 4, 5, 6, and 7 V. An N-bit data converter has 2^N possible discrete output states and $2^N - 1$ analog decision points (see Fig. 12-7).

Another source of inherent error is present in real data-converters. No data converter operates in zero time; all require some finite amount of time to make a conversion. But, the analog signal can take on any given time; so it is not limited by the data converter's problems. Figure 12-8 shows a sampled signal. The analog signal varies in its own way, completely oblivious to the data converter problems. Sampling pulses, in the form of *start conversion signals* to the ADC, cause the signal to be sampled. Sampling does not in itself result in grabbing the data. A *sample and hold circuit* stores the values temporarily while the data converter does its job. Note that there is now some distortion present in the sampled-and-held version of the signal. As mentioned, however, a sufficiently high sampling-rate yields an output waveform from the quantizer that is very similar to the input waveform.

The measure of how well a signal can be represented is the number of samples per second, but this is limited by the conversion time of the data converter and any other time losses in the system. The measure of this phenomenon is the *aperture time*.

Aperture time can represent both time and voltage uncertainties. Figure 12-9 shows the effect of aperture time on the measurement. Notice that the signal voltage, V, can change its actual value an amount ΔV over the time required to make the measurement. If dv/dt represents this small change, and T_A is the aperture time, then:

$$\Delta V = \frac{dV(t)}{dt} \times T_A$$

This equation, in slightly different form, can be used to compute the maximum-allowable aperture-time to make any given data conversion. Again, the input signal is considered a Fourier series, and the highest frequency component in the series is used as the point of examination. First, specify the percentage of resolution required of the data converter, which is given by:

$$r = \frac{\Delta V}{V}$$

The expression that you use is:

$$T_A = \frac{\Delta V}{V} \times \frac{1}{2\pi f} = \frac{r}{2\pi f}$$

142

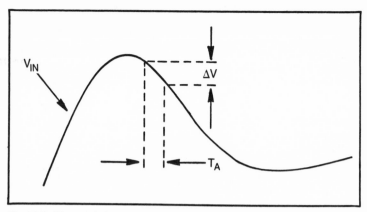

Fig. 12-9. Change during aperture time T_A.

where $\Delta V/V$ expresses the required resolution, f is the highest sinusoidal frequency in the Fourier series, and r is the resolution.

One of the most overspecified parameters in data converters is the conversion speed and the related aperture time. Many users who consider these parameters highly important are making an erroneous determination of their needs. They must analyze the signals being applied and determine if there is truly a need for high-frequency capability in the data converter. In the example given earlier, a bandwidth of 100 Hz is needed to make an acceptable recording. This means that if a 0.1 percent resolution (r=0.001) is needed (10 bits), a model with an aperture time of 150 microseconds (us) must be selected.

Resolution is a function of the data converter bit length. The smallest increment of measurement allowed is the value measured by the least significant bit (LSB) of the converter. For an eight-bit converter, there is a total of 256, or about 0.4 percent. A ten-bit converter is able to resolve one part in 2^{10}, or 1-in-1024. The resolution is therefore approximately 0.1 percent. In general, the resolution is expressed by:

$$r = \frac{100\%}{2^n}$$

where r is the resolution in percent, and n is the bit length of the converter. Table 12-1 gives some of the values for 2^N and 2^{-N} for various values of n.

CODING SCHEMES FOR DATA CONVERTERS

Data converters use one of the standard binary codes to represent data, but there are several different forms of code in common use, and you must know which one is used in any given application. Most of them are a version of either regular binary, or BCD (binary-coded decimal).

The binary number system is in base-2. Only two digits are permitted in the binary number system: 0 and 1. When binary digits are used together in the form of a weighted number, values higher than one can be represented. In this case, as in the more familiar decimal system, the position

143

Table 12-1. Resolution vs Bit Length.

n	2^n	2^{-n}	dB
0	1	1	0
1	2	.5	−6
2	4	.25	−12
3	8	.125	−18.1
4	16	.0625	−24.1
5	32	.03125	−30.1
6	64	.015625	−36.1
7	128	.0078125	−42.1
8	256	.00390625	−48.2
9	512	.001953125	−54.2
10	1 024	.0009765625	−60.2
11	2 048	.00048828125	−66.2
12	4 096	.000244140625	−72.2
13	8 192	.0001220703125	−78.3
14	16 384	.00006103515625	− 84.3
15	32 768	.000030517578125	−90.3
16	65 536	.0000152587890625	−96.3

of a digit with respect to the other digits determines its value—as a power of two. In the straight binary-code the weights are:

$$2^n + \ldots + 2^4 + 2^3 + 2^2 + 2^1 + 2^0$$
$$\infty + \ldots + 16 + 8 + 4 + 2 + 1$$

In the discussions of this chapter, assume that all binary numbers are in eight-bit format. This is actually not far from the truth in the world of eight-bit microprocessor-microcomputers!

Straight binary coding follows the ordinary binary number-system. This means that 1_{10} is represented by 00000001, while 128_{10} is represented by 01000000, etc. In the world of data conversion, the system is modified just slightly. There are 2^N different states in the binary number by which to represent data. Zero is a valid input condition; so some code must be used for zero input volts. In straight binary, it might easily be 00000000 that is used as zero. This leaves 255 remaining states ($2^8 - 1$) to represent the rest of the voltage range. Just as the maximum-allowable binary-number is $2^N - 1$, the maximum-allowable input-voltage is one bit less than full scale. For example, say that you have a 0-10 V ADC in eight-bit format. The maximum input voltage that is measured is FS-1 LSB, or:

$$E = 10 \text{ V} \times (255/256)$$
$$= 10 \text{ V} \times (0.996) = 9.96 \text{ V}$$

In general, the maximum output-voltage from any data converter in the straight unipolar binary-system is found from:

$$E^{FS} = E^M \times (2^N - 1) / 2^N$$

where E^{FS} is the full-scale input voltage, E^M is the maximum voltage in the desired range, and n is the converter bit length.

The first LSB voltage is found from:

$$E^{LSB} = \frac{1}{2^n} \times E^M$$

Table 12-2 shows the associated binary coding for a 10 V positive (unipolar) data-converter in straight binary and complemented binary. The complement of a binary number is found by changing all of the ones to zero and all of the zeros to ones.

Unipolar coding means that the converter can represent voltages in one quadrant only. While this is satisfactory in some cases, data often needs to be represented in two quadrants. Here you run into a couple of decisions. For one thing, you still have only a finite number of bits to represent the numbers. In unipolar operation each voltage level that can be represented is different by one LSB from the adjacent allowable levels. For example, in Table 12-2 for straight binary the first positive LSB voltage is 0.04 V. Every time the input voltage changes by 0.04 V, the binary number at the output (with opposite reasoning for DACs) changes by one count. The 0-10 V range is represented by 256 states. However, when you try to use the same format to represent -10 to $+10$ V, the span becomes 20 V. The single-LSB voltage is then calculated to be 80 mV (0.08 V). The data converter gains something in its operating range only at the expense of lost resolution.

Another problem is how the zero condition is treated. There are an even number of allowable states; after all, this is a binary system. If zero represents one of the states, an odd number of different states is left. This means that there is one more allowable state on one side of zero than on the other.

Consider Table 12-3, which shows the output states of a ±5-V data converter in which zero input volts is represented by the half-scale binary number, 10000000. The full-scale voltage on the minus side is -5 V and is represented by 00000000. On the positive side, though, there are only 127 different states. The maximum allowable voltage is +4.96 V. This type of encoding scheme is known as offset binary, because the allowable codes are offset about zero to accommodate a zero condition. In offset binary, the zero condition is usually represented by the half-scale code.

Also shown in Table 12-3 is the *two's complement* code. The two's complement of any binary number is formed by adding one to the LSB of the

Table 12-2. Unipolar Coding.

Scale	+10VFS	Straight Binary		Complemented Binary
		MSB	LSB	MSB LSB
+FS−1LSB	+9.96	1111	1111	0000 0000
+¾FS	+7.50	1100	0000	0011 1111
+½FS	+5.00	1000	0000	0111 1111
+¼FS	+2.50	0100	0000	1011 1111
+⅛FS	+1.25	0010	0000	1101 1111
+1LSB	+0.04	0000	0001	1111 1110
0	0.00	0000	0000	1111 1111

Table 12-3. Offset Binary Bipolar Coding.

Scale	±5VFS	Offset Binary		2's Complement	
		MSB	LSB	MSB	LSB
+FS −1LSB	+4.96	1111	1111	0111	1111
+¾FS	+3.75	1110	0000	0110	0000
+½FS	+2.50	1100	0000	0100	0000
0	0.00	1000	0000	0000	0000
− ½ FS	−2.50	0100	0000	1100	0000
− ¾ FS	−3.75	0010	0000	1010	0000
−FS + 1LSB	−4.96	0000	0001	1000	0001
−FS	−5.00	0000	0000	1000	0000

complement of the number. For example, to find the two's complement of 11010101:

Original number	1 1 0 1 0 1 0 1
Complement	0 0 1 0 1 0 1 0
Add 1	+1
Two's complement	0 0 1 0 1 0 1 1

The two's complement is used to make binary addition easier. Some data converters form the two's complement code in order to ease the software load placed on the CPU to which the data is fed.

Table 12-4 shows an alternate method for representing bipolar voltages. Zero is not represented with a specific voltage. Instead, the code is placed symmetrically about zero, so that each polarity has an equal number of allowable states. You must select which condition (10000000 or 01111111) to designate as zero. These conditions are known as plus-zero and minus-zero: plus zero is +0.04 V, while minus-zero is −0.04 V. No code uniquely denotes 0.00 V.

Whether you want to use offset or symmetrical binary depends in part upon which end of the scale is most important. If the upper end is needed more desperately than the lower end, go for symmetrical binary. On the other hand, if it is more important to know the zero condition accurately, an offset binary code is needed.

Some data converters honor some of the other binary codes, including sign magnitude. For the most part, however, the codes listed in these tables are the most popular.

One more code used is binary-coded decimal (BCD). In this system decimal-equivalent digits are formed by grouping the binary digits into four-bit groups. An eight-bit binary format accommodates two BCD-digits:

DIGIT 1	DIGIT 2
DCBA	DCBA

Table 12-4. ± Zero Coding.

+FS	11111111	+9.92 V
+Zero	10000000	+0.04 V
−Zero	01111111	−0.04 V
−FS	00000000	−9.92 V

The bits of the least significant digit are weighted 8, 4, 2, and 1, while those of the most significant digit are weighted 80, 40, 20 and 10. Table 12-5 lists the decimal, binary, and BCD representions for the numbers 0 through 33_{10}.

A typical encoding scheme for a 0-10-V unipolar-positive data-converter is shown in Table 12-6. Because 0 V is represented with the BCD code 0000 0000, the maximum code is 99_{10}, or 1001 1001. This represents +9.9 V.

SPECIFICATIONS

Specifications for any product, especially devices such as data converters, are extremely important. It is, therefore, a good idea that you understand what some of these specifications (specs) actually mean. Some of the lesser manufacturers often manipulate specifications, or indulge in what could charitably be called "creative spec writing," in order to leave a false impression about the capability of their products.

Take the matter of slew rate, for example. Some companies use the unit of volts per microsecond, others use millivolts per millisecond or some other system of measurement. One way to make valid comparisons is to convert the slew rates of all units under consideration to a common set of units. For example, $V/\mu s$ the standard of measurement. How would you convert a slew rate of 500 mV/ms to $V/\mu s$? (Here, s means second(s).)

Decimal	Binary	BCD
0	0000	0000 0000
1	0001	0000 0001
2	0010	0000 0010
3	0011	0000 0011
4	0100	0000 0100
6	0101	0000 0101
6	0110	0000 0110
7	0111	0000 0111
8	1000	0000 1000
9	1001	0000 1001
10	1010	0001 0000
11	1011	0001 0001
12	1100	0001 0010
13	1101	0001 0011
14	1110	0001 0100
15	1011	0001 0101
16	10000	0001 0110
17	10001	0001 0111
18	10010	0001 1000
19	10011	0001 1001
20	10100	0010 0000
21	10101	0010 0001
22	10110	0010 0010
23	10111	0010 0011
24	11000	0010 0100
25	11001	0010 0101
26	11010	0010 0110
27	11011	0010 0111
28	11100	0010 1000
29	11101	0010 1001
30	11110	0011 0000
31	11111	0011 0001
32	100000	0011 0010
33	100001	0011 0010

Table 12-5. Binary and BCD Equivalents for Decimal Numbers 0 Through 33.

Table 12-6. BCD Coding.

Scale	+10VFS	BCD	
		MSD	LSD
+FS−1LSD	+9.9	1001	1001
+¾FS	+7.5	0111	0101
+½FS	+5.0	0101	0000
+¼FS	+ 2.5	0010	0101
+1 LSD	+ 0.1	0000	0001
0	.0.0	0000	0000

$$\frac{500 \text{ mV} \times \frac{1 \text{ V}}{10^3 \text{ mV}}}{1 \text{ ms} \times \frac{1 \text{ s}}{10^3 \text{ ms}}} = \frac{0.5 \text{ V}}{0.001 \text{ s}} = 500 \text{ mV/ms}$$

By converting the units, you gain an appreciation of the relative slew rates of two differently specified devices. While this can sometimes be used to the advantage of the manufacturer, it is just as often merely a difference in the way two engineers write a specification.

You must also be cognizant of differences in definitions. Most of the definitions of this chapter are relatively universal and are adopted from a manual by Analog Devices, Inc., called *Analog-Digital Conversion Notes.* It is usually a good sign when a manufacturer publishes the definitions on which the specs are based. Some products look worse at first glance—until you find out about the spec definition.

For example, one product is rated to have a conversion time of several microseconds. But once the truth is known, this is for a current-input mode that effectively by-passed the input amplifier. When the settling time of the input amplifier is factored in, this converter is actually no better than those by mainline manufacturers.

DIGITAL-TO-ANALOG CONVERTERS

A digital-to-analog converter (DAC) is a circuit or device that pro-duces an analog current or voltage output that is proportional to an analog reference (voltage or current) and an N-bit binary word. In general, the DAC produces an output that is:

$$X = k \times A \times B$$

where X is the output voltage or current, k is a constant (which is often 1), A is the analog-reference voltage or current, and B is the applied binary word.

Figure 12-10 shows a block diagram of the principal components of the DAC system. The analog-reference source is a precision digital-converter reference power-supply that produces a voltage or current output. Some DACs have the reference supply inside the package, while others are found external to the DAC package. Those DACs in which the reference source is external are called multiplying DACs. In actuality, all DACs multiply, by

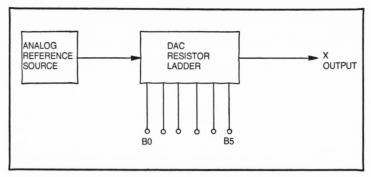

Fig. 12-10. Basic DAC diagram.

virtue of the previous equation; the designation multiplying-DAC always refers to a model in which the user can apply an external reference. In many models, incidentally, the internal reference source is brought outside and must be connected to the reference input. These models seem to offer the best in both multiplying and nonmultiplying DACs.

There are two different types of DAC circuits, and both are based on current-output resistor-ladders: *Binary weighted* and *R-2R* ladders. Figure 12-11 shows the basic binary-weighted resistor-ladder circuit. It consists of a series of resistors that can be connected to either the reference voltage, V_{REF}, if the digit is 1, or ground if the digit is 0. In this example the resistors are connected to 1 and 0 levels with ordinary switches, although in actual DACs electronic switches do the job.

The operation of this circuit becomes more apparent when you note that the resistor values are power of 2 multiples of each other. The value of R1 is taken to be R, so R2 is 2R, R3 is 4R, and so forth, until you see that R_N has a value of $2_{(N-1)}R$. When these resistors are connected to ground, the current associated with the particular resistor is zero. If the resistor is connected to V_{REF}, the current flow equals the quotient of the reference voltage to the resistance of that resistor (E /R). The currents from each branch are summed in a summation junction; so the output current, I_{OUT}, is the sum of all branch currents. Expressed mathematically:

$$I_{OUT} = V_{REF} \sum_{i=1}^{n} \frac{a^i}{2^{(i-1)}R}$$

Where I_{OUT} is the output current in amperes, a^i is the binary digit for that input (1 or 0), and R is the value of the first resistor in the ladder; i.e., R1.

The circuit shown in Fig. 12-11 is merely an example. Most DACs use electronic switching to connect the various resistors to the summation node. Figure 12-12 shows electronic switching used in a four-bit DAC. A series of transistors are used as the switches. The binary inputs are isolated from the transistors by diodes, and the transistors are biased by a current source. When the bit is low, the diode for that bit is forward biased; so the emitter of the PNP transistor is grounded. When the bit is high, the diode is reverse biased, and the emitter of the PNP transistor is biased by the reference-source main-supply, $+V_S$. In this case, the current source can

149

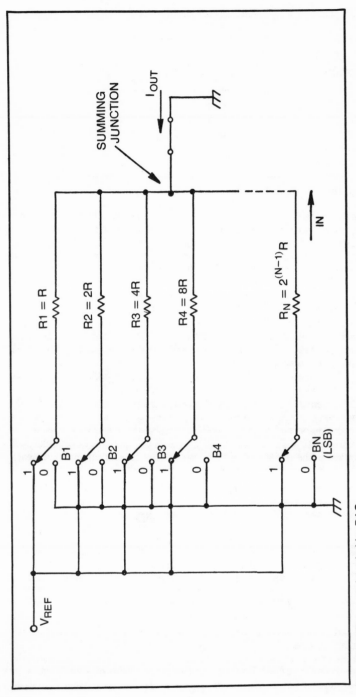

Fig. 12-11. Binary resistor-ladder DAC.

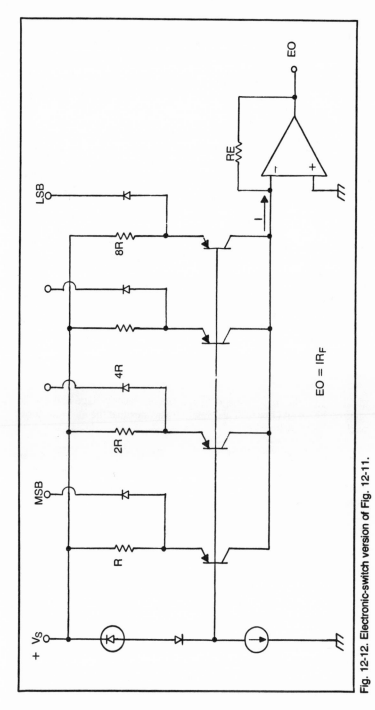

Fig. 12-12. Electronic-switch version of Fig. 12-11.

$$EO = IR_F$$

151

bias that transistor and adds its current to the total applied to the input of the operational amplifier. The purpose of the amplifier is to provide a voltage output, E_{OUT}, which is equal to the product of the ladder-output current, I, and the feedback resistor.

The binary-weighted resistor-ladder has problems if the bit length is longer than about eight: the resistor values at the ends of the ladders become out of line. For example, if R is set to 10K ohms, bit 8 is $2^{(8-1)}$ (10K ohms), or 1.28 megohms. Consider what happens when the reference voltage is + 10.00 V. Current I^8 is 10.00/1.28 megohms, or 7.8 microamperes. Finding operational amplifiers that respond to input currents of this level becomes a little difficult, unless cost is no object. Only premium devices amplify such a current. In lower cost devices, the LSB current of the circuit is down in the noise and does not produce an output.

Similarly, if you try to extend the range by making R very small, you run into exactly the opposite problem. For those circuits, the current may be too large. If resistance is set to 100 ohms, then for $V_{REF} = 10.00$ V, current I_1 will be 100 mA. This is more than most operational amplifiers want to see. Reducing the value of R to 10 ohms produces a current of 1000 mA (1 ampere).

A solution to this problem is the R-2R ladder (Fig. 12-12). All of the resistors have a value of either R or 2R. If you assume that the output load (R^L) has a resistance that is so much higher than 2R that its contribution to dropping the ladder output-voltage can be considered negligible, then you can claim that:

$$E_{OUT} = V_{REF} \sum_{i=1}^{n} \frac{a^i}{2^i}$$

where E_{OUT} is the output voltage, V_{REF} is the reference voltage, and a_i is the value of the ith bit (1 or 0). This equation assumes that the load resistor is much larger than R or 2R.

FULL-SCALE OUTPUT VOLTAGE

Most commercial DACs are made using the R-2R resistor-ladder technique. The maximum, or full-scale, output voltage depends on the reference voltage and the bit length:

$$E = \frac{V_{REF} (2^N - 1)}{2^N}$$

where E is the full-scale output potential, V_{REF} is the reference potential, and n is the bit length. See Fig. 12-13.

The output potential or current of a DAC can exist only in certain discrete states because one of the inputs is binary word. Each successive binary number changes by one LSB. The smallest increment of voltage output allowed at the output of a DAC is that produced by a single LSB change of the binary word. This voltage is expressed mathematically as:

$$\Delta E_{OUT} = \frac{V_{REF}}{2^N}$$

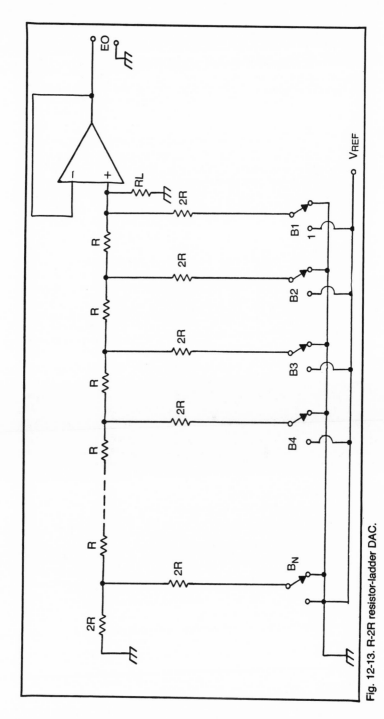

Fig. 12-13. R-2R resistor-ladder DAC.

AMPLIFIER SETTLING-TIME

One of the principal limits in any commercial DAC is the *settling time* of the output amplifier. Figure 12-14 shows an R-2R ladder DAC with an amplifier output. Any change in the input state is not reflected as an output state change immediately. There is always some sort of *lag* between the two events. This lag, incidentally, determines the maximum operating frequency of the DAC. Assume in Fig. 12-15 that an input bit-change occurs at time t^1. The output voltage increases rapidly to the correct value, but is limited by the slew rate of the amplifier(s). The voltage overshoots the mark in most cases and then settles down to the correct value. The "correct" value, incidentally, is actually a small voltage band clustered around the desired output potential. This is due to normal circuit errors. The settling time of the amplifier is the time difference between the onset of the input change t time t_1 and point t_2 where the output voltage finally settles into the normal uncertainty-band. The setting time is t_2-t_1.

Since electronic switching is already pretty fast, it is best to concentrate on the settling time of the amplifier when trying to achieve faster speeds. In many cases the DAC manufacturer produces a current-output DAC in order to keep the operating speed high. When trying to operate near the rated operating speed of the DAC (very often in the megaHertz range, if it is a current-output type), it is necessary to keep the settling time of the output amplifier, external to the DAC, less than $1/f$, where f is the operating frequency of the DAC.

Similarly, when using the output of the DAC to drive a comparator, as is often the case in ADC circuits, to try keeping the total operating speed at a level that is high enough to do the job. Comparators can be operated in both the current and voltage modes. The current mode (one input grounded and both comparison currents applied to the same input) is usually faster.

ANALOG-TO-DIGITAL CONVERTERS

Analog-to-digital converters (ADCs) are circuits or devices that examine an analog input—in other words, a current or a voltage—and then convert it to an equivalent binary word. The ADC has an encoded output in which each change of one LSB in the output word represents some given increment of the input voltage or current.

ADCs are used to interface digital instruments and computers to devices in the analog world. In a typical instrumentation system, some form of amplifier output must be applied to the computer. The amplifier output can represent the amplified version of some naturally occurring potential or it might be created by a transducer of some sort. But analog voltages and currents cannot be directly input to a digital computer. Some form of interface is needed to convert the voltage or current to a binary word.

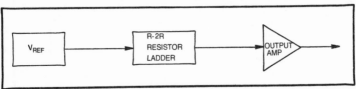

Fig. 12-14. Required stages in DAC.

154

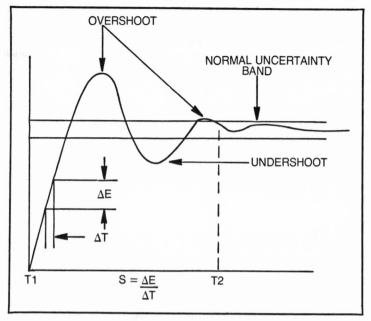

Fig. 12-15. Definition of settling time.

Although ADCs use almost all of the major digital codes, most of them are in straight (offset or symmetrical) binary, BCD, or two's complement binary.

There are several basic approaches to ADC design: *integrating, servo (ramp), successive approximation, parallel,* and *voltage-to-frequency conversion.* The more popular integrating ramp, parallel, and successive approximation (SA) converters are covered here. In a later chapter, you will be introduced to some of the commercially available ADC devices on the market and some circuits that perform the analog-to-digital function using ordinary IC devices.

Integration ADC Circuits

Integration ADC circuits use an analog operational-amplifier integrator to create a ramp voltage from the input voltage being measured. Three basic types are known: *single-slope, dual-slope,* and *multiple-slope.* Multiple-slope is composed of two different categories: triple-slope and quad-slope.

Figure 12-16 shows the basic operational amplifier integrator circuit. The op amp is a perfect—well, nearly so—amplifier that I discussed in Chapter 11 in greater detail. A resistor is connected in series with the input, and a capacitor is connected in the feedback loop between the output and input.

Because the output is an integral over time, the output is said to be proportional to the time average of the input signal. The proportionality factor will be the term 1/RC, which also describes the gain of the circuit.

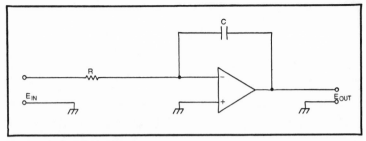

Fig. 12-16. Op-amp integrator.

Note that very low values of capacitance charge more rapidly with any given resistor; so the maximum value is reached rapidly. The gain of an integrator can become very high, very quickly, as the resistance-capacitance time constant is reduced.

Single-Slope Integrators

The simplest form of integrating ADC circuit is the single-slope integrator of Fig. 12-17. The principal components of this circuit are: integrator, voltage comparator, gate, clock, and the gate generator. The gate generator keeps the timing of the circuit straight.

The integrator circuit is the operational amplifier just discussed. Switch 1 is used to initially discharge the capacitor; so the integrator output begins the conversion cycle at zero. This switch is usually an electronic field-effect transistor that is turned on by ordinary digital logic-level signals. When switch 1 is closed, the capacitor is shorted out, and its charge goes to zero. But when switch 1 is open, the capacitor can function normally, and the circuit integrates the input voltage.

A comparator is a device that compares two analog voltages and issues an output that indicates whether the voltages are equal to each other, or which of the two is the higher. Figure 12-18 shows the operation of a voltage comparator. Figure 12-19 is a graph of the output-versus-input voltage.

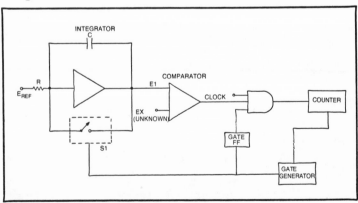

Fig. 12-17. Single-slope integrating ADC.

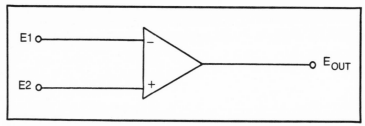

Fig. 12-18. Comparator.

The comparator is basically a differential-input operational-amplifier with too much gain. In fact, an op amp can easily be used as a comparator if no negative feedback is supplied. When $E1 = E_X$, the differential input-voltage seen by the amplifier is zero; so the output E_{OUT} is zero. When E1 is greater than E_X, however, the output of the comparator is a constant negative-voltage. When E1 is less than E_X at the input, the output of the comparator is a high positive-voltage. In most bipolar comparators the absolute values of $+E$ and $-E$ are equal. In comparators usually used for ADC work the output is monopolar; i.e., only the $E1 = E_X$ and $E1 < E_X$ conditions are needed.

The gate and clock sections of the single-slope integrator circuit are the same as in any digital electronic circuits; a three-input gate is specified here. The counter is an ordinary binary counter, although it might be in BCD in some applications, such as digital voltage-measurement.

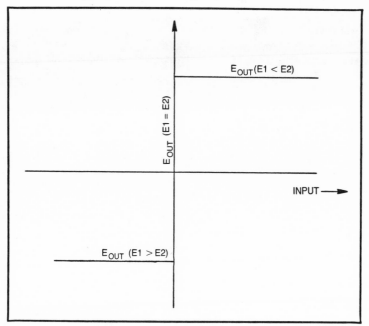

Fig. 12-19. Transfer function.

157

The operation of this circuit can be seen by examining the timing diagram in Fig. 12-20. The gate generator circuit issues a *start-conversion pulse* that resets the integrator output to zero by turning on switch 1 for a brief instant. It also insures that the counter is in the zero state by issuing a reset pulse to the counter circuit.

Immediately after the reset pulse is received, the output of the integrator begins to rise in response to the input voltage (analog signal). As soon as this process begins, the gate to the counter opens, and the clock pulses begin to accumulate in the counter. The comparator output is high at this time because E1 is less E_X. The process began at time t_1 in Fig. 12-20. At time t_2, however, $E1 = E_X$, so the comparator output drops low; turning off the flow of clock pulses to the counter. The count accumulated in the counter is then proportional to the input voltage, and if properly decoded, correctly reflects that voltage in binary form.

There are some problems with the simple single-slope converter circuit. One is that certain noise impulses tend to cause an error in the integrator output-voltage. Another error class is the normal-circuit errors in the integrator design: values of resistance and capacitance, bias currents, etc. It is also necessary that the clock frequency be accurate and stable over the conversion period.

The advantages of the single-slope converter are that it is simple and low-cost. In fact some of the lowest cost digital voltmeters use the single-slope ADC circuit. If you use the single-slope ADC, however, be prepared to put up with the errors inherent in the design. Because of these problems, the single-slope ADC has been eclipsed (although there has been a recent comeback) by the dual-slope ADC.

Dual-Slope Integrating Converters

Figure 12-21 shows a block diagram for the basic dual-slope integrator ADC circuit. The principal parts are: integrator, comparator, main gate,

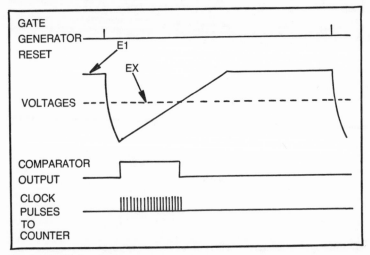

Fig. 12-20. Timing diagram.

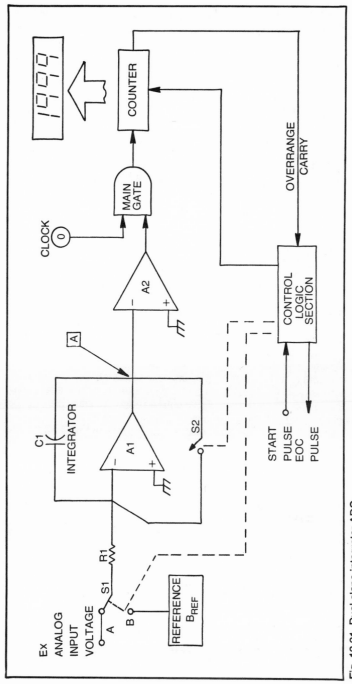

Fig. 12-21. Dual-slope integrator ADC.

counter, control-logic section, reference voltage or current, and an input switch that is controlled by the logic section. Some of the component parts of the dual-slope circuit are the same as those of the single-slope circuit; so their description is not repeated here.

The reference section is a precision analog voltage or current to which the unknown input signal is compared. First the unknown signal is integrated, much in the manner of the earlier single-slope circuit. However, this signal is then compared with the precision reference by integrating the reference in the same manner.

When a start pulse is received by the control-logic section, several things occur. One is that switch 1 connects to the input signal, switch 2 momentarily closes to reset the integrator output to zero, and a reset pulse is applied to the counter to insure that its starting state is zero.

The analog input signal is applied to the input of the integrator, so the voltage at point A begins to rise. The comparator is ground referenced in this case; so its output snaps high as soon as the integrator output is more than a few millivolts (the comparator has a small hysteresis; so it does not respond until E_A is more than a few millivolts). The instant the comparator output is high clock pulses begin to flow into the counter. The counter is allowed to overflow, and the carry signal is applied to the control logic. When the overflow occurs, the output of the integrator is proportional to the input signal (see Fig. 12-22). At this time the control logic section switches the integrator input to the precision reference source. The polarity of this source is selected such that it discharges the integrator capacitor that has been charged by the unknown signal. Because the reference has a constant level, though, the slope of the discharge is constant, yet proportional to the analog input signal. The counter state at the instant the switching of the input occurs is 0000 (overflow plus one count is zero). The counter continues to increment all during the period when the integrator is discharging and stops only when the integrator output returns to zero, causing the comparator output to snap low and turning off the gate.

To reiterate the operation of this circuit (refer to Fig. 12-22) is as follows:

1. At time 0 switch 2 is closed momentarily to dump any residual charge in the integrator capacitor, the counter is reset, and switch 1 is set to the analog input.
2. The integrator begins to charge due to current E_{IN} /R1, so E_A begins rising from zero.
3. As soon as E_A is greater than zero, plus a small hysteresis, the comparator output goes high, which enables the main gate to pass clock pulses into the counter.
4. The counter increments until it overflows at time 1. The overflow pulse generated by the counter causes switch 1 to switch to the analog reference source (position B). This applies the reference voltage to the input of the integrator. The count of the counter at this instant is 0000.
5. Between times 1 and 2 the integrator discharges under the influence of current (E_{REF} /R1). The counter continues to increment during this period.
6. At time 2, the comparator shuts off the flow of clock pulses through the main gate. The count accumulated during the period $t^2 - t^1$ represents the input voltage.

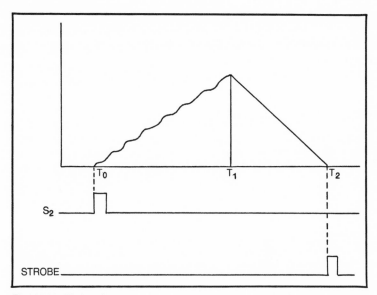

Fig. 12-22. Timing diagram.

7. The control logic section now issues an end-of-conversion (EOC) pulse to let the outside world know that the data at the output is valid. This pulse can also be used to update the output display if the ADC is being used as a digital voltmeter.

Although the dual-slope integrator is one of the slowest forms of ADC circuits, it has certain advantages: relative immunity from noise errors on the input signal and immunity to error caused by inaccuracy of the clock frequency (only the stability during the conversion cycle is important to the clock frequency). In many applications the 10-50 ms conversion-times are of little consequence, relative to the advantages.

Triple-Slope Integration

The triple-slope integrator is basically the same as the dual-slope integrator, except that one additional slope is added. As in the case of the dual-slope integrator, the triple-slope integrator (Fig. 12-23) converts the analog input voltage to a time interval, as measured by a digital pulse-counter. The first ramp, (V_A /RC) and fine ($-V_{REF}$ /2_kRC). The coarse ramp has a much steeper slope that the fine ramp. The coarse ramp, then, rapidly integrates the first portion of the signal until it is in the ball park. When the coarse ramp drops to a level of approximately V_T, the fine ramp is switched in to provide greater resolution. The high resolution is not needed in the coarse ramp; so the circuit goes for speed instead. The triple-slope integrator is capable of providing the advantages of integration analog-to-digital conversion, as outlined in the section on dual-slope circuits, yet reduces the speed from the normal 10-50-ms speed to 1-10-ms. Some triple-slope designs are capable of operating as fast as successive-approximation converters.

161

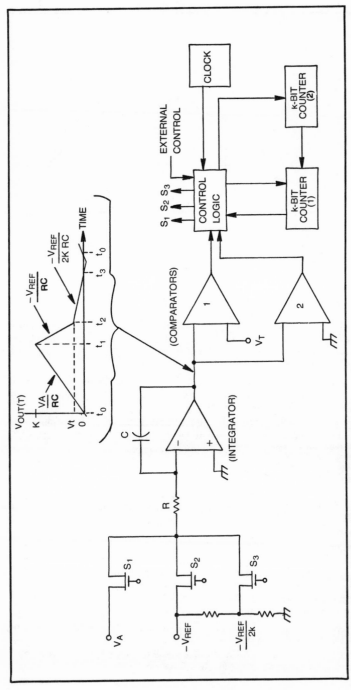

Fig. 12-23. Analog Devices Quad-Slope Integrator ADC.

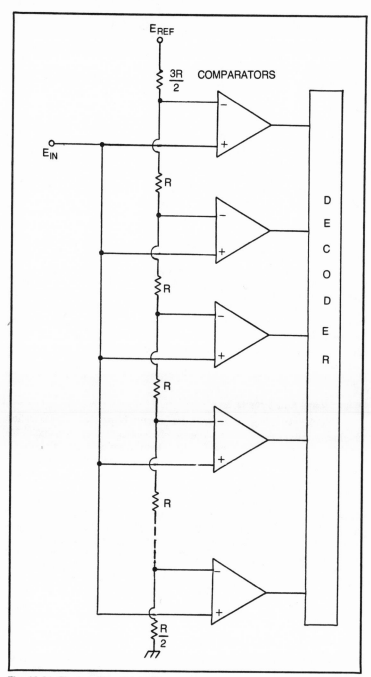

Fig. 12-24. Flash or Parallel ADC.

163

Analog Devices, Inc. offers integrating ADCs of all types. One of them is a refinement of the multiple-slope idea called a Quad-slope® ADC.

Parallel ADC Circuits

Very few ADC circuits are as fast as the parallel converter. This converter operates at such blazing speeds that it is sometimes called the flash ADC. Figure 12-24 shows a parallel ADC circuit. It consists of a stack of voltage comparators. One input of each converter in the stack is connected to the analog input signal. The other inputs are biased by a dc reference source. Each comparator is biased one LSB higher than the next one down in the chain. A simple precision-resistor network is used to accomplish the biasing scheme.

Why have any other converter circuit if the flash converter is so rapid? After all, speed is a critical parameter, isn't it?

There are actually a couple of disadvantages to the parallel converter. One of them is that the coder is limited as to the number of bits of resolution that can be accommodated. Normal problems with real voltage comparators limit the value of the LSB and this, of course, limits the total bit length.

The second problem is that the output is not encoded in any of the standard binary codes. A decoder logic circuit at the output of the comparators is needed in order to make the unit compatible with the outside world. Of course, if you have a computer, and the parallel ADC is sending data to the computer, the decoding can be done in software. But software decoding merely increases the program overhead of the CPU and might prove more costly in the long run. Only a few companies are making parallel converters. TRW, for example, offers some video ADC circuits that depend upon the speed of the parallel circuit in order to broaden bandwidth.

Binary Ramp ADC Circuits

The binary-ramp, or servo, ADC circuit is part of a class called feedback-ADC circuits. Most of the members of this class use a digital-to-analog converter (DAC) in the feedback loop to make the comparison.

The circuit for a basic servo ADC circuit is shown in Fig. 12-25. The major components are the DAC, comparator, main gate, binary counter, reference source, and control logic section.

The DAC used could be either a binary weighted resistance ladder, or an R-2R ladder design. Both current-output and voltage-output models are used in ADC circuits. The example shown in Fig. 12-25 is a voltage output design. Designs that use current-output DACs usually have both the DAC output-current and the analog input-current (or the voltage converted to a current by passing it through a resistor) applied to the same comparator input. The other comparator input is either grounded or connected to a small current source to compensate for any errors in the circuit. Current operation of the DAC and the comparator is generally faster than voltage operation.

When a start pulse is received by the control-logic section, the binary counter is reset and a gate-on signal is applied to the main gate. The binary outputs of the counter are connected to the digital inputs of the DAC; so when the main gate is opened, pulses that increment the counter have the effect of causing the DAC output to ramp upwards from zero toward E_{IN}.

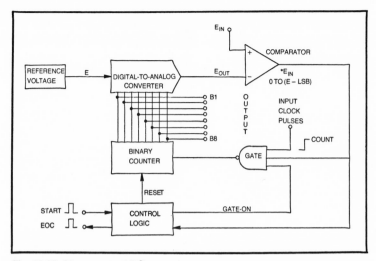

Fig. 12-25. Binary ramp ADC.

When DAC output E0 is equal to analog input voltage E_{IN}, the output of the comparator drops low, turning off the main gate. This stops the flow of clock pulses into the counter. The count remains at the level existing when the counter dropped low. This count is proportional to the value of the analog input voltage. When this occurs, the control logic section issues an *end of conversion* (EOC) pulse (see Fig. 12-26). To reiterate, the operation of the ramp ADC circuit is as follows:

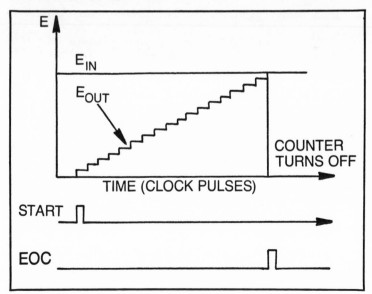

Fig. 12-26. Timing diagram for binary ramp conversion.

1. When a start pulse is received the control logic section resets the counter to zero and places a high on one input of the main gate.

2. The clock pulses now pass through the open main gate to begin incrementing the binary counter.

3. The DAC output voltage begins to ramp upward because the digital inputs of the DAC are connected to the counter output.

4. When DAC-output E_{OUT} is equal to the analog input-voltage E_{IN}, the comparator output drops low, causing the gate to close.

5. The counter output remains in its present state, which is proportional to the analog input-signal.

6. The control-logic section issues an end-of-conversion pulse to let the outside world know that the data on the outputs is valid.

The EOC pulse is also sometimes used to strobe the data into an output latch. The computer that is receiving the ADC data always sees this latched data; so all data appearing at the output of the converter is valid. Without the latch the incrementing counter data appears at the output and thus is not valid.

The converter circuits shown so far require a separate start and EOC pulse to operate properly. These lines can be tied together, however, if you want to make a continuous-operation ADC. The EOC pulse from one conversion becomes the start pulse for the next converion. Note that some designers use a set-reset flip-flop, or a pulse delay (one-shot) between the EOC output and the start input to give one clock-pulse to the external device (that is using the data) to either latch the output or input the data.

The binary-ramp ADC is faster than most integration methods. The time required to make a conversion depends upon the input voltage. The closer the voltage is to full scale, the longer the conversion time (of course, 0 V requires zero time). The time required for a full-scale conversion is the benchmark against which I often measure ADC performance. For the servo type, this time is 2^N clock pulses, where N is the bit length.

Binary ramp, servo, ADC circuits are very easy to implement. Consequently, they have become very popular. Modern IC and hybrid DACs are capable of operating to clock speeds of at least 200 kHz, with many capable of operation to 4 MHz. These clock speeds, which are easily compatible with TTL and CMOS binary-counters, allow very rapid conversions. The principal operating limitation seems to be comparator settling-time, which is similar to amplifier settling-time. Of course, this is assuming that no output-amplifier problem exists with the DAC itself.

Despite the speed of the DAC, there are still limitations that must be of concern to some users. For longer bit lengths, 2^N clock pulses can be a problem. The successive-approximation ADC of the next section solves some of the speed problems because it makes a complete conversion in N + 1 clock pulses.

Successive-Approximation ADC Circuits

The successive approximation (SA) analog-to-digital converter makes use of a technique that more nearly resembles the way you measure most physical quantities; i.e., trial and error. The successive approximation ADC makes a trial conversion, tests the results, and then modifies the output

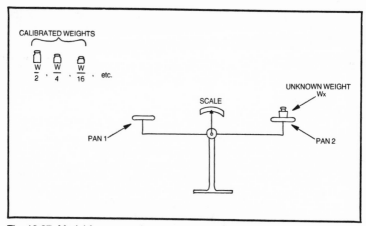

Fig. 12-27. Model for successive-approximation measurement.

according to the results of the test. It continues to make trials until the available bits are exhausted or it scores a finished conversion.

Figure 12-27 shows the successive-approximation technique in analog form. Here you have an ordinary platform-balance. The unknown weight is placed on one pan, while different trial weights are placed on the other pan. When the trial weights match the unknown weight, the scale is in balance, and the pointer is exactly in the center of its scale. The technique for making a measurement is simple. The trial weights are calibrated so that they are related by powers of two; i.e., W2, W4, W8, W16, etc. Begin the measurement by placing the heaviest trial weight (W2) on the lefthand pan and the unknown on the righthand pan.

If W_x is greater than W2, the scale pointer tilts to the right. But if the trial weight is less than the unknown, the scale tilts to the left. This is the

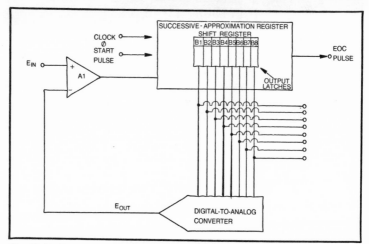

Fig. 12-28. Successive approximation ADC.

test you must make, and its result determines whether you increase the trial weight or make another trial with the next lower weight. In the successive-approximation ADC circuit the trial is made with a voltage comparator and the result is either to set or reset a bit in a register.

The trial process continues until the scale is in balance. At each trial, a weight is placed on the scale and the test performed. If the test shows that W_x is still higher, the operator adds additional weights. If W_x is less, however, the trial weight must be reduced.

Figure 12-28 shows the block diagram of a successive-approximation ADC circuit. The main components are the voltage comparator, DAC, control logic, shift register, and output latches. The last three of these are usually part of a successive-approximation register (SAR), integrated or hybrid. The output latches are needed so that the bit affected can be set or reset according to the results of the trial. When a start pulse is received by the successive-approximation ADC, all bits are set to zero (they are in the reset condition). Bit 1 is connected to the most-significant-bit input of the DAC. When the first clock pulse after the start pulse arrives, bit 1 is temporarily set high. This makes the output to the DAC 10000000, or half scale. If the unknown analog input-voltage (E_{IN}) is greater than this voltage, the output latch is set to 1 (high). If the input voltage is less than this value, however, the bit-1 latch is reset low. The first bit would be 1 in the former case and 0 in the latter. The successive-approximation ADC then shifts one bit to the right, and another trial is undertaken. At each bit the test is

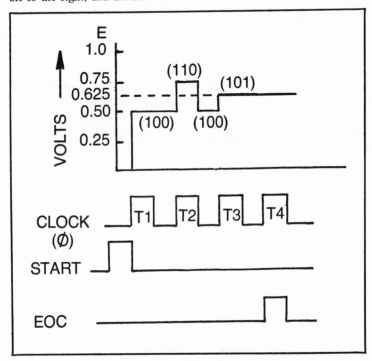

Fig. 12-29. Successive-approximation timing diagram.

performed and the output latch is set or reset, depending upon the result. When the final bit has been tested, the SAR overflows on the next clock pulse. If N is the bit length, the total conversion time is $N + 1$ clock pulses.

The operation of this circuit may become a little clearer if you follow a sample-conversion through the process. In the example of Fig. 12-29, the full-scale range is 1 V, and the value of the unknown E_{IN} is 0.625 V.

1. At time t^1, the successive-approximation ADC receives a start pulse. Register B1 goes high. The output word is now 100, so the half-scale output of the DAC is 0.5 V.
2. The test indicates that E_{IN} is still greater than E_{OUT}, so the latch for B1 is set high. The output following the first trial remains 100.
3. At time t^2 (receipt of the next clock pulse), register B2 is set high. The output word is now 110. Voltage E_{OUT} is now 0.75 V. In this case E_{IN} is less than E_{OUT}, so the output register latch for B2 is reset to zero. The output word is now 100.
4. At time t^3 output bit 3 is set high, so the output word becomes 101. The value of E_{OUT} is now 0.625 V, so $E_{OUT} = E_{IN}$. The latch for bit B3 is set HIGH, making the output word 101.
5. At time t^4 overflow occurs; so the outside world knows that the data contained on the output lines is valid. The control logic issues an EOC pulse.

Because the sample given was a three-bit successive-approximation ADC, the conversion time would be 3+1, or 4, clock pulses. Let's compare the relative conversion times of two 10-bit ADC circuits, one a servo and the other an successive-approximation. An 8-bit, 2 MHz servo ADC requires 512 microseconds to make the conversion. The successive-approximation is considerably faster—about 2 ms are required to make the conversion!

The successive-approximation ADC is 512/2, or 256, times faster than the servo ADC for the 10-bit word length. The successive-approximation becomes even more favorable as word length increases.

In the past development of successive-approximation ADC circuits was limited by the large amount of logic required to make the successive-approximation circuit work. This required a lot of TTL devices; so it was only used when high speed was necessary and the coding problems of the parallel circuit were too much trouble.

Today ADC designers can implement the successive-approximation design a lot easier because semiconductor makers offer appropriate DACs, comparators, and (best of all) IC successive-approximation registers that do all of the logic once relegated to a huge pile of TTL ICs. Motorola Semiconductor Products, Inc. makes the MC14459, while Advanced Micro Devices makes eight-bit (Am-2500) and 12-bit SAR ICs.

Chapter 13

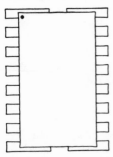

Practical Digital-to-Analog Converters

I have discussed the basic theory for the two main types of digital-to-analog converters (DACs). These devices output an analog voltage or current (depending on the type) that is proportional to the product of the analog-reference voltage or current and a binary word applied to the digital inputs. The output is a fraction of the reference level, with that fraction being $A/2^n$, in which A is the applied binary-word and n is the bit length of the converter.

FERRANTI ZN425E

Ferranti Electric of England markets the ZN425E 8-bit DAC through Ferranti Semiconductors, Ltd. of New York, NY. This DAC is shown in Fig. 13-1. It uses the R-2R ladder and an internal +2.5-V reference source. This reference is derived internally and output through pin 16. The reference input to the R-2R ladder is via pin 15. If you desire to use the internal reference, you need to short these two terminals together. If you want to use an external reference source, apply it directly to pin 15.

This particular DAC has one feature that makes it desirable for many different applications: an internal binary-counter (eight-bit) can be connected to the DAC digital inputs through some electronic switches. When the select input is low, the switches disconnect the counter, and the digital inputs control the DAC output. But when the select input is high, the counter output is connected to the DAC inputs, and the counter controls the DAC. When this occurs, the counter output-state appears on the DAC package terminals (B1 through B8). In this case B1 is the most significant bit and B8 is the least significant bit.

The internal counter can be used for several different applications. One is an analog-to-digital converter discussed in a later chapter. Another is to make a binary-ramp generator. If a clock is applied to the input of the counter, the select input high is set, and the analog output is monitored; a ramp voltage that is determined by the reference and the binary counter is seen. The frequency of the output sawtooth is determined by the clock rate, while its amplitude is the full-scale output of the DAC.

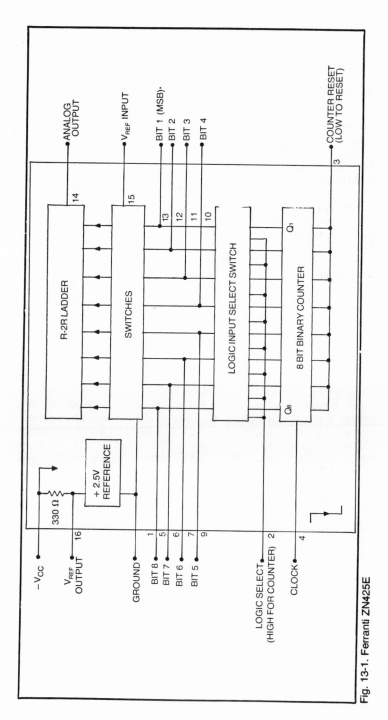

Fig. 13-1. Ferranti ZN425E

The accuracy of the ZN425E is 0.2 percent full-scale voltage per the reference (FSR) at room temperature with a one-half-LSB linearity. The E-suffix device operates over the commercial temperature range of 0-70 degree C, while the J-suffix device is mil-speced over −55-+125 degree C. The power supply is a monopolar +5 V (TTL) supply. Settling time for this DAC is typically 1 μs.

Figure 13-2 shows a typical circuit using the ZN425E. The internal reference is used, and the output voltage is applied to the noninverting-follower operational-amplifier. Zero and full-scale-output adjustments are provided. The calibration is shown below:

1. Set all input bits low.
2. Adjust potentiometer R2 (Fig. 13-2) until the output voltage is zero.
3. Set all input bits high.
4. Adjust R1 until the output voltage full-scale reference is one LSB.

In this case, the full-scale reference is 3.840 V, so the one LSB is 3.840/256, or 0.015 V, or 15 mV. The maximum output voltage at which this adjustment is made, then, is 3.84 − 0.015 V, or 3.825 V.

PMI DAC-08

The DAC-08 is an eight-bit current-output digital-to-analog converter manufactured by Precision Monolithics, Inc. and second-sourced by Advanced Micro Devices (AMD). The DAC-08 requires an external reference source; so it is a multiplying DAC. It contains the R-2R ladder, the electronic switching and current sources, and reference amplifier. The multiplication feature of this DAC makes it useful in a number of applications in which the nonmultiplying DAC could not operate.

The block diagram for the DAC-08 is shown in Fig. 13-3, while the pinouts are shown in Fig. 13-4. Most of the pins are self-explanatory, but several require a little explanation. There are two current-output terminals, and these are complements of each other. The I_{OUT} rises from zero to full scale as the input increments from 00000000 to 11111111. The I_{OUT} drops from full scale to zero as the digital inputs increment over the same range: 00000000 to 11111111.

The DAC-08 offers very fast settling-time, on the order of 85 nanoseconds (current-output DACs typically have fast settling times) and operates to 1 MHz. The output currents are matched within ±½ LSB and is low-drift (i.e., ±10 pulses-per-minute/°C). The required dc power supplies are typically 12-15 V, but the DAC-08 can operate over the range ±4.5-±18 volts. At ±5 V the device power-dissipation is a low 33 milliwatts (mW).

The output current is determined by the expression:

$$I_{OUT} = I_{REF} \ (A/2^n)$$

where I_{OUT} is the current output in mA, I_{REF} is the reference current in mA, A is the binary word applied to the digital inputs (expressed as a decimal), and n is the bit length (i.e., 8 bits, n = 8).

There are two current outputs on the DAC-08: I_{OUT} and $\overline{I}_{OUT}$. These currents are complementary and are each a fraction of the full-scale current. The relationship is:

$$I_{FS} = I_{OUT} + \overline{I}_{OUT}$$

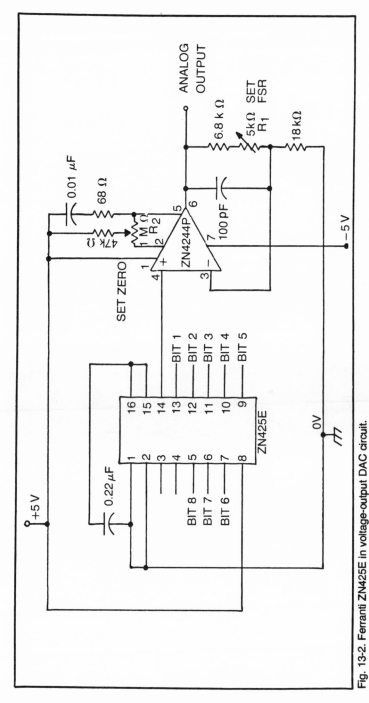

Fig. 13-2. Ferranti ZN425E in voltage-output DAC circuit.

173

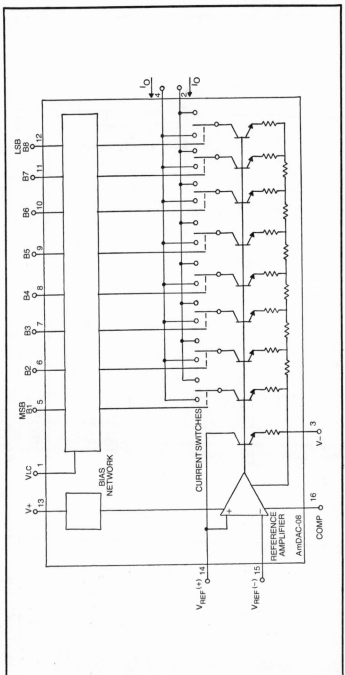

Fig. 13-3. DAC-08 block diagram.

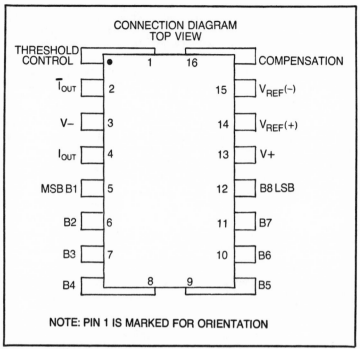

CONNECTION DIAGRAM
TOP VIEW

THRESHOLD CONTROL — 1   16 — COMPENSATION

$\overline{I}_{OUT}$ — 2   15 — $V_{REF}(-)$

V− — 3   14 — $V_{REF}(+)$

I_{OUT} — 4   13 — V+

MSB B1 — 5   12 — B8 LSB

B2 — 6   11 — B7

B3 — 7   10 — B6

B4 — 8   9 — B5

NOTE: PIN 1 IS MARKED FOR ORIENTATION

Fig. 13-4. DAC-08 pin-outs.

where I_{FS} is the full-scale current from the equation, $I_{OUT} = I_{REF}$ (255/266); I_{OUT} is the current flowing in pin 4 of the DAC-08, and $\overline{I}_{OUT}$ is the current flowing in pin 2 of the DAC-08.

The DAC-08 is monotomic over the full temperature range for which the device is rated and is capable of operation over a 32 dB range. The 85-ns settling-time is possible provided that good layout practices and grounding techniques are followed. The DAC-08 is available in several different models that have different quality levels and temperature ranges. These are detailed in Table 13-1.

Table 13-1. DAC-08 Versions.

Order Number	Temperature Range	Nonlinearity
DAC-08AQ	−55°C to +125°C	±.1%
DAC-08Q	−55°C to +125°C	±.19%
DAC-08EQ	0°C to +70°C	±.19%
DAC-08CQ	0°C to +70°C	±.39%

The basic circuit connections for positive unipolar-operation are shown in Fig. 13-5. The power-supply connections shown here are deleted in most of the illustrations to follow; so pay attention here and assume that these connections are made in the later circuits. The negative and positive-voltage terminals are connected to the negative and positive dc power supplies, respectively. Each dc power-supply terminal is bypassed to ground through a 0.1-μF disc-capacitor, and these should be mounted close to the body of the DAC-08. The fast settling time of this DAC makes such layout practices somewhat more important than in slower devices. The compensation input is used to mold the ac frequency-response properties of the circuit. In most TTL applications this input is bypassed to the negative-voltage power-supply through a 0.01-μF capacitor.

The reference inputs go to the inverting (−) and non-inverting (+) inputs of an internal operational-amplifier. In the position-quadrant operation shown, the reference current is applied to the noninverting input and the inverting input is grounded through R15. In most cases it is specified that R15 be made equal to R14 and that the value of R14 be used to set the level of the reference current:

$$I_{REF} = V_{REF}/R14$$

Resistor 14 is sometimes called R_{REF}. For TTL compatibility set R14 and R15 to 5K ohms, C_c is 0.01 μF, and the reference voltage is 10.000 V. This potential is usually derived from an REF-01 PMI reference IC.

One feature of this DAC that makes it compatible with almost any logic protocols, regardless of whether it is standard (TTL, DMOS, etc.) or one of your own concoction. The threshold voltage terminal (V_{LC}) controls the voltage levels that are recognized as high and low by the digital-input terminals. When the power-supply voltages are maximum, the logic levels that are recognized are between −10 and +18 V dc. The logic levels for different digital circuits are quite different.

The TTL device, for example, wants to see a potential of less than 800 mV (the closer to zero, the better) for low and a potential greater than a certain threshold (1.4-2.4 V, depending on the spec sheet) for high. Similarly, the CMOS devices can operate with TTL levels, at which the low is zero and the high is greater than 2.5 V. But CMOS can operate with negative voltages to −15 V for low and positive potentials to +15 V for high. Popular are ±5 and ±12 V for the logic levels. The transition between the two states is $(V_{DD}-V_{SS})/2$.

The DAC-08 can also be interfaced to some of the older, now obsolete logic levels. DTL and RTL use zero for low and 5.6 and 3.6 V, respectively, for high. Some older instruments that predate IC technology are still in daily operation, especially in school laboratories. These devices might easily have home-brew logic-levels that are unique to one manufacturer. Common are −9 or −12 V for low and +5 or +12 V for high. Most commercial DAC ICs are not capable of interfacing these instruments, since they are designed for TTL or CMOS. But the V_{LC} terminal permits you to adjust the threshold value of the transition from high to low. The threshold voltage is controlled by the voltage applied to the V_{LC} terminal of the DAC-08. The threshold voltage is approximately:

$$V_{TH} = V_{LC} + 1.4 \text{ V}$$

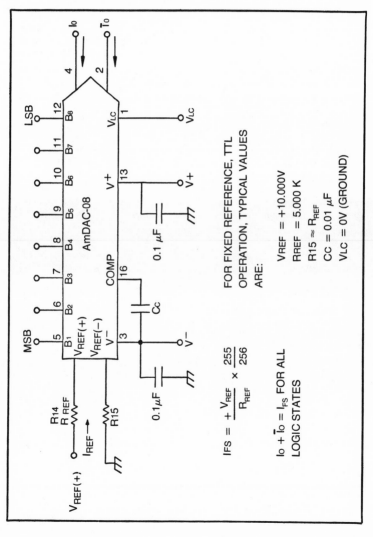

Fig. 13-5. Basic connections for the DAC-08.

177

The threshold voltage is also expressed by

$$V_{TH} = (V-) + 2.5 + (I_{REF} \times 1000 \text{ ohms})$$

where for both equations, V_{LC} is the potential applied to pin 1 of the DAC-08, V_{TH} is the logic threshold voltage, $V-$ is the negative power-supply potential, and I_{REF} is the reference-current expressed in amperes.

If this same example is working for TTL, the 1.4-V transition point of TTL requires you to make V_{LC} zero. In that case, ground pin 1. This same arrangement works for the obsolete DTL circuitry.

The reference-current input can be anything between 0.2 and 4.0 mA, but the manufacturer recommends 2 mA for TTL-to-DTL operation and 1 mA for compatibility with the high-speed ECL family. The inputs of the DAC-08 require only 2A of current and, therefore, load the digital outputs of the driving device very little.

The circuit shown in Fig. 13-5 is for positive operation. Negative reference-operation can be accomplished with a negative voltage supply and reversal of the roles of the two inputs. In negative reference operation, connect R_{REF} to ground and R15 to the $-V_{REF}$ power supply.

The resistors used in the reference input should be low-temperature coefficient-precision types. Otherwise, large errors are likely to result due to ordinary temperature-drift phenomenon.

You can trim the output current of the DAC-08 by varying the reference current. This is done by the balancing circuit of Fig. 13-6. A low-temperature, coefficient, 4500-ohm resistor is connected between the noninverting reference input and the 10.00-V power-supply. The inverting input, however, is connected to a potentiometer wiper. The ends of the potentiometer are connected to the 10.000-V supply and ground, respectively. The correct adjustment point is when the resistance to ground seen by the inverting input of the DAC-08 is approximately 5000 ohms. This circuit can be used as a full-scale output adjustment.

Although not always strictly necessary, the manufacturer recommends that a slightly modified reference-resistor circuit be adopted when there might be a noise problem. In these cases, split the total reference resistance into two portions and connect the two half-value resistors in series between the 10.00-V supply and the DAC-08 input. A 0. 1μF bypass capacitor is then connect between the junction of the resistors and ground.

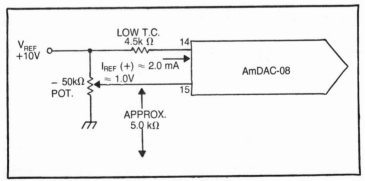

Fig. 13-6. Variable-bias current-circuit for reference supply.

Of course, both of the resistors should be low-temperature coefficient-types of equal value.

It is necessary to keep the reference current as precise as possible. The output current is directly proportional to this current; so changes in the reference current are directly reflected as output errors. The need for precision, low-tempco resistors in the reference circuit has already been mentioned. It is also necessary to mention that the reference-voltage power-supply is also subject to some specifications. Use only a reference-type power-source for this voltage—never the negative or positive-voltage power-supply. This last rule must apply even when the negative and positive voltages are regulated. The ordinary transients present on these lines from normal operation cannot be allowed into the reference current input of the DAC-08. Always use one of the precision sources shown earlier for the reference voltage used to create the current I_{REF}. The manufacturer of the DAC-08 also makes two different reference-voltage ICs. Use the REF-01 for 10.000-V supplies and REF-02 for 5.000 V.

It is usually not sufficient to use a simple zener diode for the reference. Besides thermal drift, these diodes also exhibit large, untrimmable, errors in the actual output voltage. In addition, they can also produce an excessive noise component in the output. In fact, radio-frequency engineers some-times use zener diodes in noise generator circuits of certain types of receiver and amplifier test equipment.

Thus far only the primary mode of operation has been considered: current output. But many applications require voltage-output operation. Thanks to Ohm's law, however, that operation can be provided with the DAC-08. The simplest method is to cause the output currents to flow through a resistance and use the voltage drop across the resistor as the output potential. Figure 13-7 shows the connections for unipolar negative-operation. A 2-mA reference current is applied to the noninverting input of the DAC-08. This current can be generated with a 10.00-V REF-01 and a 5000-ohm, precision, low-tempco resistor.

Both output currents are passed through pulldown resistors to ground. Both resistors have a 5000-ohm value. Because the full-scale output current is 2 mA, the output voltages are:

$$E_{OUT} = I_{OUT} \times R$$
$$= (0.002) (5000)$$
$$= 10.000 \text{ V}$$

The two output voltages are complementary to each other. This does not mean that one is positive while the other is negative; it means that both are negative. The difference is that one is at full scale (−9.96 V) when the other is zero, and vice versa. A chart of the output coding is shown in Fig. 13-7. This is the regular binary coding in which the zero condition ($E_{OUT} = 0$) is designated by 00000000. The full output is the maximum full-scale reference current less one LSB; i.e., −9.96 V. For the eight-bit, 10-V operation, the first LSB voltage is 40 mV; so the output is 10.000 − 0.040, or 9.96.

The circuit for bipolar voltage-output operation is shown in Fig. 13-8. In this case, the output currents are connected to the +10.00-V reference-supply through 10.000K ohm pull-up resistors. The DAC-08 outputs are operating as 2-mA current-sinks. The output coding, also shown in Fig. 13-8, is the offset binary scheme. The zero scale is represented by the

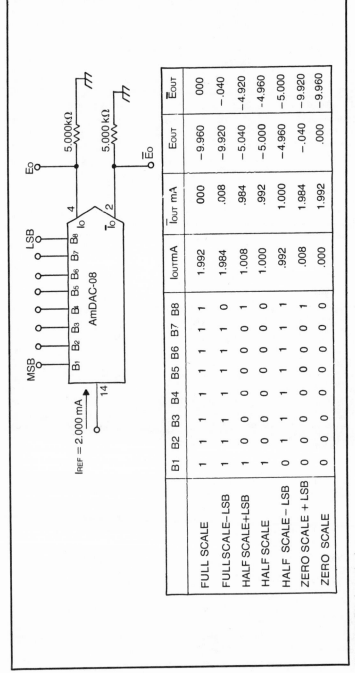

Fig. 13-7. Bipolar output.

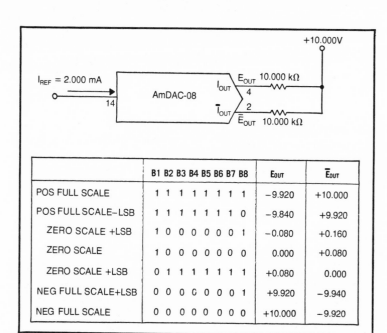

	B1 B2 B3 B4 B5 B6 B7 B8	E_{OUT}	$\bar{E}_{OUT}$
POS FULL SCALE	1 1 1 1 1 1 1 1	−9.920	+10.000
POS FULL SCALE−LSB	1 1 1 1 1 1 1 0	−9.840	+9.920
ZERO SCALE +LSB	1 0 0 0 0 0 0 1	−0.080	+0.160
ZERO SCALE	1 0 0 0 0 0 0 0	0.000	+0.080
ZERO SCALE +LSB	0 1 1 1 1 1 1 1	+0.080	0.000
NEG FULL SCALE+LSB	0 0 0 0 0 0 0 1	+9.920	−9.940
NEG FULL SCALE	0 0 0 0 0 0 0 0	+10.000	−9.920

Fig. 13-8. Bipolar output.

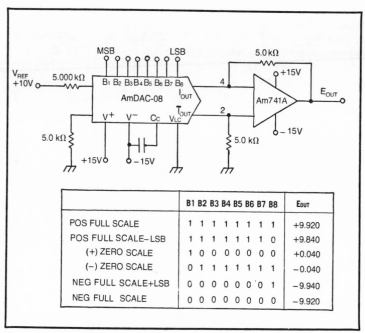

	B1 B2 B3 B4 B5 B6 B7 B8	E_{OUT}
POS FULL SCALE	1 1 1 1 1 1 1 1	+9.920
POS FULL SCALE−LSB	1 1 1 1 1 1 1 0	+9.840
(+) ZERO SCALE	1 0 0 0 0 0 0 0	+0.040
(−) ZERO SCALE	0 1 1 1 1 1 1 1	−0.040
NEG FULL SCALE+LSB	0 0 0 0 0 0 0 1	−9.940
NEG FULL SCALE	0 0 0 0 0 0 0 0	−9.920

Fig. 13-9. DAC-08 in low-impedance bipolar-output.

half-scale condition, 10000000. This code produces an E_{OUT} of 0.00 V, but this creates a glitch in the coding. In a binary system an even number of binary word states can be used. Because one is used for zero, this leaves an odd number to represent the positive and negative output voltages. The negative full-scale voltage output is -10.00 V, created by input code 00000000. Look at the positive full-scale output-voltage, though: $+9.92$ V. The unevenness of the positive and negative output voltages is a reflection of the decision to use one state to represent zero. Note one other aspect to this code: the one-LSB quanta are twice as high as in the unipolar case. The range is now twice as large for the same number of binary code states; so each increment must represent a voltage jump twice that in the unipolar circuit. Range is gained for resolution.

The decision about the input code and output range is a matter of design in the system. If it is more important to correctly specify the zero state and less important to have the exact full-scale value, use the offset binary shown in Fig. 13-8. If the full range is more important than rigorously defining zero, however, then use the symmetrical-offset binary-circuit and coding shown in Fig. 13-9. This circuit applies the output currents to a differential amplifier of the 741 class. Note the coding chart. Both positive and negative full-scale have the same magnitude of 9.96 V, but there is no clear definition of zero. There are two possible zero states, arranged symmetrically about true zero. These are called plus and minus zero. Plus zero is $+40$ mV and is created by input code 10000000. Minus zero is -40 mV and is created by code 01111111.

Low-impedance voltage-output operation is shown in Figs. 13-10 and 13-11. The circuit in Fig. 13-10 is for positive-output voltages. The I_{OUT} of the DAC-08 and the noninverting input of the amplifier are grounded. The I output of the DAC-08 is connected directly to the inverting input of the DAC-08. Feedback resistor R_L provides any needed voltage gain. The maximum output voltage is given by:

$$E_{OUT} = \frac{255\ I_{REF}\ R_L}{256}$$

The negative-output operation of the DAC-08 is shown in Fig. 13-11. This circuit develops the output voltage by applying the current to a

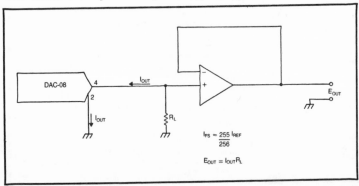

Fig. 13-10. Low-impedance unipolar-output.

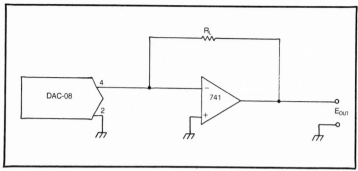

Fig. 13-11. Low-impedance output.

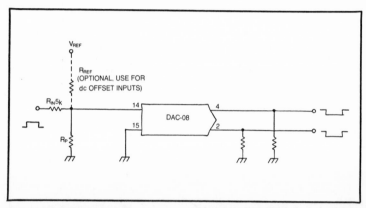

Fig. 13-12. Pulsed operation.

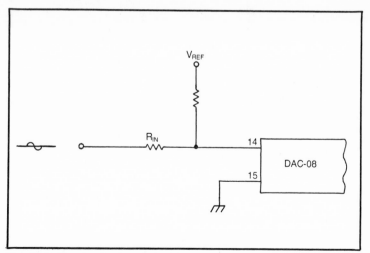

Fig. 13-13. Regular circuit ac operation.

183

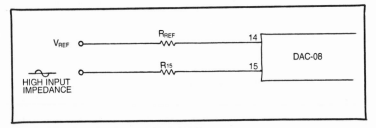

Fig. 13-14. Ac operation with offset signals.

precision resistor. The voltage drop across this resistor is applied to the noninverting input of the unity-gain 741 op-amp follower. The 741, in this case, is used mostly for the impedance-transformation available in the noninverting circuit.

Operation with pulsed and alternating-current reference-inputs is shown in Figs. 13-12 and 13-13, respectively. These circuits find use in cases where you want to control the amplitude of the output sine-wave or pulse using the binary inputs of the DAC. In these applications the DAC-08 is used as a *variable attenuator.* The pulsed-referenced operation is shown in Fig. 13-12. In this circuit the series resistor to the noninverting

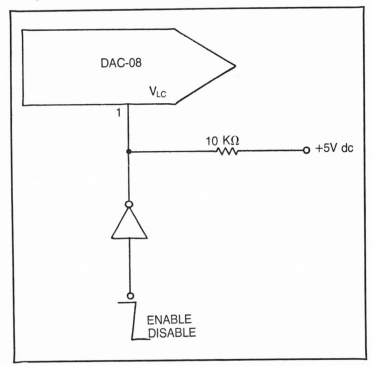

Fig. 13-15. Strobing the DAC-08 under control of a TTL-compatible computer output.

Rref (Ω)	Cc(pf)
1000	15
2500	37
5000	75
10,000	150

Table 13-2. Values of Resistance and Capacitance for Frequency Compensation.

reference-input is 5000 ohms, and there is a low-value resistor of 200 ohms to ground. The compensation capacitor is eliminated in order to increase the bandwidth of the DAC-08. The capacitor has the effect of dampening the bandwidth, and that is not acceptable in pulse circuits. The output currents are pulsed and converted to equivalent voltages when passed through resistances.

Ac operation is shown in Figs. 13-13 and 13-14. In the circuit of Fig. 13-13, the inverting input of the DAC-08 is grounded, and the noninverting input sees two input-currents. One is a bias current derived from a dc reference-potential. The current, I_{IN}, is created by applying voltage V_{IN} to resistor R_{IN}. The value of reference current I_{REF} must be greater-than, or at least equal-to, the greatest negative swing of I_{IN}. The idea is to use I_{REF} to bias the DAC-08 input to some midpoint. Then allow the actual DAC input-current to vary around this quiescent value, as the AC signal causes $\pm I_{IN}$ to vary the total current into that junction.

The circuit in Fig. 13-13 suffers from low input-impedance. The input impedance of the circuit can be increased by using the configuration of Fig. 13-14. The same basic rules apply here, but refer to voltage levels: $+V_{REF}$ must be greater-than, or at least equal-to, the greatest positive swing of V_{IN}.

The slew rate of the DAC-08 must be considered when dealing with ac or pulse signals. You improve the situation in pulse circuits by deleting the compensation capacitor. Some proper combinations of reference resistor and compensation capacitor are listed in Table 13-2.

The use of a 1000-ohm and 15-pF combination gives a maximum slew-rate of approximately 16 mA/μs. The pulse circuit of the previous example, with no compensation, can handle rise times on the order of 500.

The DAC-08 can also be strobed on and off under control of some external digital circuit. Just use the V_{LC} terminal (pin 1) of the DAC-08 and a 7404 TTL inverter circuit. A pull-up resistor is tied between the inverter output and +5 V. When the input to the inverter is high, the output is low, and this causes the DAC-08 input to be grounded. Under the normal rules for using the DAC-08 in TTL circuits, this turns the device on. When the inverter is low, the V_{LC} terminal of the DAC-08 is high. This places V_{LC} at 5 V, so no TTL pulse becomes high enough to turn on the DAC-08 (see Fig. 13-15).

Chapter 14

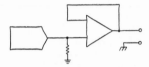

Practical Analog-
to-Digital Converters

Now we will look at some applications of the circuits we have studied.

EIGHT-BIT BINARY ANALOG-TO-DIGITAL CONVERTER

The circuit for a complete eight-bit binary ramp (servo) ADC is shown in Fig. 14-1, while a typical conversion-timing diagram is shown in Fig. 14-2. This circuit is based upon the Ferranti ZN425E digital-to-analog converter integrated-circuit.

The Ferranti ZN425E is almost unique among DAC ICs in that it contains a complete binary counter along with the voltage-output R-2R DAC circuitry. Pin 2 on the ZN425 device is the counter select. If this pin is held HIGH, the counter is connected to the input switches to the R-2R ladder. The state of the counter is output on the DAC lines. But if pin 2 is low, the digital word applied to the eight input-lines driven the R-2R ladder, and the counter outputs are disconnected. In Fig. 14-1 pin 2 is permanently tied high through a 1K-ohm pull-up resistor, so the counter is connected to the B1-B8 pin-outs and the DAC input lines.

The ZN425E contains its own built-in +2.5-V, precision, reference-voltage source, which is brought outside of the package via pin 16. The V_{REF} input (pin 15) is also brought outside of the package and can be connected either to the internal reference or to some external reference source. In the circuit shown, the internal reference is being used; so these two pins are shorted together. A 0.22-μF reference capacitor (C1) is connected between the reference and ground.

IC 2 is an operational amplifier (ZN424P) used as a voltage comparator. The DAC output voltage (E3) is connected to the noninverting input, while the sample of the analog input-voltage (E2) is connected to the inverting input of the comparator. This IC operates as a voltage comparator because no feedback loop is around the operational amplifier; the gain of this circuit is essentially the open-loop gain of the op amp. A zero adjustment for the DAC is connected to the operational-amplifier offset-null terminals. The power source for the op amp is ±5-volts dc, which is almost compatible with the TTL 7400 NAND-gate that the output drives. This device wants to see a ±5-V potential for high and 0 V for low. However, it is possible for the output of the comparator to swing negative under some circumstances—with disastrous results for the 7400! To prevent negative excursions of the 7400 input, it is necessary to clamp the output of the comparator with a silicon diode (D1, the 1N914). The maximum negative voltage is the positive-negative junction drop of this diode, which is about 0.6 to 0.7 V. In the situation where the comparator output is positive, the diode is reverse-biased and therefore becomes inert.

A full-scale adjustment is provided through the use of voltage divider R2/R6. Resistor 2 is a potentiometer that allows adjustment of E2 to any fraction of analog input voltage E1. Voltage E2, then, is a fractional sample of E1.

Three sections of a 7400-quad NAND-gate are used in this ADC circuit. Gates 1 and 2 form an RS flip-flop. Gate 3 is the main gate and controls the clock circuit. When pin 13 of the 7400 is low, pin 11 is jammed high (no clock pulses can pass through G3). When pin 13 is high, however, the output follows the clock pulses. This admits pulses into the clock terminal (pin 4) of the ZN425E.

The set input of the RS flip-flop is pin 5. When an active-low start pulse is applied to this input, the RS flip-flop goes into the set condition in which Q is high and not-Q is low. The Q output is used as a *status line*, while the not-Q is a *not-status* line (i.e., active-low). During the time when the converter is making its conversion, the status line is high. Because this line is the control signal to the main gate, the gate is opened and the clock pulses enter the DAC's internal counter. (The counter is reset to zero by the start pulse.)

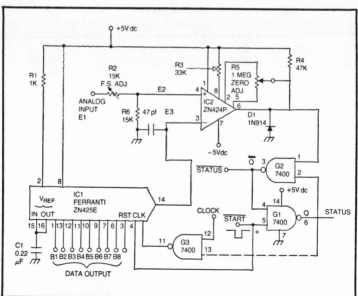

Fig. 14-1. Ferranti ZN-425E as an ADC.

187

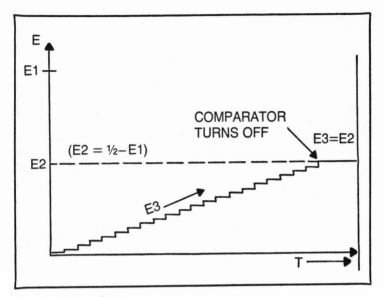

Fig. 14-2. Timing diagram.

Opening the main gate causes the binary counter to increment, and this in turn causes DAC output-voltage E3 to ramp upward in a staircase fashion (Fig. 14-2). As long as E3 is less than E2 (the sample of the analog input-voltage), the comparator output is high. It remains in this condition until the counter increments the DAC output enough to make E2-E3. At that instant the output of the comparator drops low, and this applies a reset pulse to the input of the RS flip-flop (pin 1 of the 7400). The RS flip-flop immediately goes to the condition in which Q is low and not-Q is high, shutting off the flow of clock pulses to the counter.

The state of the counter, which appears on the B1-B8 lines, reflects the value of the analog input-voltage applied (E1). The count remains on these outputs because no new reset pulse has been issued.

The speed of this circuit is limited by the operational amplifier used as a voltage comparator. If the ZN424P is used, the speed is 100 kHz or less. But, replacing this operational amplifier with either a higher-frequency operational amplifier or a high-speed IC comparator results in operation to 250 kHz.

The conversion time of this circuit depends upon the clock frequency. For a full-scale conversion, the value of T_C is:

$$T_C = \frac{256}{f}$$

where T_C is the conversion in seconds, and f is the frequency of the clock in hertz.

The outside world needs to know when the output data is valid. During the active-conversion period the output lines (B1-B8) have a continuously changing binary number, which is valid only when the counter ceases incrementing. The status and not-status lines can be used for this purpose. If an external device, such as a computer, is used, it can interrogate these lines. It would not, for example, accept any data from the ADC when it found that the status line was high or the not-status line was low.

Two adjustments are permitted in this circuit: *zero adjust* and *full-scale adjust*. The best accuracy is obtained when the input voltage is known to four decimal-places of resolution. Use a 4½-digit or better voltmeter or a precision-reference source with output resolution to 100 V. The procedure is as follows:

1. Apply a continuous train of clock pulses to the ADC circuit.

2. Apply an analog input-potential equal to the full-scale potential less 1.5 LSB. In this case the full-scale input voltage is 4.00 V. The first LSB voltage of the circuit, then, is 4.00 V/256, or 15.63 mV. One point five LSB, then, is 23.45 mV. The applied input voltage is (4.00 − 0.02345)V, or 3.9765 V.

3. Potentiometer R2 is adjusted until all bits except the LSB bobbles back and forth between high and low.

4. Apply a voltage equal to the ½-LSB potential (7.82 mV) to the analog input.

5. Adjust potentiometer R5 (zero adjust) until all bits are low—except the LSB (00000001)—and the LSB is bobbling back and forth between HIGH and LOW.

6. Repeat all adjustments until no further improvement is possible. Most, simple, ADC circuits have full-scale and zero adjustments that are somewhat interactive.

The full-scale input voltage can be changed by varying the resistor voltage-divider between the analog input and the noninverting input of the operational amplifier.

This type of circuit can be implemented using any of several DAC-comparator combinations. In the case of DACs other than the ZN425E, however, an external eight-bit binary counter must be connected to the DAC inputs. A pair of 7493 TTL counter chips (each four bits) connected in cascade provides this counter. Also, in the case of a current-output DAC (PMI DAC-08 or Motorola MC1408), it is necessary to either operate the comparator in the current mode or convert the DAC output to a voltage.

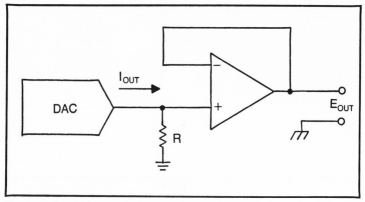

Fig. 14-3. Op-amp output for low-impedance buffering.

Figure 14-3 shows the case where the current output, I_{OUT}, from the DAC is converted to an equivalent voltage, E1. The voltage is created by passing the output current through a precision resistor ($E1=I_{OUT}R$). The amplifier is connected in the unity-gain, noninverting-follower configuration, so $E_{OUT}=E1=I_{OUT}R$.

The alternative case operates the comparator in the current mode. In the circuit of Fig. 14-4 the non-inverting input of a PMI CMP-01 comparator is grounded, placing the inverting input at virtual ground. The output current I_{OUT} from the DAC is applied to the inverting input. Also applied to this input is current I_{IN}, which is proportional to the analog input voltage E_{IN}. The value of this current is $E_{IN}/R=E_{IN}/5000$ ohms. When $I_{OUT} = I_{IN}$, the output of the comparator drops low.

EIGHT-BIT BINARY RAMP ADC

The Precision Monolithic DAC-100 is a 10-bit digital-to-analog converter. This converter is used in the feedback loop of a binary ramp ADC circuit, shown in Fig. 14-5. The principal components of this circuit are the DAC-100, a PMI CMP-01C voltage-comparator, a pair of 8284 four-bit up/down counters, and a 7474 type-D flip-flop. This circuit is a tracking ADC, so it follows changes in the input signal.

The comparator continuously examines the voltage for polarity and always drives the output code of the counter in the direction that causes the ac output voltage to approach zero. Once a balance is achieved, the circuit becomes locked and therefore changes only when analog voltage changes a certain minimum amount. The ADC tracks input signal-changes as long as the slew rate of the loop is not exceeded.

The comparator is operated in the current mode and is designed such that the comparator output is high when the DAC-100 output-current is nonzero (i.e., the noninverting input of the CMP-01C is grounded). This operation allows faster conversion times because the slew rate of the comparator in the current mode is faster and the settling time is slower.

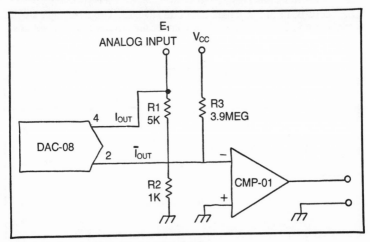

Fig. 14-4. Constant-impedance-input circuit.

190

Full-scale adjustment is provided by a 200-ohm potentiometer at the reference terminal inputs of the DAC-100. A full-scale (10.00 V) signal is applied to the analog input, and this potentiometer is adjusted to find all bits high, except the LSB, which bobbles back and forth between high and low.

The printed-circuit layout and the parts list are given in Fig. 14-6 and Table 14-1, respectively. This board is a double-sided PC card; so some care in the top-to-bottom registration is needed. The clock frequency is obtained off-board and can be as high as 3 MHz. A sine wave to 4 kHz can be accommodated at the analog-input terminal. If desired, a clock can be made from a pair of 7400 NAND-gates, a 240-ohm resistor, and a feedback resistor. The period is given by resistance-capacitance 3; so the output frequency is RC/3.

SUCCESSIVE APPROXIMATION IN ANALOG-TO-ANALOG CONVERTERS

The successive approximation (SA) ADC technique uses a special register and a DAC to make a conversion. The MSB of the register is set high; so the DAC output is half-scale. This output is compared with the analog input-voltage, and the subsequent action taken by the register is determined by the result of the test. If the trial DAC output-value is less than the analog input-signal, the MSB is then set to the high state, and the register proceeds to repeat the procedure with the MSB-1 bit. But if the trial output is greater than the analog input signal, the MSB is reset low. The register control then transfers the actions to MSB 1. This activity continues until all bits have been tried and the DAC output matches the analog input.

The successive-approximation for analog-to-digital conversion is faster than the binary-ramp method. The binary ramp requires 2^N clock pulses to implement a full-scale conversion, while successive approximation needs only $N+1$ pulses (N is the bit length). Consequently, the successive-approximation technique is more rapid. The successive-approximation technique, however, is more sensitive to input voltage changes during the conversion period, often requiring designers to sample and hold the analog input-signal for the duration of the conversion period.

An eight-bit successive-approximation ADC is shown in Fig. 14-7, and a 12-bit version is shown in Fig. 14-8. Both are based on PMI's CAC ICs and

Table 14-1. Parts List.

Quantity	Description
1	DAC-100CCT1
1	CMP-01CJ comparator
2	8284 up / down counters
1	7474 dual d-type flip-flop
1	7400 quad gate
1	200Ω trimpot, bourns 3359P
4	IN4148 diodes
5	Ceramic capacitors
1	Carbon composition resistor
1	PC board

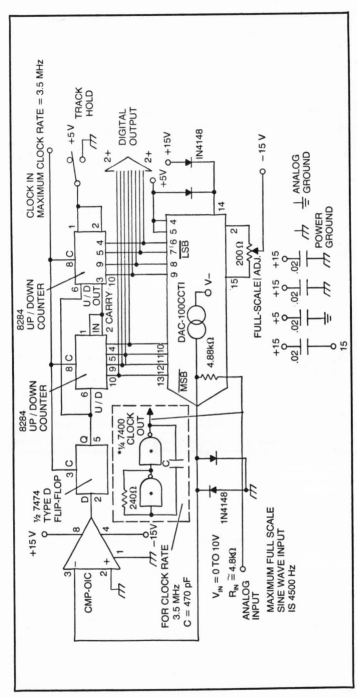

Fig. 14-5. Tracking ADC.

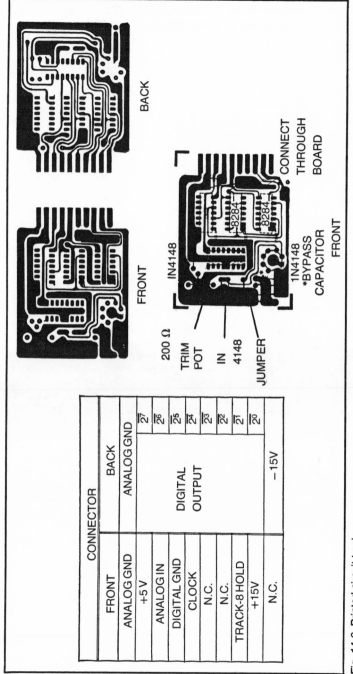

Fig. 14-6. Printed-circuit tracks.

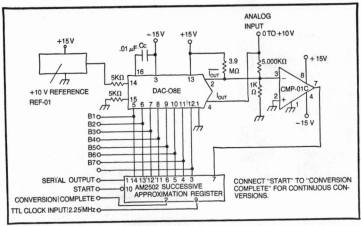

Fig. 14-7. Eight-bit low-cost successive-approximation ADC.

Advanced Micro Devices successive-approximation-register (SAR) IC's. The AM2502 is the 8-bit SAR, while the AM2504 is the 12-bit model. They are very similar to each other, except for bit length.

The 8-bit circuit is shown in Fig. 14-7. The digital inputs of the DAC-08 DAC are connected to the latched outputs of the AM2502 SAR. The reference current is provided by a 10.00-V REF-01 precision reference-source and a 5K-ohm precision-resistor to pin 14 of the DAC-08. A zero or full-scale adjustment for this circuit can be provided by using the adjustment potentiometer for the REF-01 or by making the 500-ohm resistor to pin 14 a potentiometer and fixed-resistor combination centered on 5K ohms.

The comparator, a PMI CMP-01, is connected in a current mode similar to Fig. 14-4. The analog input voltage, which can take on a full-scale value of 10 V, is converted to a 0-2 mA current by the series 5K-ohm resistor to the inverting input of the comparator. The I_{OUT} current output from the DAC is connected to the inverting input of the comparator, while the I_{OUT} complementary output is connected to the analog input voltage. This maintains a constant input-impedance of 5K ohms. A 3.9 megohm and 1K-ohm resistor voltage-divider from the positive voltage is designed to keep the comparator slightly above actual zero, which can be a little noisy. The performance is improved, however, by the slight bias-current provided by these resistors.

A full-scale adjustment can be provided by placing the 5K-ohm resistor in series with the input a potentiometer and fixed-resistor combination. If the reference current adjustment is used for full-scale instead of zero, you must depend on the circuitry for zero set. In an example to follow, however, I introduce a method that can be adapted for this circuit, in which the noninverting input of the comparator is given a slight bias to account for zero effects.

The 10-bit successive-approximation circuit of Fig. 14-8 is essentially the same idea, with a 10-bit DAC and 12-bit (wired for 10-bit operations) SAR instead of the 8-bit devices. There are two other differences in this circuit. One is that the reference voltage is internal to the DAC-100, while the analog input voltage is applied to the comparator through a resistor that is internal to the DAC-100. Full-scale adjust is provided by a 200-ohm potentiometer at the reference input-terminals of the DAC-100.

The operation in both cases is similar, even though specific pin assignments are different for the two SARs. An active-low start-pulse is applied to the SAR. The SAR contains the internal logic necessary to produce the successive-approximation conversion, each step taking place on the receipt of a clock pulse. When the trial value on the DAC output cancels the current caused by the analog-input signal applied to pin 1 of the DAC-100, the comparator sees the input equality needed to make its output drop low. This level is applied to an input of the SAR and tells the SAR that the conversion is completed or that the next trial will now take place on the next clock pulse. When the conversion has finally been completed, the conversion-complete (another name for end-of-conversion) pulse is issued from the CC output.

In both circuits continuous conversion can be achieved by connecting the $\overline{CC}$ output to the $\overline{S}$ (start) input. The end of conversion pulse for the current conversion then becomes the start pulse for the next conversion. If these lines are separated, however, synchronous operation with some external device is possible. The other device (i.e., a computer or data logger) issues a start pulse when it is ready and looks for the end of conversion pulse before it accepts the data as valid.

In the eight-bit version, a 1.125-MHz clock-speed results in an eight microsecond conversion time. The 10-bit conversion is a little longer by two additional bit times, or in this example, 9.78 μs.

An 8-bit successive-approximation ADC is shown in Fig. 14-9. This circuit is based upon two Motorola integrated circuits, the MC1408 current-output DAC and the MC14559B successive approximation regis-

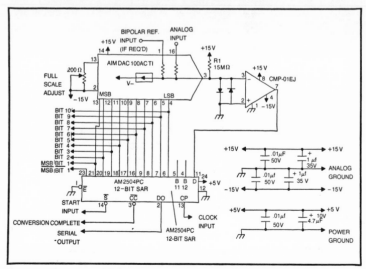

Fig. 14-8. Twelve-bit ADC.

195

ter. For the hobby or small-scale science-engineering lab, this successive approximation seems to be a little easier to obtain in unit quantities than the AMD device. This circuit operates from the commonly available − 15 V and +5 V dc power-supply voltages and requires approximately 200 mW of power. The conversion rate is 2 μs per bit.

As in the two previous cases, the DAC used in this circuit is a current-output type. Current I_{OUT} is proportional to the reference current ($I_{REF} = V_{REF}/R1$) and the binary word applied to the digital inputs. These inputs are connected to the latched register output lines and become the ADC output lines once the data conversion is completed.

The analog input-signal is applied through a unit gain, noninverting follower. The operational amplifier selected for this purpose has a faster slew rate and shorter settling time than the 741 class of device you might be tempted to use.

The following relationship holds true for values of I_{REF} between 0.5 mA and 4.0 mA:

$$\frac{V_{REF}}{R1} = \frac{V_{IN(FS)}}{R2}$$

Operational amplifier 2, another 301, is used as current-mode comparator. The inverting input is operated as close to ground potential as possible. But more about this input later. The signals are applied to the noninverting input. When the output current from the DAC and input current generated by V_{IN} are equal, the comparator output drops low. If these currents are not equal, the comparator output is high. The output of the comparator is applied to the successive-approximation register, which uses this signal to determine the outcome of each trial and to find the end of a conversion.

As in the previous circuits, there are two modes of operation. In this circuit, however, a switch selects them. In the triggered mode an outside

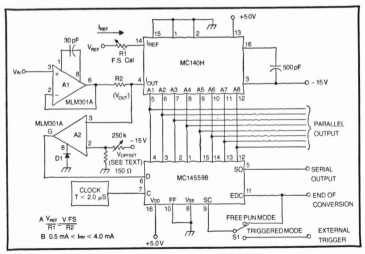

Fig. 14-9. Eight-bit successive-approximation ADC.

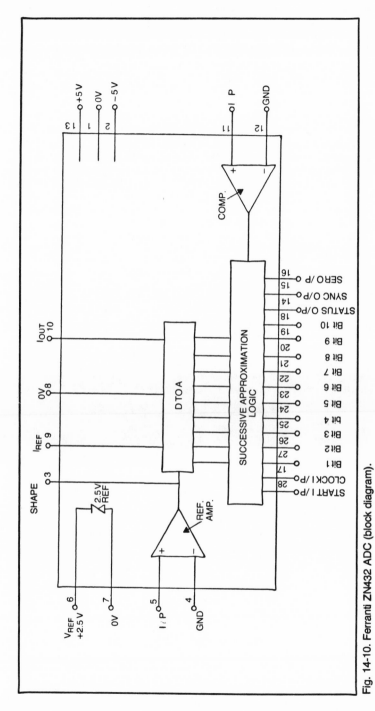

Fig. 14-10. Ferranti ZN432 ADC (block diagram).

start-pulse is required to initiate a conversion. But in the free-running mode, the EOC pulse becomes the start pulse for the next conversion cycle. The speed of this circuit is 18 μs for an eight-bit full-scale conversion. The full-scale value of the analog input-signal can be set by resistors 1 and 2.

The calibration of this circuit is similar to that of the previous circuits; in fact, it is adaptable to other ADCs of similar design. You must apply an input voltage equal to the full-scale input, minus ½ LSB. The full-scale adjustment potentiometer (R1) is adjusted to make the output data bobble from 11111110 to 11111111. Next, a ½-LSB signal is applied to the input, and the zero-offset potentiometer is adjusted for an output data bobble of 00000000 to 00000001. Again, make these adjustments several times until no further improvement is possible.

The zero-adjust circuit in Fig. 14-9 allows the comparator bias-point to be shifted slightly to account for minor differences from the ideal performance. It also permits you to overcome the hysteresis present in all comparators, allowing more precise triggering when the two currents applied to the noninverting input of A2 are cancelled out, indicating equality of the two currents.

FERRANTI ZN432

Figures 14-10 and 14-11 show the Ferranti ZN432-series ADC chips. This device is packaged in a 28-pin DIP format. It operates from ± 5 V dc power-supplies and provide 20-μs conversion-times. 8-, 9-, and 10-bit accuracy is available. The ZN432 is compatible with both TTL and CMOS logic.

The device is a successive-approximation ADC circuit. It contains an internal SAR, a DAC, a comparator, a reference power-supply, and a reference amplifer. Figure 14-10 shows the block diagram of the internal circuitry.

An example circuit is shown in Fig. 14-11. The reference amplifier must be connected to the reference power-supply through external connection. Although this method of applying the reference requires external connections, it makes the IC more versatile by allowing external reference sources to be used.

Resistors 3 and 5 must be of high quality to allow gain and offset stability. Resistors 1 and 2 are used to compensate for the amplifier-input bias-currents. It is necessary, therefore, that R1=R2 and these be equal to the parallel combination of R3, R4, and R5. This is standard operational amplifier practice. The reference current is 0.5 mA; so the value of resistor R3 is $V_{REF}/0.005A$. Current I_{OUT} is four times the reference current. The values of the other two resistors are:

$$R4 = \frac{-V_{REF}R_5}{V_{IN(MIN)}}$$

and

$$R5 = \frac{V_{IN(MAX)} - V_{IN(MIN)}}{I_{OUT\ (FS)}}$$

where V_{REF} is the reference voltage, $V_{IN(MIN)}$ is the analog input voltage to make output code 00000000, $V_{IN(MAX)}$ is the analog voltage required to make output code 11111111, and $I_{OUT(FS)}$ is the full-scale output current.

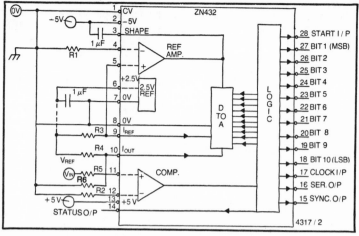

Fig. 14-11. ZN-432 circuit connections.

The calibration of this circuit is pretty much the same as in the previous case. Place an input voltage on the analog terminal that is 1½-LSB less than the maximum input voltage.

INTERSIL ISL7109 12-BIT BINARY ADC

Figure 14-12 shows the Intersil ICL7109 12-bit binary output ADC specifically designed for interfacing with microprocessor circuits. This circuit offers 12-bit binary, with polarity and overrange bits. It uses the noise-immune dual-slope integration technique. This device permits as many as 30 conversions per second.

Timing is supported by an on-chip internal oscillator that can be connected with a resistor or capacitor network that sets the clock frequency. It is also possible to use a standard 3.58-MHz crystal (standard because it is the color-subcarrier crystal-oscillator frequency from television receivers). This arrangement allows seven to eight conversions per second and is less susceptible to 60-Hz interference.

One thing that makes this converter microprocessor compatible is that it has TTL three-state data outputs. This is a necessary feature, regardless of whether I/O or memory-mapped organization is selected. If the ADC and non-Tri-state outputs, it could not be connected directly to the data bus without loading the bus down. A low condition on one of the data bits would be effectively short out that data line, even when the ADC was not being addressed.

But in the ICL7109, the outputs are Three-state. This means that the third state, which allows the outputs to float across the data bus, creates a high impedance to both the +5-V supply and ground. Normal TTL outputs are a low impedance to +5 V in the high condition and a low impedance to ground in the low condition.

There are two basic sections to the ICL7109 device: analog and digital. The analog input contains a buffer amplifier, integrator, and comparator stage; plus internal switching to effect the dual-slope system. The digital section contains the oscillator-clock circuit and handshake logic ($\overline{\text{LBEN}}$, $\overline{\text{HBEN}}$, and $\overline{\text{CE/LOAD}}$). There are also a 12-bit binary counter, 14 latches, and 14 Three-state outputs (12 for the output data bits, with one each for polarity and overrange).

$\overline{\text{LBEN}}$ is the *low-byte enable* terminal. If the mode-pin (21) is low and the $\overline{\text{CE/LOAD}}$ pin 20 is low, making this pin low activates the low-order byte (bits 1-8). If the mode pin is high, the $\overline{\text{HBEN}}$ pin serves as a flag-output bit for handshaking with the computer.

$\overline{\text{HBEN}}$ is the high-byte version of the $\overline{\text{LBEN}}$ pin. If this pin and the $\overline{\text{CE/LOAD}}$ pin are low, making $\overline{\text{HBEN}}$ low activates B9-B12 and the polarity and overrange bits. With a high on the mode pin, this pin becomes the high-byte handshake output.

$\overline{\text{CE/LOAD}}$ is the chip-enable/load pin. If the mode pin is held low, then the $\overline{\text{CE/LOAD}}$ is the master output enable; i.e., it turns on the Three-state outputs. If this pin is high, then the 12-output bits, overrange bit, and polarity bit are three-stated. If the mode is high, this pin is the load strobe for handshake operations.

Analog Section

The analog section uses three operation phases: *auto zero, signal integrate,* and *deintegrate* (or *reference integrate*). The auto-zero phase initializes the circuit. The two analog-inputs are disconnected from the pins and are then shorted to the analog to common-ground. Next, the reference capacitor is charged to the reference voltage. Finally, a feedback loop that charges the auto-zero capacitor is closed. This compensates for the normal offset-voltages in the buffer amplifier, integrator, and voltage comparator. The offset can be nulled to 10 mV.

The signal-integration phase causes the input of the integrator to be connected to the analog-input signal for a fixed time period. Exactly 2048

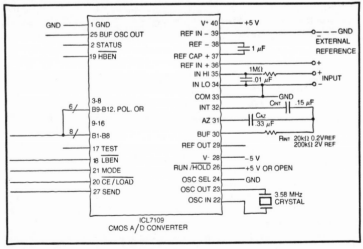

Fig. 14-12. Intersil ICL7109 ADC.

clock pulses are occupied by the signal-integrate phase of operation. The polarity of the input signal is determined in this phase of operation, and this sets the polarity bit.

The reference-integrate phase is the second slope of the conversion cycle. In this phase the charge in the integrator capacitor is discharged by applying a reference signal to the input of the integrator. The polarity of the reference is selected to deintegrate the charge. The rate of the deintegration is fixed by the reference-voltage value; so the time required to make the integrator charge zero again is determined by the level of the charge. This level is in turn set by the value of the analog-input signal. The time period occupied by the deintergrate phase is then directly proportional to the analog value applied to the ADC. The time is measured by the binary counter, which supplies the digital output to the computer through the three-state section.

Digital Section

The digital section contains the 12-bit counter, 14 output latches, and 14 three-state TTL outputs. It sends four signals to the analog section, namely, auto zero, integrate, and deintegrate (plus/minus). The particular deintegrate signal that is used depends on the polarity of the integrator voltage at the end of the signal-integration period. The analog section returns the comparator output to the digital section. The inputs to the digital section that are available to the outside world are compatible with several logic families, as defined in the ICL7109 spec sheet. But, for TTL compatibility, use a 3-5K ohm pull-up resistor.

The mode input terminal is used to select direct output or UART modes. When the mode input is held low, the ICL7109 is in the direct mode. The output data is directly controlled by the chip-enable and byte-enable pins. When the mode input is high, the converter is placed in the UART mode. This mode allows handshaking with the outside world and outputs the data in two independent bytes. If the mode input is *pulsed* high, this transfer occurs once, and the chip returns to the direct mode. If the mode is held high, the ADC outputs data at the end of each conversion cycle.

The mode input is considered low when left open-in distinct contrast with other chips. The ICL7109 contains an internal pull-down resistor that sets the input low on open.

The status output tells the outside world when the new data is available on the output latches. This terminal goes high when the ADC enters the signal-integrate phase and remains high until after the new data is stored in the output latches. The time period required for this is roughly one-half clock period after the end of the deintegrate period.

The status output is used to signal interrupts to the microprocessor or to strobe data into some other digital circuits. The conditions are high for conversion in progress and low for conversion completed.

The run/hold controls the conversion cycle. If this input is left high, the converter continuously cycles; it performs a new conversion as soon as the old conversion is completed. The conversions each require 8192 clock periods. Bringing the run/hold low causes the ADC to become dormant. If the converter is in the middle of a conversion, the conversion is completed.

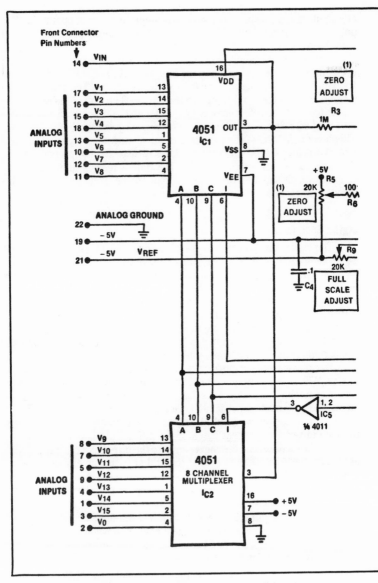

Fig. 14-13. Multi-channel data-acquisition system.

The new data is stored in the output latches. The ADC then jumps to the auto-zero mode and stays there until the run/hold goes high again.

The direct mode allows ordinary parallel-output operations of the data converter. When the mode control is left low, the outputs remain under control of the chip-enable and byte-control bits. In the handshake mode, the

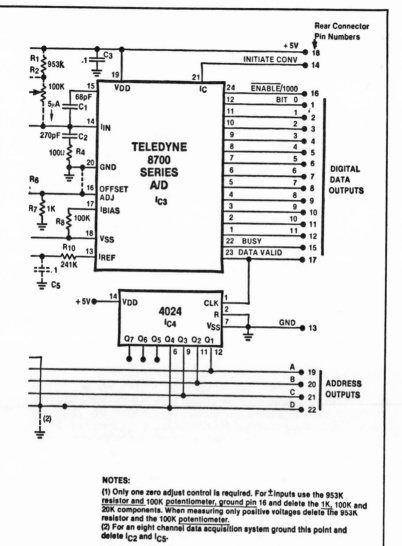

NOTES:

(1) Only one zero adjust control is required. For ±inputs use the 953K resistor and 100K potentiometer, ground pin 16 and delete the 1K, 100K and 20K components. When measuring only positive voltages delete the 953K resistor and the 100K potentiometer.
(2) For an eight channel data acquisition system ground this point and delete I$_{C2}$ and I$_{C5}$.

ICL7109 can be connected directly to the industry-standard UART (universal asynchronous receiver-transmitter) chips. The ADC sends the $\overline{CE/LOAD}$ signal to the UART and receives back SEND, RUN/HOLD and MODE signals.

TELEDYNE 8700

The Teledyne 8700, 8701, and 8702 ADC chips provide 8-, 10-, and 12-bit operation, respectively. These are full self-contained CMOS,

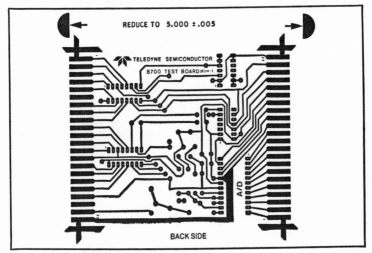

REDUCE TO 5.000 ±.005

TELEDYNE SEMICONDUCTOR

8700 TEST BOARD

A/D

BACK SIDE

Fig. 14-14. PC pattern.

monolithic, integrated-circuits in the 24-pin DIP package. The conversion technique is a variation on the dual-slope integration theme, in which the deintegrate phase takes place under pulsed increments of current rather than a continuous flow. This is called a charge-balancing integration. The circuit counts the number of pulses (each deintegrating a given charge) required to bring the integrator back to near-zero after the analog signal caused it to charge to some value.

Figure 14-13 shows the circuit for a complete data-acquisitions system based on the Teledyne 8700 ADC chip. This self-contained circuit is capable of either 16 single-ended analog-input channels or 8 differential-input channels. Zero adjust and full-scale adjust controls are provided.

Input multiplexing is provided by a pair of CMOS 4051 analog-switches that are controlled by a CMOS 4024 binary-counter. The clock terminal is controlled by the data-valid (an EOC or status output) terminal of the 8700. Each time a conversion is completed, the data-valid terminal drops low, and this increments the binary counter. The 4024 is a seven-bit binary-counter, of which only the four LSDs are used in this application. This circuit can, therefore, be expanded in multiples of eight channels by adding a 4051 for each bank of eight channels. It is also necessary to provide the decoding of the 4024 outputs needed to insure the correct 4051 being turned on. The 4051 control input weighted 1 is used to turn on the chip.

The circuit shown in Fig. 14-13 is used in the I/O mode of the computer. The eight output-bits are connected to a computer input-port in a manner similar to those shown in the chapter on interfacing. If you want to directly interface the circuit to a microprocessor, using the memory-mapping technique, then substitute the 8703 device for the 8700. The 8703 is identical to the 8700, except that it uses three-state outputs. Pin 24 is used as an active-low chip-enable. When this terminal is brought low, the 8703 outputs become active and pass data directly to the microprocessor data-bus.

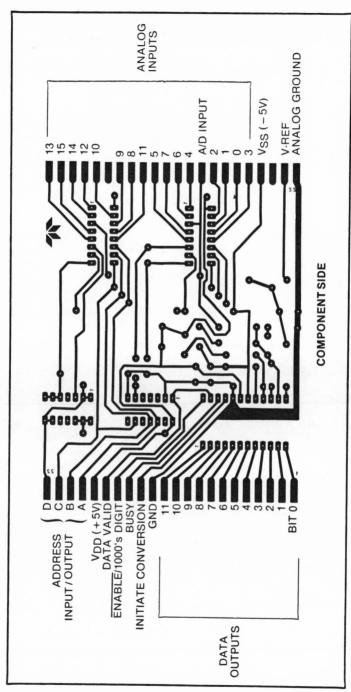

ANALOG INPUTS

13
15
14
12
10

9
8
11
5
7
6
4

A/D INPUT
2
1
0
3

VSS (−5V)

V-REF
ANALOG GROUND

COMPONENT SIDE

ADDRESS
INPUT / OUTPUT

D
C
B
A

VDD (+5V)
DATA VALID
ENABLE/1000's DIGIT
BUSY
INITIATE CONVERSION
GND

11
10
9
8
7
6
5
4
3
2
1

BIT 0

DATA
OUTPUTS

Fig. 14-15. Printed-circuit layout.

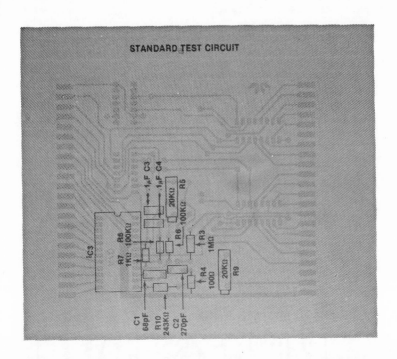

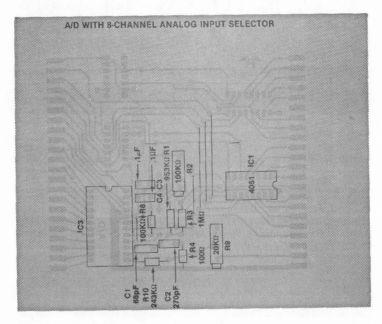

Fig. 14-16. Components layout.

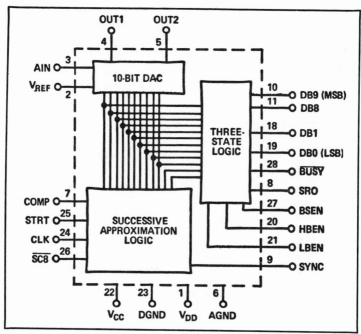

Fig. 14-17. AD 7570 block diagram.

Figure 14-13 shows the circuit for making an eight-channel or 16-channel data acquisition system based on the Teledyne 8700 and 8703 ADC ICs. If you want to make the circuit into an eight-bit ADC, ground the Q4 output of the 4024 (pin 6) and delete one of the 4051s (IC 2) and the 4011 inverter (IC 5).

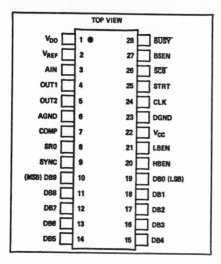

Fig. 14-18. AD 7570 pinouts.

The printed circuit foil-pattern for this circuit is shown in Fig. 14-14. This pattern can be used for either eight-bit or 16-bit versions of the circuit. This pattern can be duplicated photographically for making the PCB by using standard techniques. The pin-outs are shown in Fig. 14-15. The pattern is shown from the component side of the board.

The component layouts are shown in Fig. 14-16. The pattern in Fig. 14-16B is for the 16-channel version.

ANALOG DEVICES' AD7570

The Analog Devices model AD7570 is a ten-bit monolithic successive-approximation analog-to-digital-converter. The internal circuitry (Fig. 14-17) contains the ten-bit DAC, SAR control-logic and Tri-state output logic. The use of three-state outputs permits direct interface with microprocessor buses. One feature of this circuit makes it more versatile than some others: there are two enable-controls. One of them controls the two MSBs, while the other controls the lower eight-bits. This arrangement allows it to be interfaced directly with eight-bit microprocessor data-buses.

The AD7570 is capable of serial output. The serial output (SRO) is used in conjunction with the serial synchronization line to output data. The internal sync clock operates as high as 600 kHz or can be driven externally. The frequency of the internal clock is set by an external resistance-capacitance time-constant. At a 600-kHz clock-rate the AD7570 can perform an eight-bit conversion in approximately 20 μs. There is a short-cycle terminal that is used to stop the conversion after eight bits.

The pin-outs for the DIP package used for the AD7570 are shown in Fig. 14-18, while Table 14-2 gives the functions and mnemonics used to described each pin function.

Pin-Function Description

● Convert Start (pin 25, STRT). When the start input goes to logical 1, the MSB data-latch is set to logic 1, and all other data latches are set to logic 0. When the start input returns low, the conversion sequence begins. The start command must remain high for at least 500 ns. If a start command is reinitiated during conversion, the conversion sequence starts over.

● High-byte-enable (pin 20, HBEN). This is a Tri-state enable for the bit 9 (MSB) and bit 8. When the control is low, the output data lines for bits 9 and 8 are floating. When the control is high, digital data from the latches appears on the data lines.

● Low-byte-enable (pin 21, LBEN). This is the same as the high-byte-enable pin, but controls bits 0 (LSB) through 7.

● Busy Enable (pin 27, BSEN). This is an interrogation input that requests the status of the converter, i.e., conversion-in-process or conversion completed. The converter status is addressed by applying a logic 1 to the busy enable.

● Short-cycle 8-bits (pin 26, SC8). With a logic 0 input, the conversion stops after 8 bits, reducing the conversion time by 2 clock periods. This control should be exercised for proper operation of the version. When a logic 1 is applied, a complete 10-bit conversion takes place (L version).

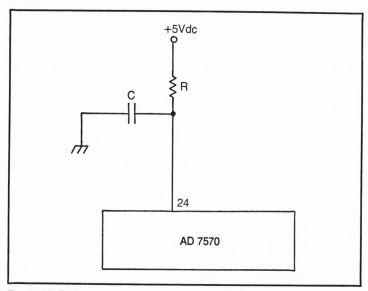

Fig. 14-19. Resistor-capacitor circuit for generating clock frequency.

● Clock (pin 24, CLK). With an external resistor-capacitor connected, as shown in Fig. 14-19, clock activity begins on receipt of a CONVERT-START command to the ADC and ceases on completion of the conversion. An external clock (CMOS or TTL/DTL levels) can directly drive the clock terminals, if required. If V$_{CC}$ is less than 4.75 V, the internal clock does not operate.

● V$_{PP}$ (pin 1). V$_{PP}$ is the positive supply for all analog circuitry plus some digital-logic circuits that are not part of the TTL compatible I/O lines (back gates to the positive-channel devices). Nominal supply-voltage is +15 V.

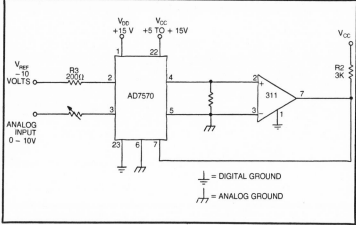

Fig. 14-20. AD7570 circuit.

Table 14-2. Pin-Outs.

PIN NO.	MNEMONIC	FUNCTION
1	V$_{DD}$	Positive Supply (+15 V)
2	V$_{REF}$	Voltage REFerence (±10V)
3	A$_{IN}$	Analog INput
4	OUT1	DAC Current OUTput 1
5	OUT2	DAC Current OUTput 2
6	AGND	Analog GrouND
7	COMP	COMParator
8	SRO	SeRial Output
9	SYNC	Serial SYNChronization
10	DB9	Data Bit 9 (MSB)
11	DB8	Data Bit 8
12	DB7	Data Bit 7
13	DB6	Data Bit 6
14	DB5	Data Bit 5
15	DB4	Data Bit 4
16	DB3	Data Bit 3
17	DB2	Data Bit 2
18	DB1	Data Bit 1
19	**DB0**	Data Bit 0 (LSB)
20	HBEN	High Byte ENable
21	LBEN	Low Byte ENable
22	V$_{CC}$	Logic Supply (+5V to +15V)
23	DGND	Digital GrouND
24	CLK	CLocK
25	$\overline{STRT}$	STaRT
26	$\overline{SC8}$	Short Cycle 8 Bits
27	$\overline{BSEN}$	BuSy ENable
28	BUSY	BUSY

● V$_{CC}$ (pin 22). V$_{CC}$ is the logic power supply. If +5 V is used, all control I/O (with the exception of comparator terminal) are DTL/TTL compatible. If +15 V is applied, control I/Os are CMOS compatible.

● Busy (pin 28 $\overline{BUSY}$). The busy line indicates whether conversion is complete or in process. Busy is a Three-state output and floats until the busy-enable line is addressed with a logic 1. When addressed, busy indicates either a 1 (conversion complete) or a 0 (conversion in process).

● Serial Output (pin 8, SRO). Provides output data in serial format. Data is available only during conversion. When the ADC is not converting, the serial output line floats. The serial sync (see next function) must be used, along with the serial output terminal, to avoid misinterpreting data.

● Serial Synchronization (pin 9, SYNC). Provides 10 positive-edges which are synchronized to the serial output pin. Serial sync is floating if conversion is not taking place. Note that all digital I/Os are TTL/DTL compatible when V$_{CC}$ is +5 V and CMOS compatible when V$_{CC}$ is +15 V.

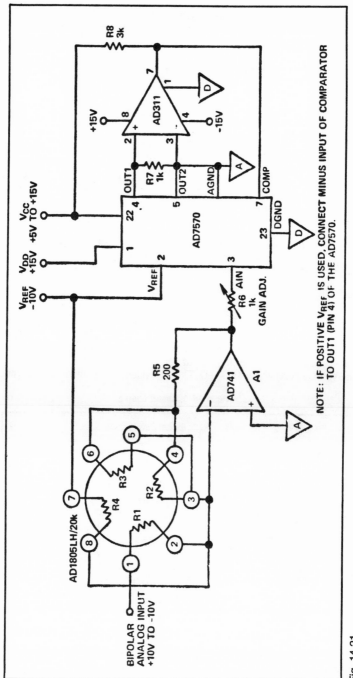

NOTE: IF POSITIVE V_{REF} IS USED, CONNECT MINUS INPUT OF COMPARATOR TO OUT1 (PIN 4) OF THE AD7570.

Fig. 14-21.

211

Table 14-3. Output Coding.

Analog Input (AIN) Notes 1, 2, 3	Digital Output Code	
	MSB	LSB
FS − 1 LSB	1 1 1 1 1 1 1 1 1 1	
FS − 2 LSB	1 1 1 1 1 1 1 1 1 0	
¾ FS	1 1 0 0 0 0 0 0 0 0	
½ FS + 1LSB	1 0 0 0 0 0 0 0 0 1	
½FS	1 0 0 0 0 0 0 0 0 0	
½ FS − 1 LSB	0 1 1 1 1 1 1 1 1 1	
¼ FS	0 1 0 0 0 0 0 0 0 0	
1 LSB	0 0 0 0 0 0 0 0 0 1	
0	0 0 0 0 0 0 0 0 0 0	

NOTES:
1. Analog inputs shown are nominal center values of code.
2. "FS" is full scale, i.e., $(-V_{REF})$.
3. For 8-bit operation, 1 LSB equals $(-V_{REF}) (2^{-8})$; for 10-bit operation, 1 LSB equals $(-V_{REF}) (2^{-10})$.

Operation

Figure 14-20 shows the circuit needed for unipolar operation. In the particular configuration shown, the circuit operates over the range of 0-+10 V. If the input is always positive the reference potential must be negative. Similarly, if the input range is negative, the reference must be positive. It is also necessary in the negative-input version to reverse the connections to the voltage comparator (AD311). The digital data and control lines are not

Table 14-4. Output Coding.

Analog Input (AIN) Notes 1, 2, 3	Digital Output Code	
	MSB	LSB
+(FS − 1LSB)	1 1 1 1 1 1 1 1 1 1	
+(FS − 2LSB)	1 1 1 1 1 1 1 1 1 0	
+(½ FS)	1 1 0 0 0 0 0 0 0 0	
+(1LSB)	1 0 0 0 0 0 0 0 0 1	
0	1 0 0 0 0 0 0 0 0 0	
−(1 LSB)	0 1 1 1 1 1 1 1 1 1	
−(½ FS)	0 1 0 0 0 0 0 0 0 0	
−(FS − 1LSB)	0 0 0 0 0 0 0 0 0 1	
−FS	0 0 0 0 0 0 0 0 0 0	

NOTES:
1. Analog inputs shown are nominal center values of code.
2. "FS" is full scale; i.e., (V_{REF}).
3. For 8-bit operation, 1 LSB equals $(-V_{REF}) (2^{-7})$: for 10-bit operation 11 SB equals $(-V_{REF}) (2^{-9})$.

shown in Fig. 14-20 and must be inferred. The range of the ADC input can be changed by varying the reference-voltage input. In the case shown it is −10 volts; so the input range is 0-+10 V. Reference voltages in the 1-10-V range are useful, following the polarity rules given above.

The calibration procedure for this device is similar to the usual calibration procedure for unipolar alignment.

1. Apply a continuous-start command to the STRT input of the AD7570.
2. Apply an analog-input voltage equal to 1½-LSB to AIN.
3. Adjust gain-potentiometer R4 or the reference-voltage until the LSB bobbles back and forth between high and low. This can be seen on the serial-output terminal.

The circuit in Fig. 14-21 shows what is needed to offer bipolar conversion with the AD7570. This circuit uses a resistor-voltage divider (in this case, a monolithic IC containing four 20K ohm-resistors), the AD1805LH/20K by Analog Devices. The 741 operational amplifier is used in the inverting-follower configuration. A current applied to the inverting input from the reference potential biases the amplifier to a midpoint. The analog-input signal then modulates this fixed point, causing the 741 output to vary up and down from the quiescent point in response to the ±10-V analog-input signal.

The following is the calibration procedure for bipolar alignment.

1. Apply continuous-start command to the STRT terminal of the AD7570.
2. Apply an analog-input voltage equal to the 1½-LSB less than full-scale (i.e., $V_{FS} = V_{REF}$) to the bipolar input of the AD7570.
3. Adjust gain potentiometer for the LSB to bobble between high and low. This can be seen on serial-output terminal.

The output codes for the AD 7570 are shown in Tables 14-3 and 14-4. Both unipolar and bipolar versions are shown. The unipolar circuit uses straight binary in which the zero-input voltage creates an output code of 0000000000. This means that the maximum allowable input signal is one LSB less than the reference voltage (i.e., 9.96 V in an eight-bit device).

The bipolar code is the offset binary, which means that the zero-input voltage is represented by the code 10000000000. The +1-LSB voltage is then 1000000001, and the −1-LSB is 0111111111. The code for $+V_{FS}$ (FS-1LSB) is 1111111111, while that for $-V_{FS}$ is 0000000000.

HYBRID ADCs

Monolithic circuits are true ICs. Hybrid circuits are built along slightly different lines and may include ICs (in chip rather than packaged form) along with discrete components such as resistors and capacitors. But, the components do not look like those you are familiar with from ordinary discrete-component electronics construction. They are thick film, chip, form and are microcircuits in their own right.

Also, in this class, for purposes here, are *analog function modules*. Some function modules are hybrid devices, while others are made from individual discrete components. The printed-circuit card can contain both discrete components and hybrid modules (this might be called hybrid-hybrid, or hybrid², construction). This device is intended as a standalone module, i.e., a subsystem among other components in the overall system. See Table 14-4.

Chapter 15

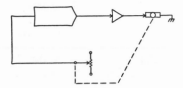

Interfacing Motors, Triacs, and Relays

The microprocessor is one of those truly remarkable devices that seems to have an almost endless range of applications! There is a growing tendency to find applications that are outside of traditional roles. In some cases the microprocessor is used to control real-world devices. The analog output of the DAC, for example, which is controlled by a binary input, can be used to allow a computer to control such things as motor speed or the position of some mechanical device.

MOTOR CONTROL

If you want to control the speed of a dc motor with a computer, it is necessary to create a dc output voltage that is proportional to the speed that the motor should attain. This is done by controlling the output of a DAC with the computer that controls the motor. The DAC output is then usually amplified in a power amplifier (most DACs cannot directly drive a heavy load such as a motor), before being applied to the motor. The voltage across the motor-winding determines the speed, while its polarity (in a dc motor) controls the direction of rotation.

While this application is interesting, it is also somewhat trivial. The computer and DAC combination is capable of a lot more than merely setting the speed of a motor. Figure 15-1 shows an elementary circuit in which the DAC is used by the computer to move some mechanical object to a specified position. A single-quadrant system is constructed in which the object moved by the motor can take on any position in the range of Y_0 to Y_1.

This circuit is based upon three main sections: power amplifier, voltage comparator, and a DAC. The input of the power amplifier always sees one of three possible values: zero, positive voltage, or negative voltage. The direction of the rotation of the motor is determined by the polarity of the amplifier-input signal. Because this signal is also the output of a comparator, the amplitude is constant (only its polarity changes) or zero.

The comparator sees two input-signals. One input is from the DAC, which is under control of a computer. The other input is from a position

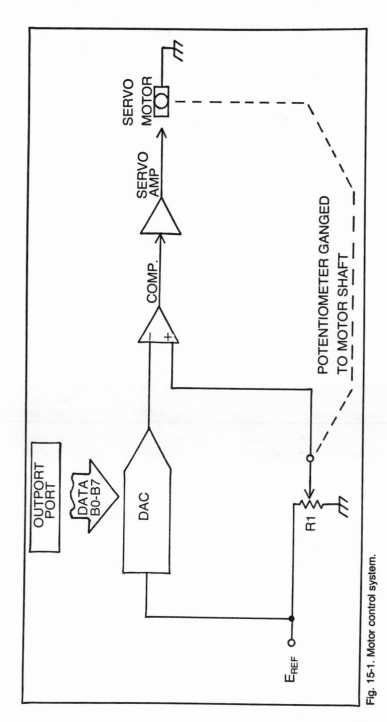

Fig. 15-1. Motor control system.

215

transducer directly connected to the object being moved. The position transducer is merely a linear potentiometer connected to a precision-voltage reference-source. The transducer output-voltage E1 is a linear function of the position of the object to which the transducer is attached. When the object is at position Y_0, the output at E1 is zero. But if the transducer/object is advanced to position Y_1, the output of the transducer E1 is the full-reference voltage, E_{REF}. At intermediate positions the value of E1 reflects the position of the object as a percentage of E_{REF} greater than zero.

The computer determines where it wants the object to be located. It then calculates the binary value required to create this position. There is a certain range of motion allowable, and the computer has N bits of resolution. If, for example, an eight-bit computer is used, then there are 256 different locations possible. Assuming that 00000000 represents Y_0 and 11111111 represents Y_1, you can locate the end points of motion and 254 locations in between them.

Assume that the computer wants the object to be located at the midpoint $(Y_1 - Y_0)/2$. It then outputs 10000000 to the DAC, which creates a midscale voltage, E0. This voltage is applied to the inverting input of the voltage comparator. The comparator now has the new position. If it is the same as the old position, then the E0 = E1. If E1 is less than E0, then the comparator output is positive. The amplifier sees a constant-amplitude positive-polarity signal. It moves the object being controlled at a constant speed towards the correct position. Similarly , if E1 is greater than E0, the comparator output is negative voltage. The absolute values of negative and positive voltage are usually the same. The motor speed is the same regardless of the direction of travel. In the case of the negative-voltage output, the motor rotation is opposite from that of the positive voltage case, but the speed is constant. Again, the motor propels the object toward the correct point at a constant speed.

When the object reaches the correct point, the values of E1 and E0 are the same. This means that the comparator output is zero which shuts off the motor.

There is another variation on this theme that uses an *analog summer* to control the motor. This is shown in Fig. 15-2. The advantage of this is that

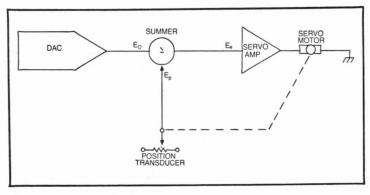

Fig. 15-2. Basic control system.

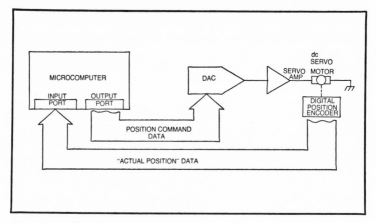

Fig. 15-3. Using a digital-position controller.

the speed of the motor is not constant. If the motor is far away from the commanded position, the servo amplifier controlling the motor sees a higher input signal than exists when the position difference is small. The principal parts of this circuit are the DAC, a servo power-amplifier to control the motor, a position transducer, and a summer circuit. The summer can be an inverting-follower operational-amplifier in which two input currents are created or a differential amplifier.

The following signal voltages are in this circuit: E_0, E_E, E_M, and E_P. These are defined as follows:

● E_0 is the DAC output voltage.
● E_M is the motor-control voltage (amplitude controls the speed, polarity controls the direction of rotation of the motor).
● E_P is the position signal generated by the potentiometer position-transducer.
● E_E is the error voltage and is proportional to the difference between the commanded position signal and the actual position signal ($E_0 - E_P$). If the object being controlled by the motor is in the correct spot, then E_E is zero.

The circuit operates as a simple control system. When E_0 changes, indicating that the computer wants to move the object to a new position, then $E_0 = E_P$, so E_E (the error signal) is no longer zero. This signal is applied to the input of the servo amplifier, which in turn controls the speed and direction of travel of the object. If E_E is less than zero, the motor turns in one direction. If E_E is greater than zero, the motor turns in the other direction.

The advantage of this system is that the speed of travel depends upon the value of E_E. If the new position is close to the old position, E_E has a small magnitude. The motor turns slowly, and the object, therefore, approaches the new position cautiously. If the error between old and new positions is great, however, the speed of approach is rapid at first. The speed becomes less and less at the correct position is approached. This allows it to chew up distance while far away, yet slow down sufficiently to make the same, precise, cautious approach as in the previous case.

Figure 15-3 shows the same type of circuit in which the summer is actually the computer and the position transducer is a digital type. Several different types of transducers are available that output a digital code which indicates the position of a device. In some cases a binary, BCD, or *Gray code* is used. The Gray code has the advantage that only one bit changes for every increment of position, a subject that I will return to shortly. The computer issues a command to the DAC to turn on the servo amplifier, thereby moving the motor, if the position data does not agree with the commanded position. In this circuit the comparison is made totally inside the computer, using software instead of hardware.

The circuit in Fig. 15-4 uses two DACs and a differential-input servo amplifier to make the comparison. Again, the position transducer is a digital type. In this case the Gray code or binary type is usually recommended, with Gray code preferred. The computer applies the data for the desired position to the input of DAC 1, producing output voltage E1. The position transducer applies its signal to the input of DAC 2, creating voltage E2. If the position agrees with the commanded position, then E2-E1 is zero, and the amplifier output is zero. If there is a discrepancy, the amplifier sees a nonzero signal and, therefore, produces output signal E_M. This voltage drives the motor and brings the object closer to the commanded position. Again, the speed is greater when the position difference is great and then slows down as the two positions becomes closer together.

It is important that the computer and the digital-position transducer use the same digital-code scheme, or there is a discrepancy in output voltage when the object is at the correct position. The operation of this circuit improves if the DAC voltage or current references are the same for both DACs. This means using an external reference supply or using one of the types that output the reference voltage source so that other DACs can be driven from the same source. Most of those DACs use an internal reference supply that must be connected to the reference amplifier of the DAC through an external connection. In these you merely select one of the DACs as the reference and connect the reference amplifier inputs of both DACs to the selected reference-supply.

You might also find an application in which a single DAC performs both jobs. Remember that a multiplying DAC (which uses an external reference source), obeys the function:

$$E_{OUT} = E_{REF} \times \frac{A}{2^n}$$

Where E_{OUT} is the DAC output voltage, E_{REF} is the reference voltage, n is the DAC input's bit-length, and A is the value of the binary word actually applied to the DAC inputs.

Figure 15-5 shows how a single DAC, which obeys the expression in the previous equation is used to make the comparison. The digital inputs of the DAC are connected to the computer output-port. The position transducer is a potentiometer type; so it produces a position signal, E_P. This signal may or may not be amplified. If the value of the reference voltage on the transducer is correctly selected, however, no scaling is needed.

Motor speed can also be controlled by the computer. You need some type of transducer that indicates the motor speed. Three types are avail-

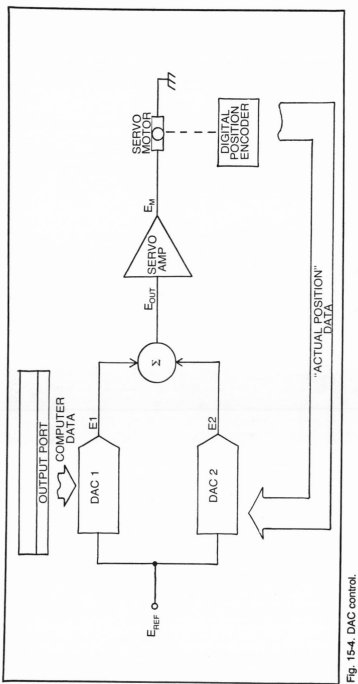

Fig. 15-4. DAC control.

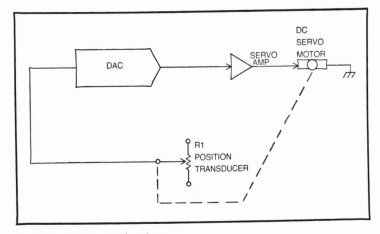

Fig. 15-5. Analog-control system.

able: dc generator, ac tachometer-alternator, and pulse. The dc generator produces a dc voltage that is proportional to the motor speed. The alternator produces an ac signal with a frequency that is proportional to the speed. A *zero-crossing detector* or Schmitt trigger produces pulses from the ac signal that the computer can use to read motor speed. The pulse type uses a wheel on the motor shaft to interrupt the optical path between an LED and photocell. If there are six holes in the rim of the wheel, then produce six pulses from the photocell for each motor revolution. A second LED and photocell combination, and a single hole on another line allow you to also know shaft position; you can reset a counter in the computer every time this position pulse comes along. You then know that the shaft has

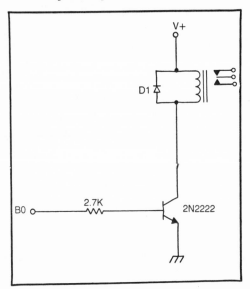

Fig. 15-6. Relay driver.

rotated one-sixth the circumference when one of the six other holes inter-rupts the other LED/photocell. Of course, any number of holes can be used, depending upon the required resolution.

CONTROLLING EXTERNAL LOADS WITH RELAYS

In some cases it is desirable to control an external load with an electromechanical relay. Although I know some electrical engineers who would consider that statement to be heresy, the truth remains that relay control is often the very best method.

Figure 15-6 shows one method of interfacing a relay to a microcom-puter. Here we are using a single transistor switch to turn the relay on and off under command from bit B0 of an output port of the microcomputer. This scheme, incidentally, leaves the other bits of the port free to be used in other applications. Some microcomputers allow the independent setting of bits on specific ports; so you need not lose control of one load just because it becomes necessary to turn on another.

The 2N2222 transistor (almost any suitable NPN transistor can be used instead) is connected as a grounded emitter switch. The relay is connected between the collector of the transistor and positive voltage (which need not be the computer +5 V line, although it could be). When bit B0 of the selected output is low, the base of the transistor is at ground potential so the transistor does not conduct. Under this condition the relay is turned off. If, however, the computer decides to turn on bit B0 of the output port, the transistor conducts and energizes the relay.

The diode in parallel with the coil of the relay is used to prevent high voltage spikes from damaging the transistor. When the transistor is turned back off, after having energized the coil of the relay, there is a magnetic field built around the coil. This field collapses at that time, creating a large counter EMF, which means a high voltage spike. The diode is reverse biased for the normal dc operating potentials; so it is forward biased for the *inductive kick* spike. This condition causes the spike to be suppressed; it has an amplitude equal to the forward-conduction voltage-drop of the diode.

CONTROLLING A TRIAC OR SCR WITH THE MICROCOMPUTER

One frequent control application is turning on a TRIAC or SCR from one bit of a microcomputer. This type of circuit is used in applications that include home heating-cooling environmental control; burglar frustration (light control); burglar alarms; and certain types of industrial, scientific or engineering applications.

Figure 15-7 shows the basic interfacing-circuit for connecting the TRIAC to the microcomputer. In this case I have selected bit B0 of the output port for the control bit. The ac line is not compatible with the microcomputer output (sigh); so you must isolate these two circuits from each other. The optoisolator (OP 1) accomplishes this trick for us. When bit B0 of the microcomputer goes high, the LED in the optoisolator is turned on and causes the transistor to be forward biased. This causes the dc collector-voltage to appear across the emitter resistor, thereby turning on the TRIAC-gate circuit.

The TRIAC, you recall, is turned off until the gate is energized. It turns off again the next time the ac line voltage goes through zero, unless the gate is reenergized.

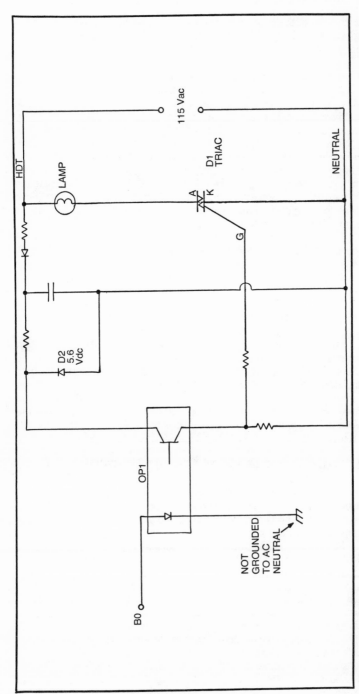

Fig. 15-7. Driving a TRIAC Circuit.

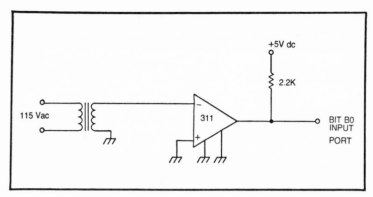

Fig. 15-8. Power line sync.

The circuit shown in Fig. 15-7 turns on the SCR/TRIAC, but the TRIAC extinquishes 8.3 ms later when the 60 Hz ac sinewave goes through zero! You could, of course, keep the output bit high, thereby reenergizing the TRIAC gate. But, this only turns the TRIAC on full-blast every half cycle. In that case you would have a half-baked relay and nothing more. If you want to control the current in the load (e.g., the brightness of the lamp),

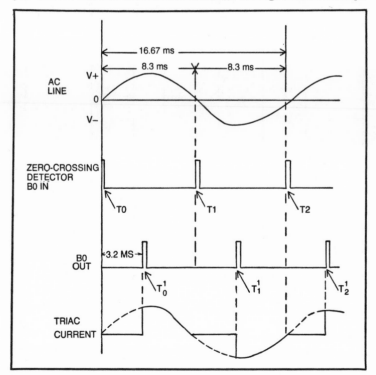

Fig. 15-9. Timing diagram.

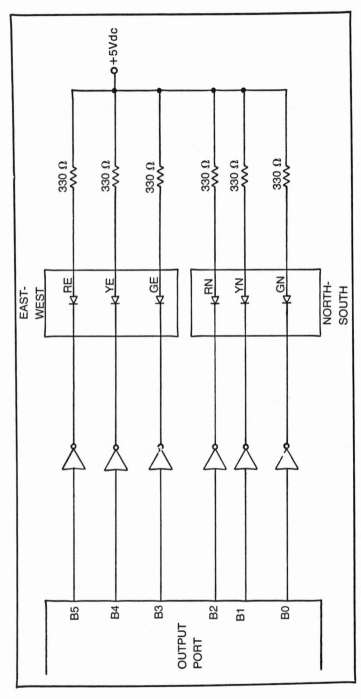

Fig. 15-10. Traffic-light system.

224

then you need to find a way to turn the TRIAC on for a specified portion of each half cycle. The way to do this is shown in the preceding figures.

Figure 15-8 shows a zero-crossing detector (some ICs are designed for this application, but this uses a LM-311 comparator and transformer) that outputs a pulse every time the ac sine wave goes through zero. Route this pulse to bit B0 of an input pulse. A program must be written for the microcomputer that will cause it to loop while looking for the high condition on B0 of the appropriate input port. When the zero-crossing pulse is received, the program branches to a timer subroutine that causes a delay equal to the portion of the half-cycle that you want the lamp off. After that time expires the program outputs a high on B0 of the output port, thereby turning on the TRIAC.

Figure 15-9 shows the timing diagram of this problem. The top trace is the ac voltage from the power line. The second trace is the zero-crossing-detector output, while the third trace is the TRIAC-gate signal-pulse. The bottom trace is the TRIAC current. Note that current flows in the lamp only for a portion of each cycle. This means that the lamp glows at reduced brilliance. In the case shown here, the TRIAC is gated-on just a little short of halfway through each half cycle, i.e., 3.2 ms after the zero-crossing. You can control the brilliance of the lamp or the current in any other type of load by controlling the duration of the loop timer in the program that determines when the TRIAC-gate signal is generated.

TRAFFIC-LIGHT CONTROLLER: AN EXERCISE

Figure 15-10 shows the circuit for a simulated traffic light array. Of course, in a real traffic light the computer would control either relays or TRIACS; one of the previous circuits might be used. Here, however, I simply want to demonstrate a programming concept. The lights are actually red, yellow and green light-emitting diodes (LEDs). There is an east-west bank and a north-south bank. The individual LEDs are designated RE, YE, and GE in the east-west bank; and RN, YN, and GN in the north-south bank (guess how I came up with those designations!).

The LEDs are controlled from open-collector TTL inverters (e.g., 7416) connected to one output port of the microcomputer. Try and program three different cases:

Case 1: Try red blinking east-west and yellow blinking north-south one second intervals:
a) Both blinking simultaneously (R-Y) . . . (R-Y) . . . (R-Y) . . .
b) Blinking out of phase with each other (R) . . . (Y) . . . (R) . . . (Y)

Case 2: Go through the normal American system: green 25 seconds in one direction, a five-second yellow on the green side, green for the other direction for 25 seconds, and so forth ad infinitum.

Case 3: Operate in the north-south direction permanently unless a car comes from either the east or the west. One bit of an input port can be used to represent the east-west sensor. Have the light wait an additional 25 seconds after the sensor pulse if there are two or less cars and go immediately if there are three or more cars waiting. If you want to add something interesting, try adding a pedestrian button that turns on the appropriate light scheme for a crossing of the north-south street while walking along the east-west street.

Chapter 16

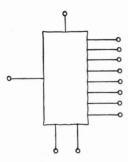

Interfacing ADCs and DACs
to the Microprocessor

Microcomputers and microprocessors are frequently used in applications that require an interface with the analog world. It seems that many electronic instruments produce an analog voltage or current signal as the relevant output. Similarly, transducers and other sensors usually produce only an analog output signal. For example, the popular solid-state temperature-sensors (those based on PN junctions) produce an output potential of 1 or 10 mV/^{0}K. Interfacing that sensor to your microprocessor, e.g., for environmental control or measurement-data logging, requires that you convert the analog signal to a digital signal. This is the function of an analog-to-digital converter (ADC). Similarly, there are other devices, such as oscilloscopes, strip-chart recorders, X-Y recorders, electrical motors, and proportional heaters that need to see an analog signal at the input. If the microcomputer is used as the central controller of the instrument, then a digital-to-analog converter (DAC) is needed.

How are these devices interfaced? How do they work? Well, for the work part of the question, let me refer you to another of my books: *Microprocessor Interfacing: A/D and D/A,* TAB Book No. 1271.

INTERFACING DACs

The DAC is a device that accepts a binary word at the input and produce an analog voltage or current at the output that is proportional to the product of that word and an analog reference-voltage or current. For example, the popular DAC-08 device has a reference-current input (e.g., 2 mA) and produces an output current of 2 mA × (n/256), where n is the 8-bit binary value applied to the input.

Some DACs (like those by Ferranti Semiconductor) have their own internal data latches. These you can connect directly to the data bus and then activate the chip enable with a device select pulse (see chapter 4). But, most DACs that you will use have no internal latches; so they must either be connected to a latched output port or be equipped with an external latch.

Figure 16-1 shows the connection of a DAC to a latched output-port. It seems that nothing could be simpler! Just connect the lines from the output port to the appropriate input lines on the DAC, remembering to keep LSB and MSB separated! Also, keep the line short (under 24 inches) if a fast-settling high-frequency DAC is planned. Note that most microcomputers have latched output-ports. This term means that the data remains on the output port to which it is written, even after the microcomputer has passed by the output instruction. The data remains as the last written until and unless it is overwritten by a new command or the power fails (in which case all bets are off).

The circuit for including an external output-latch is shown in Fig. 16-2. This circuit can be used when the microcomputer has unlatched output-ports, when the data is loaded sometime prior to being used at the DAC inputs, or when the DAC is connected directly to the data bus.

The latch is a TTL-74100 integrated-circuit. This is a dual four-bit latch. Data at the output lines remains at the last valid value when the strobe lines are low and will follow the inputs when the strobe lines are high. To latch data onto the 74100 outputs, apply the data to output port 1 and then produce the device-select pulse on the strobe lines. When this pulse goes high, the data at the output port is transferred to the 74100 outputs. When the device select pulse goes away, the data remains latched on the 74100 outputs until another device-select pulse is received.

Notice that the device-select pulse is generated in Fig. 16-2 by one bit of another output port. It can also be generated in a circuit such as those of Chapter 4 (and, in fact, is so-generated if the 74100 inputs are connected directly to the data bus). The device-select pulse is created by writing a high to bit B0 for a period of a few microseconds (or more) and then writing a low to the port:

1. Write 00000001 to port 2 (i.e., set B0).

2. Loop for several microseconds (at least the settling time of the output port).

3. Reset bit B0 of port 2 by writing 00000000 to port 2.

The unused bits of port 2 can be used for other purposes in most microcomputers. You need not lose an entire output port for the sake of one device-select pulse.

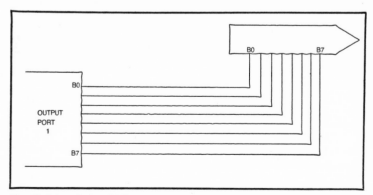

Fig. 16-1. Interfacing DAC to an output port.

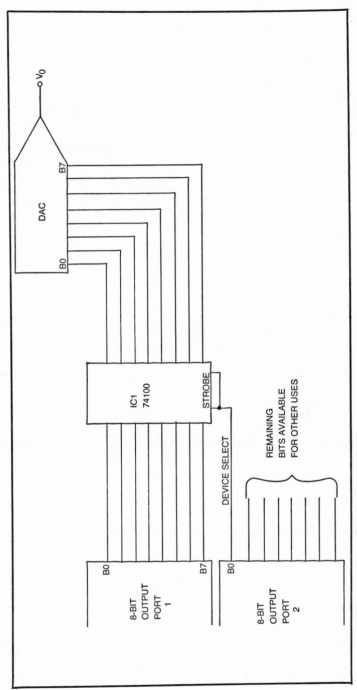

Fig. 16-2. Interfacing to an unlatched output-port.

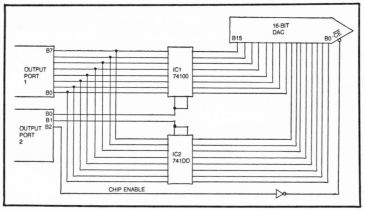

Fig. 16-3. Interfacing an eight-bit microcomputer to 10, 12 and 16-bit DACs.

INTERFACING 10-, 12- and 16-BIT DACs TO THE 8-BIT MICROCOMPUTER

Most of the microcomputers that you use are 8-bit machines. The typical microcomputer has an 8-bit data bus; so it will also have 8-bit I/O ports. How do you go about interfacing with a 10-, 12-, or 16-bit digital-to-analog converter? It's easy—double-clutch it!

Figure 16-3 shows the basic method for interfacing an 8-bit I/O port (or memory-mapped port) with a larger-than eight-bit DAC. This particular scheme is for those DACs that have a built-in latch or a chip-enable line. Although the chip-enable method is shown here, the method is essentially the same for the latched type. The only probable major difference is that the latched-input type probably use an active-high strobe, while most chip-enable pins are active-low. The other difference is that most chip-enable types float the DAC output at one extreme or the other (ground or supply rail), while the latched type maintains the DAC at the last valid data-level.

Two output-ports are used in this application. Alternately, if the DAC is memory-mapped, two memory-locations must be assigned to the project. I call these two output-ports 1 and 2 for convenience sake.

The two eight-bit data-latches, IC 1 and IC 2, are connected such that their inputs are to the eight-bit lines of output-port 1. The strobe lines, however, are controlled by separate bits of port 2. The loading sequence is programmed into the computer and follows this pattern:
1. Set both ports 1 and 2 low (i.e., 00000000).
2. Output the high order byte to port 1.
3. Write 00000001 to output port 2; this brings the strobe line of IC 1 high, transferring the high-byte data into the 74100 register.
4. Write a 00000000 to port 2, thereby latching the data onto the outputs of IC 2.
5. Write the low-order bytes (or bits, if it is not a 16-bit DAC) to port 1.
6. Write 00000010 to output port 2. This brings the strobe line of IC 2 high, causing the data on the common input-lines to be transferred to the 74100 output.
7. Write 00000000 to output port 2, latching the data onto the 74100 outputs.

8. Write 00000100 to output port 2. This causes the CE line, connected to the output of the inverter, to go low, thereby turning on the DAC. The output of the DAC is proportional to the binary word appearing at the output of the 74100 latches.

The circuit shown in Fig. 16-3 works only when the DAC is equipped with either an internal input-data latch or if it has a chip-enable line. Although more and more commercial ICs and hybrid DACs are equipped with these features, there are still a large number which have neither. For these devices, another tactic is needed.

The double-buffered-latch system shown in Fig. 16-4 works with any type of DAC, regardless of whether or not it has internal latches or CE lines. This system is essentially the same as that of Fig. 16-3, except that a second pair of eight-bit latches is interposed between the primary latches (IC 1 and IC 2) and the DAC inputs. The operation is:

1. Clear both output ports by writing 00000000.

2. Write the high-order byte of the word to be applied to the DAC to port 1.

3. Write 00000001 to port 2. This causes the strobe line of IC 1 to go high, placing the data on port 1 on the IC 1 outputs.

4. Write 00000000 to port 2, thereby latching the data on IC 1.

5. Write the low-order byte (or bits) to output port 1.

6. Write 00000010 to port 2, causing the strobe line of IC 2 to go high.

7. Write a 00000000 to port 2.

8. Write 00000100 to port 2. This causes the strobe lines of IC 3 and IC 4 to go high, transferring the data from IC 1 to the output of IC 3, and from IC 2 to the output of IC 4.

9. Write 00000000 to output port 2. This latches the data onto the outputs of IC 3 and IC 4. Note that the DAC output changed state shortly after step 8 was initiated.

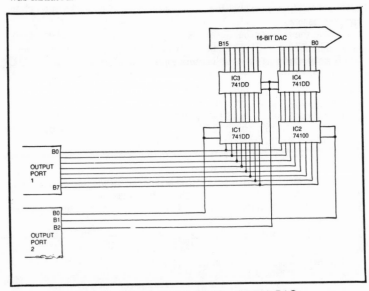

Fig. 16-4. Double-latched interfacing for 10, 12 and 16-bit DACs.

The circuit shown in Fig. 16-4 works for any DAC up to 16-bit word-length. Longer DACs can be accommodated by adding additional latches. If fewer bits are used, then either use fewer bits of the 74100 devices or use another latch such as the 7475.

INTERFACING THE ADC TO THE MICROPROCESSOR

The purpose of the ADC is to convert an analog voltage or current to a proportional binary word. Most ADCs are 8-, 10-, 12-, or 16-bit devices, although both shorter and longer converters are known. Figure 16-5 shows a block form of a typical ADC. There is an analog input line (V_X), plus at least two control-lines, and the N-bit binary-output lines.

Most ADCs have a start input, and either an end-of-conversion (EOC) output or a status line. The start input initiates the conversion process when an appropriate pulse is seen. Both active-high and active-low start inputs are known. The difference between the EOC and status lines is that the EOC generates a pulse (usually for one clock period) and then returns to the dormant state. The status line, on the other hand, goes to the busy condition while the converter is making the conversion and then drops to the data-valid condition when the conversion is completed. The line remains in this condition as long as no additional start pulses are received. Both methods have their own unique advantages and vocal supporters. In one of the methods to follow, I demonstrate how to make an EOC ADC think that it's a status-line type.

The simplest method for interfacing the ADC is to connect it to an input port on the microcomputer. The start line connects to one bit of an output port, while the EOC or status line connects to one bit of an input port—not the same input port as the data lines! The programmer initiates a conversion by outputing a pulse to the start line. Use a loop until the EOC pulse is received. At that time the data on the binary lines is valid; so the microcomputer will input the analog-to-digital data.

There is a problem with this system. The ADC outputs may not be latched; so the microcomputer must be much faster than the ADC clock. For

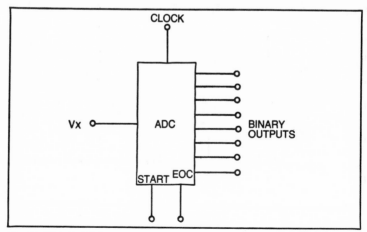

Fig. 16-5. Basic ADC connections.

231

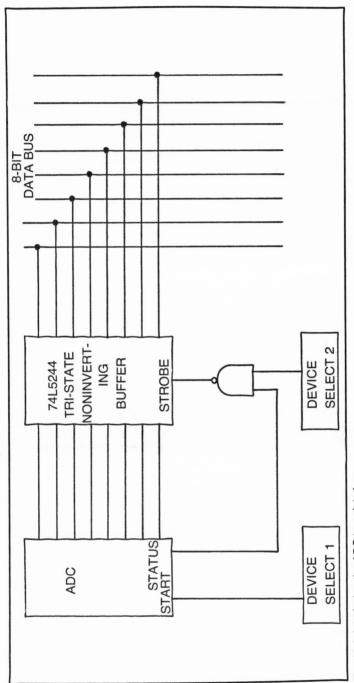

Fig. 16-6. Interfacing the ADC to a data bus.

example, if the computer clock is 1 MHz, its clock period is 1 μs. A typical loop program may take as many as 15 clock pulses to execute; so it inputs data in 15 μs. If the ADC also has a 1 MHz clock, the EOC pulse might disappear (the data, too) after 1 μs. The trick in this case is to use a clock speed on the ADC that is 15 times slower than the time required for the microcomputer to execute the input operation. This is not the most palatable method of doing the job! Of course, if the ADC is the type that uses a status line, it probably contains its own, internal, data latch. Lacking this latch, you can make one by using a 74100 between the outputs of the ADC and the input port of the microcomputer. The EOC pulse can then be used to strobe the data to the outputs of the 74100.

In some cases it is necessary to connect the ADC directly to the computer data bus. You might lack an available output port or may wish for one reason or another to memory-map the ADC (i.e., treat it as a location somewhere in memory). In that case, you cannot simply connect the output lines of the ADC to the data-bus lines unless they are three-state. The Tri-state output line has low impedance to ground for low, a low impedance to +5 V for a high, and a high impedance to both ground and +5 V when disabled. This condition lightly loads the data-bus lines, allowing you to connect the ADC directly to the data bus without feat of fouling up the other operations of the computer. If the ADC lacks Three-state outputs, you must provide them. In that case (see Fig. 16-6); you must interpose a Tri-state buffer between the ADC outputs and the data bus. The 74LS244 device consists of two banks of four Three-state noninverting-buffers (tie pins 1 and 19 together to make the strobe line). Also useful are the 74125 (noninverting), 74126 (inverting), Intel 8216 (inverting—two of four bits are required, and 8226 (noninverting version of the 8216 device). The timing diagram is shown in Fig. 16-7.

In Fig. 16-6 the start and status lines are shown connected to device-select circuits. These are essentially address-status decoders for the CPU and are used for any I/O port or memory location used. They were covered in Chapter 4. In this discussion I assume that the outputs of the device-select circuits are active-high.

The microcomputer can select the device by either writing to the output port represented by the circuit or by writing to the memory location represented (depending upon whether or not the circuit is I/O or memory-mapped oriented). Let's assume that the circuit is I/O oriented and represents ports 1 and 2, respectively.

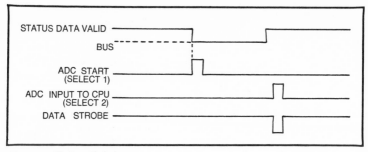

Fig. 16-7. Timing diagram.

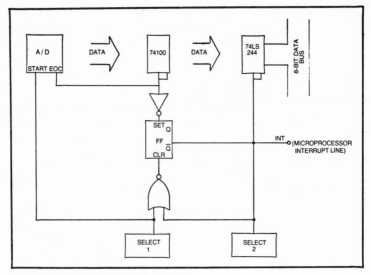

Fig. 16-8. Using the interrupt line, reset.

To initiate a conversion, the computer produces an output to port 1. It doesn't matter what data is in the accumulator at this time. It is output down the data bus, but is not used. When the computer produces an output to port 1, the device-select pulse 1 is generated. This pulse is applied to the start line of the ADC. The status line drops from the valid state to the busy state on seeing the leading edge of the start pulse.

When the ADC is finished making the conversion, the status line snaps high again, indicating valid data. But, the computer might not be in a position to receive the data yet. So, the NAND gate must be used to keep the ADC waiting until the computer indicates that it will receive the ADC output. It does this by writing an output to port 2. This applies a high to the other input of the NAND gate, causing the output to drop low. This condition activates the 74LS244, causing the outputs of the noninverting buffers inside the chip to be connected to the lines of the data bus.

Microcomputers are capable of executing thousands, even hundreds of thousands, of operations per second. In contrast some ADC are very slow. Some of the integrating converters, often selected for their ability to reject noise, take as much as 50 ms to complete a conversion. A little arithmetic demonstrates that a 400,000-operations-per-second microcomputer is wasting a lot of time if it has to sit and loop for 50 ms while the ADC huffs and puffs through a conversion! You would lose 8000 operations per conversion. In some cases this is not too much of a problem, because you might make one conversion per minute and really don't overload the computer at that rate. If you are taking data at more rapid rates, the 8000 operations lost per conversion becomes a real headache.

In one case for example, an engineering graduate student was making 128 conversions-per-second using a relatively slow converter (faster than 50 ms, however!). He was doing some electroencephalographic averaging (evoked potentials) during some medical studies. The computer was pro-

234

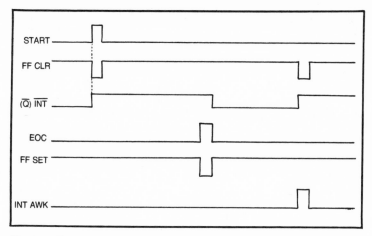

Fig. 16-9. Timing diagram.

grammed to perform part of the averaging between each conversion. The ADC interrupted the computer when it was ready. The computer could then temporarily abandon the data crunching and go to input operation.

Figure 16-8 shows a method for interfacing the ADC to the interrupt line of the microcomputer. The analog-to-digital output data is latched into a 74100 by the EOC pulse. This same pulse is inverted and applied to the SET input of a TTL flip-flop. In this condition Q is high and the not-Q is low—the condition demanded by most microcomputer interrupt-lines. Figures 16-9 and 16-10 show the timing diagram and power-on reset. The operation of the circuit is:

1. The start pulse is initiated by writing an output to port 1. This same pulse is propagated through the NOR gate to the CLR line of the flip-flop, causing the interrupt line to go high.

2. The converter makes its conversion. When the conversion is finished, an EOC pulse appears and sets the flip-flop (not-Q=low). The computer sees this as an interrupt.

3. When the computer acknowledges the interrupt it writes an output to port 2. This pulse turns on the Three-state buffer (74LS244) and (through the NOR gate) resets the flip-flop.

In some cases, you want to ensure that the ADC interrupt-line is in the reset condition when the power is applied to the system. You can ac-

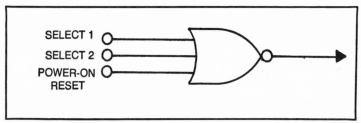

Fig. 16-10. Power-on reset.

complish this by replacing the two-input NOR gate with a three-input NOR gate (see Fig. 16-10). The third input can be connected to the system reset-line or the power-on reset-line (usually the same line).

In many cases the ADC must be connected to make continuous conversions. All of the cases shown so far require the computer to initiate all of the conversions by outputing a start pulse. You can make the circuit into an asynchronous converter by the mere expedient of connecting the EOC to the start pulse. This causes the converter to automatically initiate a new conversion each time a conversion is completed. Most ADCs are designed so that the EOC pulse serves as the start pulse.

Chapter 17

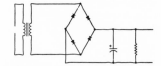

Dc Power Supplies

The dc power supply is not strictly an interfacing, but it is very important to the operation of the microcomputer. In addition typical home-built computers or the typical single-board computers of the learner class, do not include a power supply. The companies that sell these products happily sell an outboard power supply for fees that range from $30 to $100. For the most part you can easily beat these prices by building your own.

If you have a junkbox that is well stocked with items like filter capacitors, rectifiers, and three-terminal regulators, or if you can reduce costs by picking up surplus transformers at hamfests and computer fests, you can definitely beat the cost of the commercial power supply. Here are several typical construction-projects for power supplies that are suitable for a variety of microcomputer applications.

S-100 POWER SUPPLY

The S-100 computer mainframe uses distributed regulation. In this system the main low-voltage, high-current, bus is unregulated. Each printed circuit board (PCB) that plugs into the bus has its own regulators. Most S-100 boards have from one to four three-terminal regulators that are each rated at 1 to 3 A.

In the typical S-100 microcomputer the main bus-voltage is +8 V. This potential is above the minimum input-voltage required by three terminal regulators (i.e., typically 2.5 V over the rated output-voltage, which means 7.5 V in a 5-V system), yet is low enough to prevent overheating of the regulators. The power dissipated by a regulator is the product of the current drawn (1-3 A, typically) and the difference between the input and output voltages. In a 3-A regulator with an 8-V input-potential and 5-V output-potential, the difference is 3V; so the power dissipated is 3 A × 3 V, or 9 W.

If you use a 17-V rectified-dc line from a 12.6 V RMS transformer, the power dissipated is 3 A × (17-5), or 3 × 12 = 36 W. Obviously, the regulator runs a lot cooler with an 8 V input! This is the principal reason that +8 V is used for the unregulated high-current line in the S-100 microcomputer!

Figure 17-1 shows the circuit for the S-100 mainframe power-supply The rectifier is rated at 50-V or more peak-inverse voltage (PIV) at a current of 25 A or more. It is a good idea to buy heat-sinkable rectifiers and then mount them on an adequate heat-sinks (the aluminum kind with fins). You can also use a 25 A bridge-rectifier stack such as the GEBR-425 (General Electric), and it also should be heat-sinked. Use a generous smear of silicone heat-transfer grease between the rectifier bridge and the heat-sink.

There are several alternatives for the transformer. Obviously, an S-100 mainframe should have at least 10 A, and 20-25 A would not be too much. Triad makes several transformers that are particularly useful for this application. In general, though, you need a 6.3-7.4 =V filament transformer that is rated at 10-30 amperes. The Triad F-28U is rated at 6.3/7/5 volts (depending upon the primary winding selected) at 25 A. The circuit of Fig. 17-1 uses a bridge rectifier; so the current rating of the transformer is exactly half of the stated rating. This is because the transformers are rated for use in circuits that have two rectifiers (not a bridge) and a center tap for the common connection. You can use either of the Triad transformers in this manner by connecting two of them into the circuit of Fig. 17-2.

In this circuit the primaries are connected in parallel, and the secondaries are connected in series. If the output voltage is zero or very low when this connection is made, the phase of the windings is incorrect. The condition can be corrected by reversing either the primary winding or secondary winding-not both) of one of the transformers. The two diodes are 25 A, 50 piv stud-mounted types that are mounted on a heat-sink.

You can also use certain signal transformers; rectifier transformers; and other low-voltage, high current, rectifiers in this application.

The filter capacitor is 80,000 μF at 15 WVdc or more. This capacitor should have not less than 2000 μF per ampere of rated load, but the general rule is the more the merrier. As a practical matter use a capacitor in the range of 75,000 μF to 125,000 μF.

The 100 ohm, 2-watt, resistor connected across the filter capacitor is to load the rectifiers to produce a certain minimum current. Otherwise, the rectifiers do not work properly and the voltage across the 15 V filter is 18-20 V. This resistor can be connected directly to the screw-terminals on the filter capacitor.

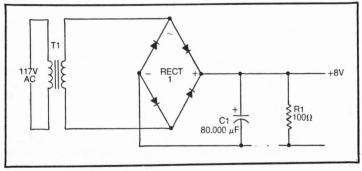

Fig. 17-1. S-100 8 V power-supply.

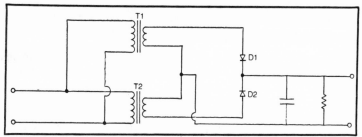

Fig. 17-2. S-100 8-V, high-current, power supply.

+5-V LOW-CURRENT POWER SUPPLY

Single-board computers and other, small, digital projects often require a +5 V dc power-supply that delivers 1-5 A. Typical requirements are 1, 3, 4, and 5 A depending on whose advertisements you read. Figure 17-3 shows the general circuit for all of these power supplies.

This circuit is based on the popular three-terminal IC-regulators. There are actually several different devices and series of devices available for this duty. The oldest, and perhaps most popular, 5-V regulator is the venerable LM-309 device. There are two versions of the LM-309 and each has a different current ratings. The LM-309H is housed in a TO-5 transistor can, and produces something on the order of 100 mA of dc output-current at 5 V. The larger LM-309K is in a diamond-shaped TO-3 power-transistor case and produces 1 A without heat-sinking and as much as 1.5 A if properly heat-sinked (and if you like living dangerously).

The other series of regulators include the 78xx and LM-340-xx devices. In each case the xx is replaced with the voltage rating of the device. Hence, a 5-V regulator in both series is a 7805 or LM-340-5. Similarly, a 12-V regulator is a 7812 and LM-340-12.

The current ratings of these regulators are given by a letter attached to the part number. The letters used are H, K and T. The H designates 100 mA in a TO-5 package, the K designates 1 A in a TO-3 package, while the T means that the device produces 750 mA and is in a plastic TO-220 (also called P-66 in some catalogs) package. Therefore, you can determine the ratings by the part number. For example, if the part number is LM-340T-12, you know that it is a positive regulator at 12 V and 750 mA and is in a plastic power-transistor package (TO-200).

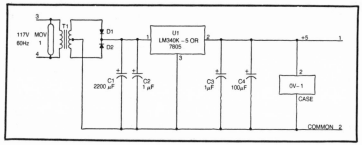

Fig. 17-3. 5-V 1-A power-supply.

The rectifier shown in Figure 17-3 is the ordinary center-tapped transformer, but a bridge rectifier works just as well. The rating of the rectifier for 5-V power-supplies should be 25 V piv or more (50 V is a better selection) at a current rating that is more than required for the regulator. Always allow some margin in the rectifier, if possible. For example, in a 1-A supply, try to use 1-5-A rectifiers.

The filter capacitor (C1 in Fig. 16-3) is selected according to the rule of 2000 μF per ampere of load current. In a 1-A power-supply use 2000 μF (2200 μF is a standard value). In a 5 A supply, however, you need 10,000 μF. Of course, the value given by the rule of thumb is a minimum value! Always select a higher value if feasible. The voltage rating of the filter capacitor should be 15 WVdc or higher. In general a 25-V or 50-V electrolytic capacitor is used for the filter.

The output capacitor (C4) is used to improve the transient response of the power supply. This capacitor serves not to filter the output, but to provide a reservoir of current (the capacitor charge) that is available to the load when there is an abrupt change that is too rapid for the regulator to follow. The regulator readjusts to produce the required output voltage, but that takes a few milliseconds. Capacitor C4 is used to provide current to the circuit during that brief instant. The value of C4 should be 100 μF per ampere of load current. The value shown in Fig. 17-3 is for the 1 A power supply. If you build the 5-A version, however, substitute a 500-1000 μF capacitor.

The two low-value capacitors (C2 and C3) are used to improve the immunity of the regulator to noise impulses. The capacitors should have a value between 0.1 μF and 1.0 μF and must be mounted on the regulator as close as possible to the body of the device. If these capacitors are placed too far away, they will be as effective as a block of wood.

The transformer selected should be a 6.3-V ac (or 7.5-V ac, if available) with a current rating sufficient to handle the output-current requirements of the load. Remember, it is generally true that the primary voltage-ampere rating of the transformer means that the secondary current rating in the bridge-rectifier configuration is exactly half of the center-tapped rectifier configuration. Typical transformers are rated at 6.3 V ac (rms) at 1-5 A. These are ordinary filament transformers. A good selection for the 5 A power-supply is the Triad F-24U, which is rated at 6.3/7.5 V ac at 8 A. In the bridge rectified configuration (necessary if a 6.3-V transformer is used) this transformer produces 4A of current. I find that pushing the transformer to 5A does not result in any noticeable overheating; so it probably works well. It would be a good idea, however, to mount the transformer (or any component that you chose to overrate) where it can be easily ventilated. An even better tactic blows a fan over the transformer.

If you prefer the center-tapped-rectifier configuration, select a 12.6-V transformer with a current rating identical to the rating of the rectifier (it may be higher and perhaps should be).

The component marked MOVl is a General Electric metal-oxide-varistor device that suppresses transients on the power line. These transients are well known to computerists as the devil that sneaks in and causes programs to bomb—and sometimes damages components. Most residential electrical services in the U.S.A. see a 1500-V (or more) transient of 20 ms or longer at least ten times per day! The MOV clips these transients and keeps them from affecting the computer. This component should be placed on the transformer side of the fuse (all power supplies should be fused).

The component marked OV-1 is an overvoltage protector. It is designed to protect the load circuitry (i.e., your computer) in the event of a catastrophic power-supply failure. The input voltage to the regulator is +8 V or more and this level kills the TTL devices in the computer. The overvoltage protector is designed to short the power supply line to ground (blowing the transformer primary fuse in most cases), if the power-supply voltage exceeds some magic number. There are two different approaches to overvoltage protection, but they both fall under the heading of *SCR crowbar* circuit (because of their brute force in dealing with the problem). One method is to buy an IC version, such as those made by Lambda Electronics. The L2-0V5 is a 2-A version for use with 1-2-A power supplies. The L6-0V5 is a 6-A, 5-V, version that works with all of the other power supplies of this section. Lambda makes versions at voltages to 15 V and currents to 35 A.

The power-supply circuit can also be used to provide currents to 5 A, if an appropriate three-terminal regulator is selected. The LM-323 device operates to 3 A, while the special Lambda LAS-1905 device operates to 5 A. Both of these should be heat-sinked.

Negative voltages can also be provided, if necessary, by substituting the 79xx and LM-320-xx devices for the 78xx and LM-340-xx devices, respectively. There are pin-out differences; so look them up or see the last project in this chapter.

Figure 17-4 shows the alternate SCR crowbar circuit. This circuit uses an SCR and a 5.6-V zener-diode. The SCR must be selected to be able to pass the full short-circuit current of the power supply; so I recommend 10-15-A models. The SCR is normally turned off unless a current is applied to the gate circuit. At that time, the SCR will turn on and act like any ordinary rectifier. The gate circuit of the SCR is controlled by the 5.6 volt zener diode. If the power supply is operating normally, then the output voltage (5 V) is too low to trip the SCR. But, if the regulator shorts out and places the full 8 V on the 5-V line, the zener diode breaks over (begins conducting) and inputs a current to the gate of the SCR. This current turns on the SCR and causes it to short-circuit the output-voltage line, thereby blowing the fuse.

5-V 10-A POWER SUPPLY

Some microcomputers require a current level of 10 A at 5 V. These computers are not generally S-100 types, but rather certain single-board computers that contain lots of memory and other functions. The circuit in Fig. 17-5 is capable of delivering 10 A at 5 V dc. The rectifier and transformer for this power supply are the same as for the S-100 power-supplies shown earlier in Figs. 17-1 and 17-2. Refer to those circuit descriptions for information regarding these components.

The main regulator consists of a 2N3771 (or HEP S7000) NPN, silicon, power-transistor, and an MC1469R (or HEP C6049R) IC regulator. The IC regulator is programmable for output voltage using the ratio of R4 and R5 (in fact, you can trim the output to exactly 5.0 V by making one of these

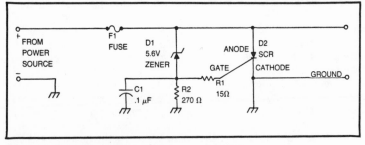

Fig. 17-4. Overvoltage SCR crowbar.

resistors variable). The IC regulator is available in two types that have different current ratings. You want the *R* version, which can pass a higher current than the *G* version. The R version is capable of producing up to 500 mA and can operate without a series-pass transistor at currents less than that figure. Higher levels of current are provided by the series-pass transistor. The IC regulator controls the base of the series-pass transistor, which in turn controls the output current.

The L35-0V5 device is a Lambda 35-A overvoltage-protection module intended for use in 5-V power-supplies. It is similar to the devices discussed in the previous section on 1-5-A supplies.

The other transistor in this circuit (Q2) is used as an output current-limiting circuit. This transistor is kept turned off during normal operation. When it conducts, it drops pin 4 of the IC regulator low, causing the circuit to turn off. The base of the transistor is controlled by the voltage drop across resistor 1. When this voltage reaches approximately 0.6 V, the current-limiter transistor becomes forward biased, and the circuit shuts down. The current at which event occurs is the rated output-current of the supply The resistor is selected from:

$$R = \frac{0.6}{I}$$

Where R is the value of R1 in ohms, and I is the rated output-current of the power supply.

In the case of the 10-A power-supply of this section the value of R1 needs to be

R = 0.6/10
R = 0.060 ohms = 60 milliohms

Because of the current drain this resistor must have a power rating of 6 W or more. You can obtain 60 milliohm by paralleling audio-amplifier or car-radio fuse-resistors. These resistors are normally used in the emitter circuit of af power-transistors and serve as a fuse and to provide a little bit of negative feedback. Two 0.12 ohm, 5-W fusistors in parallel produces the required result. Another combination is five 0.33 ohm 2-watt or 5-watt fusistors and may be more easily obtained.

The IC regulator used in this project is a feedback type. It takes a sample of the output voltage and compares it with a reference voltage inside of the IC package. The sample of the voltage is obtained through pin 5 of the

242

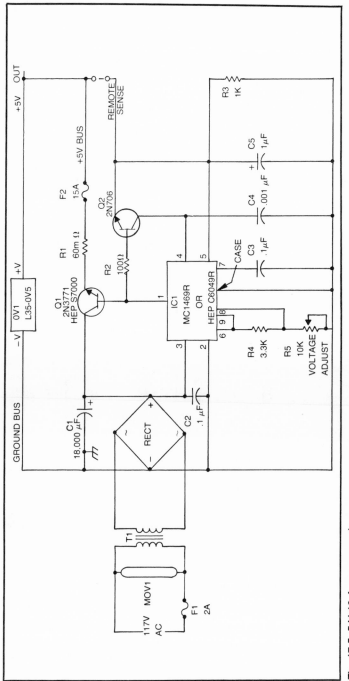

Fig. 17-5. 5-V 10-A power-supply.

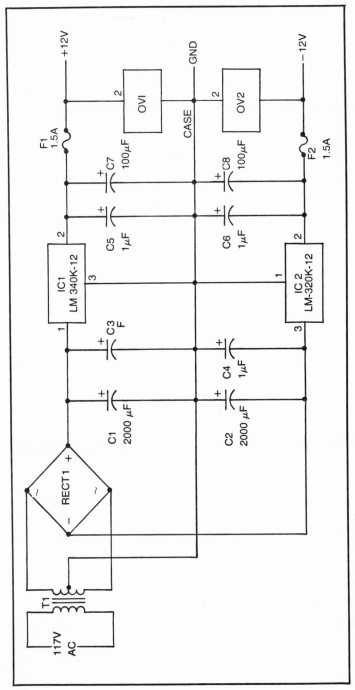

Fig. 17-6. ± 12-V 1-A power-supply.

IC regulator. You can simply strap pin 5 directly to the +5-V line. But, that could cause a problem. The current level of this supply is sufficient to cause a drop in the voltage due to copper losses in the printed-circuit tracks or other power-wiring of the computer. The delivered voltage might easily be too low to ensure proper operation of the computer circuits. You can overcome this problem by sensing the voltage at the delivery point!

To do this run a second wire to the delivery point and connect it to the sense line of the power supply. The sense line need only be a small (22 or so) conductor and does not carry high current. The main +5-V bus-wire, however, must be a large diameter. In general the largest wire that can be easily accommodated on the screw-type terminals normally used in power supplies should be used. I recommend number 10 or 12 wire.

The power-supply voltage is adjusted using potentiometer R5. Connect a load to the power supply and then adjust R5 as close to +5 V as possible.

I use this circuit in my own 26K, Z-80-based, Digital Group computer. I find that the power transistor runs very hot, even with a heat-sink. In order to keep things cool I positioned a 40 cubic feet per minute fan to flow over the heat-sink, and the overheating problem evaporated.

± 12-V 1-A POWER SUPPLY

Figure 17-6 shows a dual polarity version of the three-terminal regulator supply discussed earlier. In the earlier version the current is rated to 5 A, and the voltage is fixed at 5 V. In this version use either LM-340-12 or LM-320-12 (or 7812/7912) regulators; so the current is limited to 1 A for the K versions and 750 mA for the T versions. This power supply is used to power the other circuits in the computer (most computers require ±12 V for proper operation!).

The transformer is rated at not less than 2 A and at 25 to 26 V. Triad makes a 25.6-V, 2.8-A, transformer that is ideal for this application. Note that the center tap is used even though a bridge circuit is present. This circuit uses the bridge stack as a pair of half wave bridges, instead of a single full-wave bridge. This produces the needed dual-polarity scheme. All of the other components of this circuit are the same as in the 5-V supply given earlier. Reread that section for an explanation of the components.

Index

Edited by Dennis Thurlow